...US DIE!" CRY WOMEN AT MORGUE

PITIABLE SCENES IN THE STRICKEN DISTRICT;
340 VOICES ARE STILL AT SCHOOL ROLL CALL

ROWS OF COFFINS IN TEMPORARY MORGUE.

LATEST DEATH-ROLL.

Bodies Recovered .	533
Persons Missing . .	625
Estimated Dead .	1,200

NEGLIGENCE DOUBLED THE DEATH LIST.
DEATH AND GREED PARTNERS.

The lure of this child and many hundreds of others were sacrificed to Greed in the General Slocum disaster. Death and Greed count the profits. When will a day of reckoning come for the criminals that are responsible for the deaths?

Fire Hose Rotten.
Boats Chocked.
Preservers Old.
Fixing Blame.
Officials Act.
Charges Made.

WERE LIFE PRESERVERS ROTTEN?

TALLY-HO RUNS INTO MOURNERS

GIRL TAGGED "DEAD" REVIVED IN STATION

HOSE BURST AS THE CREW FOUGHT FIRE

MATE FLANNIGAN SAYS IT WAS USELESS

Horror Seen from Office Windows of City Skyscrapers.

LASHES HIS VESSEL TO BLAZING STEAMER;
SAVES TWO HUNDRED FROM THE SLOCUM

SHIP ABLAZ

ALSO BY EDWARD T. O'DONNELL

1001 Things Everyone Should Know
About Irish American History

BROADWAY BOOKS
NEW YORK

SHIP ABLAZE

The Tragedy of the
Steamboat *General Slocum*

EDWARD T. O'DONNELL

PRINTED IN THE UNITED STATES OF AMERICA

BROADWAY BOOKS and its logo, a letter B bisected on the
diagonal, are trademarks of Random House, Inc.

Visit our website at www.broadwaybooks.com

First edition published 2003

Book design by Jennifer Ann Daddio
Map and illustration by Laura Hartman Maestro

Library of Congress Cataloging-in-Publication Data

O'Donnell, Edward T., 1963–
Ship ablaze: the tragedy of the steamboat *General Slocum* /
Edward T. O'Donnell.—1st ed.
p. cm.
Includes index.
1. *General Slocum* (Steamboat)   2. Fires—New York (State)—
New York—History—20th century.   3. Ships—Fire and fire prevention—
New York (State)—New York—History—20th century.   4. New York
(N.Y.)—History—1898–1951.   I. Title.
F128.5.O29 2003
910'.9163'46—dc21   2002033008

ISBN 0-7679-0905-4

1   3   5   7   9   10   8   6   4   2

to the innocents lost in
the catastrophes of
6/15/04 and 9/11/01

and the brave ones
who saved so many

and the bereaved
left behind

and the city
that always overcomes

AUTHOR'S NOTE

Like any good historian, I have endeavored to tell an engaging story while remaining true to the standards of evidence and documentation. As a work of nonfiction, this book is based on the real-life experiences of real people. Every character and event mentioned is real, and their descriptions are drawn from voluminous newspaper accounts, court testimony, interviews with survivors and their descendants, and other historical sources. The same is true of all the dialogue presented in this book. Every word quoted in this book is based on these sources and none is invented.

CONTENTS

PART TWO: HORROR

PART THREE: SEARCHING

PART FOUR: FORGETTING

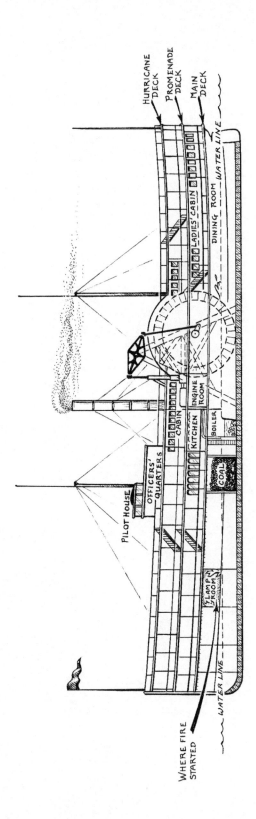

DIAGRAM OF THE GENERAL SLOCUM

HURRICANE DECK
PROMENADE DECK
MAIN DECK

LADIES' CABIN
DINING ROOM
WATER LINE

CABIN
KITCHEN
ENGINE ROOM
BOILER
COAL

PILOT HOUSE
OFFICERS' QUARTERS

LAMP ROOM
WATER LINE

WHERE FIRE STARTED

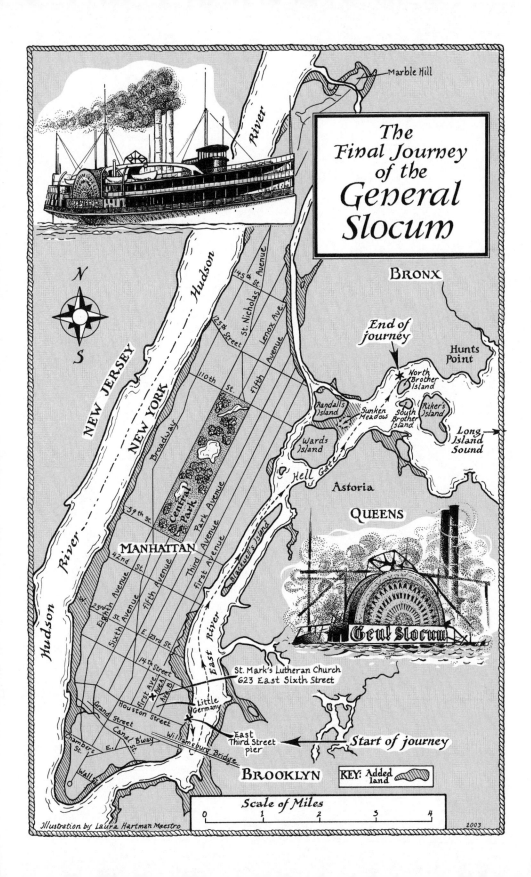

The
Final Journey
of the
General
Slocum

Marble Hill

BRONX

Hunts
Point

End of
journey

North
Brother
Island

Randalls
Island

Sunken
Meadow

Riker's
Island

South
Brother
Island

Long
Island
Sound

Wards
Island

Hell Gate

Astoria

QUEENS

N
S

NEW JERSEY

NEW YORK

Hudson

145th St.

St. Nicholas Ave.

Lenox Ave.

125th Street

110th St.

Fifth Avenue

Broadway

Central Park

Park Avenue

Third Avenue

First Avenue

Blackwell's Island

East River

MANHATTAN

59th St.

42nd St.

Eighth Avenue

Sixth Avenue

Fifth Avenue

23rd St.

E. 23rd St.

14th Street

Genl Slocum

St. Mark's Lutheran Church
623 East Sixth Street

First Ave.
Ave. B

Little
Germany

Houston Street

Grand
Street

Canal St.

B'way

Chambers
St.

E.

Wall

Williamsburg Bridge

East
Third Street
pier

Start of journey

BROOKLYN

Hudson River

KEY: Added land

Scale of Miles

0 1 2 3 4

Illustration by Laura Hartman Maestro

2003

THE ENVY OF ALL

O
UT ACROSS the slate gray expanse of swirling water, it was hard to miss. Freshly painted for the new season then just beginning, it fairly glistened in the midmorning sun. Two hundred sixty-four feet from stem to stern, topped with three vast open decks stacked one atop the other, the steamboat drew notice as it plied its way upriver. It was hardly the only boat out that morning, for today, as on every day, the East River was choked with boats of every shape, size, and purpose. Yet as a passenger steamer jammed with people bound on a pleasure excursion, it presented a majestic image as it glided on with apparent effortlessness.

This veil of grace and beauty, pleasing as it was to the eye, failed to obscure the boat's most overwhelming aspect: raw power. The signs were everywhere, beginning with the flag attached to the boat's tall staff. From a distance the stiff bit of fabric seemed frozen, pulled taut in the direction of the stern by the force of the vessel's astonishing fifteen-knot speed. All about the flag a trail of thick but fast-dissipating black smoke billowed from two stacks amidships, revealing the presence of two raging boilers belowdecks. Along the waterline, twin wakes of white, seemingly boiling water flowed alongside the hull, churned by the boat's two mighty paddle wheels.

That something weighing nearly thirteen hundred tons could be compelled to move so fast yet so gracefully was still a wonder in 1904. Steam locomotives possessed far more power and attained greater speeds, but graceful was not a word that came to mind among those who rode them. Certainly the same could be said of the newfangled contraptions now in vogue among the restless nouveau riche—horseless carriages—despite the growing numbers of them on the nation's streets. And air travel? As far as most Americans were concerned, it remained the stuff of science fiction, despite Orville and Wilbur Wright's successful test of their flying machine six months earlier. In 1904, at the peak of the age of steam, when it came to speed, comfort, and cost, no mode of transportation could rival the passenger steamboat. Every day dozens plied the murky waters in and around New York City, and every day people stood and watched. This morning was no different. From nearby vessels captains, deckhands, and passengers looked on as the radiant boat passed. Along both shorelines hardened dockworkers paused to appreciate the spectacle, if only for a quick glance. High above the river on the brand-new Williamsburg Bridge, commuters craned their necks to watch. Through the windows of the metropolis's new soaring skyscrapers, secretaries and executives broke the monotony of the emerging corporate culture to steal a glimpse. All gazed with a conflicting mixture of admiration and jealousy, as a widow might when studying a passing wedding party.

They were drawn not merely by the boat, but also by the event it clearly represented. Most who noticed the boat were too far away to hear the joyous sounds of the band aboard or to see the festively dressed passengers talking, running, and dancing on the decks. They didn't need to see it, for the scene was easily imagined.

A thousand or so people were aboard a chartered steamboat. The specific group (a church? a charity? a club?) and the occasion (an anniversary? a wedding? an annual outing?) mattered little. Nor did the particular destination, though most likely this northbound excursion was headed for one of the many recreation areas along Long Island Sound. If it was like most outings, the day would be one long endless round of food and drink, dancing and games, and for the few who knew how, swimming. Later that evening the steamer would return bearing a load of sunburned, overfed, and exhausted revelers, not a few tipsy from the plentiful drink.

On this day, those aboard such a boat were the lucky ones, the ones able to get away even if just for eight or nine hours.

None were more aware of their good fortune that day than the thirteen hundred souls now cruising up the East River. Most were German immigrants or their children, members of St. Mark's Lutheran Church on Manhattan's Lower East Side. Some of their number had scrimped, sacrificed, and saved their way into the middle class and a few were undeniably rich. The rest were working-class folk, the kind of people who appreciated every second of leisure time precisely because they had so little of it. They'd spent the previous 364 days anticipating the 17th Annual St. Mark's outing to Locust Grove on Long Island, and the day had finally arrived.

As the steamer's twin paddle wheels clawed at the water and propelled the vessel on its journey, they could be seen dressed in their best outfits moving about the vessel or gathered in clusters chatting excitedly about the fabulous weather. Everywhere little children scurried to and fro while a group of teenagers began to dance to the sounds of the German band. Hundreds more crammed against the steamer's railings on all three decks to drink in the urban panorama slipping slowly past.

For many it was a rare, perhaps even first, detached glimpse of the city that overwhelmed them day after day. Even though the unspoken theme of the day was escape, most were unable to take their eyes off the cityscape. No doubt many were struck by how calm and quiet the city seemed from the river. The familiar sounds of everyday life—clip-clopping horses, pounding hammers, grinding machinery, bellowing vendors—were barely audible on the river, especially aboard a boat humming with the drone of its engine at three-quarters throttle.

Already the excursion was having its desired effect. They were slipping, however fleetingly, from the gravitational pull of their chaotic, stressful urban world. One by one the relentlessly ordered streets passed by—14th Street, 23rd Street, 34th Street, 42nd Street, and so on—as if measuring the progress of their flight. With every passing minute their eyes drew in the enormity and complexity of their city. One moment endless rows of tenements much like their own downtown came into view, the next a cluster of upscale brownstone mansions. In the foreground along the water's edge they saw familiar collections of seemingly ancient warehouses and countinghouses, vestiges of a fast-disappearing waterfront economy. Beyond them loomed the future—dozens of skyscrapers newly opened or nearing completion.

Those first fifteen minutes aboard the steamboat put before her passengers their city in all its confusing, contradictory glory. New York was a city of hope and despair, of fabulous wealth and crushing poverty, of limitless possibilities and unimaginable pitfalls, of traditional Old World values and relentless, almost pathological newness. Every day the people of St. Mark's struggled to survive amid these competing forces. Every day, that is, except today. For one day, at least, they could leave it all behind.

Those who saw the steamboat that morning knew this, and so they looked on.

Part One

HOPE

THE CAPTAIN

H e awoke to the same familiar sounds as on every morning—the
creak and groan of a wooden vessel at pier, the persistent *lap, lap, lap* of water against the hull, the squawk of a seagull, the peal of
a distant ship whistle. Dawn was breaking over the Hudson River, and an-
other day of furious maritime activity was about to begin.

It was still dark as the captain rolled off his bunk, dressed, and stepped
out on the deck of his boat. The air was cold, but it being June 14, there
was a noticeable springlike hint in it. Out across the frigid, seemingly mo-
tionless river he could see the sources of the morning's first sounds. Dark
silhouettes of tugs and barges moved in the distance, punctuated here and
there by colored lanterns. Seagulls stood on the ship railings and soared
overhead looking for the first sign of breakfast. Closer by, the captain saw
row upon row of boats at pier, most dark and silent as though sleeping, but
a few like his with lantern light streaming from a cabin window.

Captain William Van Schaick, like a lot of old-time unmarried captains,
lived aboard his boat. He did so less because of some romantic love of the
sea and more to simply save money. At sixty-seven years of age, retirement
was not far off and he needed to save every penny of his $37.50 per week

salary if he wanted to avoid living out his last days in poverty. He still paid rent, but less than half the going rate for a Manhattan apartment. Plus you couldn't beat the commute.

The onset of warm weather meant his busy season was upon him. From late May to early October he'd work nearly every day as New Yorkers clambered aboard his boat on group outings to the shore and day trips to see the big yacht races. Today was the eighth charter excursion of the young season for him. He'd been at it now for more years than he cared to remember, including the last thirteen on this steamboat, the *General Slocum*. In fact, he had been the only captain the steamer had ever known.

Tethered to a long, weatherbeaten pier, the steamboat rolled gently back and forth with the silent rhythms of waves left by passing vessels. In the faint predawn light then beginning to brighten the sky over the Hudson, the steamer *General Slocum* presented an imposing, dark silhouette. Unlike many of its fellow passenger steamers, many of which began their careers in other port cities like Boston, Providence, or Newport, the *General Slocum* was a New York boat through and through. It was built by the Devine Burtis shipbuilding firm in the Red Hook section of Brooklyn in 1890–91. Miss May Lewis, niece of the Knickerbocker Steamboat Company's president, joined a large crowd of spectators on the day of the launch in April 1891. Moments after she broke a bottle across its bow, the steamboat slid down the ways into the chilly waters of New York harbor.

As befitting a locally built boat destined to ply local waterways, the Knickerbocker Steamboat Co. named it for Maj. Gen. Henry Warner Slocum (1827–94). A graduate of West Point, Slocum had served with distinction in the Union Army, including commands at Gettysburg and with Sherman's scorched-earth march to the sea across Georgia. Slocum parlayed his military record into a successful law practice and three terms in Congress between 1869 and 1885. Affixing the name of this much-admired elder statesman to the paddle box in large fancy lettering would, the owners hoped, lend the new steamboat an aura of respectability, honor, glory, and history.

The steamer itself, however, conveyed a very different image. The moment its sharp hull sliced into the chilly waters of New York harbor on that cold spring morning in 1891, there was no question which passenger steamer stood supreme. No steamboat in and around New York could compare with the *General Slocum* in terms of design and luxurious appointments. At 264 feet in length and weighing 1,281 tons, the *Slocum* was not the largest boat of its kind in the harbor. Even its sister ship, the *Grand Republic*, was longer. But its sleek, wooden hull that swept gracefully upward from stern to prow indicated a steamboat designed for both speed and elegance as well as size. As was the custom of the day, the *Slocum*'s hull was painted a brilliant white. Above it the three stacked decks, cabin walls, rails, doors, and benches were varying shades of brown varnished wood.

The *Slocum*'s interior was likewise designed to provide up to twenty-five hundred passengers with a maximum of luxury and comfort. Two large open rooms called "saloons" on the lower and middle decks provided passengers with wicker chairs upholstered in fine red velvet and tables at which they could enjoy good things to eat from the kitchen and bar. Lush carpeting, fine paintings, wood carvings, and ornate light fixtures here and elsewhere in the boat's several lounges added to its ambience. Abundant windows allowed for a maximum of natural light and fresh air. For those who wanted more of both, there was the vast upper or "hurricane" deck, some ten thousand square feet of open space enclosed only by a three-foot-high railing. Towering above it all stood two large side-by-side smokestacks painted a flat yellow.

In 1891 no steamboat in New York could equal the *Slocum*'s beauty and opulence. Nor could any steamboat match its combination of speed, size, and maneuverability. Deep inside the boat's hull, beneath the decks devoted to the needs and whims of the passengers, lay the enormous steam-powered engine built by the W. & A. Fletcher Company in Hoboken, New Jersey. Attached to it were two massive paddle wheels mounted on both sides of the boat. Each was nine feet wide, thirty-one feet in diameter, and studded with twenty-six paddles. With the engine running at full throttle, they could claw the water with such ferocity that the steamer reached the astonishing speed of fifteen knots. Even still, speed and size did not compromise maneuverability, for the *Slocum* was fitted with an ultramodern steam-powered steering system.

None of this was possible, of course, without steam. One deck below the W. & A. Fletcher engine were two huge boilers and an entire hold compartment full of several tons of coal. The age of steamboat travel had dawned nearly a century ago on the very waters where the *Slocum* now floated. In 1807, Robert Fulton became the first person to successfully apply steam power to a boat when he piloted the *Clermont* 150 miles up the Hudson River to Albany. Fulton's triumph announced the arrival of the industrial age, when new technology would allow man to defy nature—in this case, the relentless downward flow of a major river. More precisely, it ushered in a new era, decades before the railroad, of steam-propelled travel. And with each passing decade, subsequent inventors and engineers made enormous improvements in steamboat power, efficiency, speed, and safety. By the time of the *General Slocum*'s launch in 1891, massive steam-driven ocean liners routinely crossed the Atlantic and Pacific Oceans, carrying thousands of passengers and tons of cargo.

Much of the *Slocum*'s mechanical format was visible for all to see. Mounted amidships just aft of the smokestacks stood a tall steel tower surmounted by a diamond-shaped lever. Attached to one end of the lever was the engine's twenty-foot-high piston rod. Attached to the lever's other end were two drive rods that led to the paddle wheels (see diagram). As the rhythmic pulses of steam from the boiler caused the piston rod to move upward and downward six feet in each direction, it moved the lever, which in turn moved the wheels. Despite its deceptively simple appearance, it was a highly complex system of energy generation and transfer, the product of more than two centuries of refinement in engineering.

For its first five seasons the *General Slocum* enjoyed a reputation as one of the city's finest passenger steamers. On weekends and holidays from late May to early October, it made two round-trips from Manhattan to Rockaway, a popular seaside retreat in outermost Queens on Long Island. At fifty cents for a round-trip, New Yorkers of every class enjoyed the two and a half hours (75 minutes each way) about the commodious *Slocum* almost as much as the intervening time at the beach. On weekdays and special occasions such as the annual international yacht races off Sandy Hook, groups paid top dollar to charter the steamboat.

But in that era of incessant advancements in technology and cutthroat competition between passenger lines, the *Slocum*'s reign as the city's top steamer was short-lived. What had been cutting-edge technology and the very latest in first-class appointments in 1891 were by the mid-1890s rather unexceptional. Newer, bigger, faster steamboats with far more luxurious accommodations such as full dining rooms, lounges, and dance floors now commanded the attention—and dollars—of the city's swell set. By 1896 the *Slocum* had slipped to the second-tier rankings of steamboats, still very respectable and profitable, yet considerably less so than the day she went into service. The boat rarely sat idle during the peak season, only now it was chartered by middle- and working-class groups like unions, fraternal societies, and churches.

Today it was the latter, a church group bound for Empire Grove on Long Island Sound. An hour after the captain awoke, the steamer buzzed with activity as the crew prepared it for the excursion. Tons of coal and water were brought aboard along with ample food, drink, and ice. Deckhands spiffed up the boat's appearance using mops and rags and then hosed the whole boat down. Most crews used their own boat's fire hose and pump for this morning ritual, but not on the *Slocum*. For as long as anyone could remember, they had used a hose and hydrant from the pier. And it was just as well, for anyone could see that the *Slocum*'s weathered fire hoses were not up to the task.

It took only fifteen minutes or so to complete the wash-down. Cloudy gray torrents of water spilled from the boat's scuppers, carrying away layers of salt, seagull droppings, coal soot, and traces of fine cork dust. The latter fell every day from the twenty-five hundred tattered life preservers slowly disintegrating in their racks above the decks. Minutes later, the deckhands cast off lines and the *Slocum* headed down the Hudson River to a pier where more than a thousand passengers awaited, eagerly anticipating a day of fun at the shore, safe from the dangers of the city.

EMPIRE CITY

N ot long after the *Slocum* glided down the Hudson for its scheduled rendezvous with its church group, a ferry pulled away from
its landing in Atlantic Highlands, New Jersey. Jammed to the rails
with rush-hour commuters, the craft moved slowly through the brackish
water. In twenty minutes it would reach the landing on the Lower West
Side of Manhattan, deposit its cargo of hundreds, and return for another
load. Every morning hundreds of thousands of men and women of every
profession and class made their way to the Empire City in this manner over
the harbor, or across the Hudson and East Rivers. Every evening the
process was reversed as dozens of ferries slowly drained off a sizable portion of Manhattan's workforce, taking them to their homes in Queens,
Brooklyn, Staten Island, and New Jersey.

Most of the passengers on the ferry that morning lived permanently
outside of Manhattan. But it being June 14 and the beginning of the summer season, some were professional men commuting from summer cottages rented for one or more weeks along the Jersey Shore. Among them
was George B. McClellan, Jr., the mayor of New York City and son of the

controversial Civil War general of the same name. Commuting to his office at city hall via the Hudson River ferry was an entirely new experience for him. Only yesterday he and his wife had moved into a seaside cottage at Long Branch for the duration of the summer and early fall. The idea had been his wife's, for she was worried that the mounting stress from the day-to-day rigors of office would ruin his health. They could certainly afford it on McClellan's annual salary of fifteen thousand dollars. As an added plus, the move would give them a chance to mix with the finest kind of New York society, since in the words of one guidebook, "The Branch" had been "for many years the most fashionable summer resort in the vicinity of New York." Residents of the area's fine hotels and private cottages, the guide continued, divided their days between "bathing in the morning, driving in the afternoon, and dancing in the evening."

At thirty-nine, McClellan, known as Max to his friends, was one of the youngest men to occupy the mayor's office. Born in late 1865 while his parents were in Dresden during a three-and-a-half-year tour of Europe, he enjoyed an upbringing that was both comfortable and focused. His parents, nurses, teachers, and professors at Princeton instilled in him the habits and attitudes of an aristocrat, or what democratically inclined Americans preferred to call a gentleman. Like others of his class, he attended an Ivy League college (Princeton) where he studied history, art, and languages as well as literature, math, and science. This grooming plus a steady stream of famous personages into the McClellan household from the worlds of business and politics brought him to understand that he belonged to an American nobility, not an inherited status as in Europe, but one secured through the acquisition of wealth and training. With this status, he was informed, came certain obligations, chief among them public service. For Max, of course, there would be an additional requirement of no small magnitude—that he win the presidency and redeem the honor of the father to whom he was so devoted.

Until recently, he had seemed well on his way to doing just that. After a stint as the youngest man to serve as president of the New York City Board of Aldermen followed by several terms in Congress, McClellan's name was bandied about in 1900 as a possible Democratic nominee for vice president, perhaps even president. His youth (he was only thirty-five) and modest national profile caused the boon to fizzle, but his journey to the White House seemed only a matter of time. Three years later the gentleman politician threw caution to the wind and ran for mayor of New York. He hoped the high-profile job would give him the national exposure he needed to secure the Democratic nomination in 1904. Such a scenario seemed firmly grounded in reality, for the current occupant of the White House, Theodore Roosevelt, first gained national recognition as an anti-corruption crusader while serving as New York's commissioner of police from 1895 to 1897. Four short years later he had managed to ride that fame, boosted by his "Rough Rider" exploits in Cuba in 1898, into the governor's office, the vice presidency, and, courtesy of an assassin's bullet, the White House.

The one big difference between McClellan and Roosevelt was party affiliation. As a Democrat, McClellan's political aspirations required that he join the most notorious political machine in the nation, Tammany Hall. Political machines operated in most American cities in this era, but none could hold a candle to Tammany when it came to corruption, nepotism, bribery, and voter fraud. Active as a political organization since the 1820s, Tammany achieved international ignominy during the reign of Boss William Tweed, whose corrupt exploits in the early 1870s were stupendous even by New York standards. "Tammany Hall," thundered one outraged statesman in 1876, "bears the same relation to the penitentiary as the Sunday-school to the church." Reformers and readers of Lincoln Steffens's muckraking series "Shame of the Cities" in *McClure's* magazine that year saw little evidence that much had changed a quarter century later.

Nonetheless, when McClellan entered city hall on January 1, 1904, he was confident that any negatives derived from his association with Tammany could be overcome by a successful first six months in office. If by July 1904—the month when Democrats would convene in St. Louis to choose their nominees for president and vice president—he had shown himself to be a successful proponent of efficient and effective government, he might yet be nominated. Certainly there would be no denying him the nomination for governor of New York State in 1906. The *New York Times* agreed. "Mr. McClellan is yet young," the editors wrote in January 1904, "and he might go very far if, cutting altogether loose from evil Tammany influence and bad Tammany men, he would assert himself positively and mightily as a Mayor determined to enforce the laws impartially and to be guided by no other considerations than those of the public interest. . . . It is not merely a duty that confronts Mayor McClellan; it is an opportunity. As Mayor of this city he could make a reputation that would attract the attention of the whole country."

As of June 14 the young mayor had been in office exactly six and one-half months. Yet already the job had begun to overwhelm him. In large measure this was due to the day-to-day struggle of municipal politics. Steering a middle course between Tammany corruption and goo-goo idealism had proven far more difficult than he ever imagined. He had underestimated the power and resourcefulness of Tammany boss Charles Francis Murphy and found himself increasingly at odds with him. This was no small matter, for Murphy had the power to make—or break—a McClellan-for-president boon.

McClellan's sagging spirits also stemmed from the sheer enormity of his job, a fact made abundantly clear this morning as he approached the city from the waters of the harbor. There before him off the ferry's bow loomed the southern profile of his domain, a colossal urban civilization of 320 square miles and home to more than 4 million people. Like many a corporation in its day, the city owed its vast size to a megamerger only six years earlier that had dissolved forty surrounding towns with names like Flushing, New Brighton, and the country's third-largest city, Brooklyn, into one City of Greater New York. Consolidation, as it was called, ended once and for all any talk that New York would surrender the title of the nation's largest city. Gotham had taken the upstart city of Chicago by its broad shoulders and shoved it firmly back into second place. The ebullient attitude of the city was best expressed by the *New York Sun* on January 1, 1898, the day the merger took effect:

> *All hail to the new New York which comes into being to-day! . . .*
> *Long before the lives of many of those who read these lines are spent it*
> *will be the foremost capital of the world in population, in wealth, and*
> *in commercial and financial power. Nor can we doubt that there is to*
> *be developed a city which will surpass in grandeur any which has yet*
> *been builded by man. All hail the imperial city!*

All, it seemed, except for the man charged with running it. New York's population exceeded that of every state in the union save Illinois, Ohio, and Pennsylvania. The same could be said for its annual budget of more than $100 million. Thousands worked for the city in dozens of departments, from street sweepers and toll takers to schoolteachers and engineers. And six years after consolidation, the mayor and other officials still wrestled with the challenge of knitting together the economies, bureaucracies, and transportation systems of the five boroughs into a single, efficient unit.

More than the sheer number of people there was, of course, the diversity. Up ahead off the ferry's port rail stood the twin totems of the city's heritage as the great melting pot of the world, Ellis Island and the Statue of Liberty. Today, as on every day, thousands of newcomers would arrive on transatlantic steamers in hopes of starting a new life in America. Indeed, that very morning the city's papers informed the mayor and his constituents of a fare war among the transatlantic steamship companies that promised a surge in immigration. "Ten-Dollar Rate," proclaimed a *Times* headline, "Brings Myriads of Immigrants."

His city was famous for being what writer Edwin Hill called "the great whirlpool of the races." And it had been since colonial times, when one visitor in 1643 counted eighteen languages among New Amsterdam's five hundred residents. Three hundred sixty-one years later it was the most racially, ethnically, culturally, and religiously diverse population on the planet. Fully 75 percent of the city's population were immigrants or the children of immigrants in 1904.

Other revealing glimpses of the massive and complex municipality passed before the mayor as his ferry moved steadily toward Manhattan. Directly off the ferry's bow loomed the tip of Manhattan island, a place now known as the Financial District. Its principal place of worship, a brand-new New York Stock Exchange built at a cost of $3 million, was hidden behind a phalanx of recently constructed buildings called "skyscrapers." The first skyscrapers in the early 1880s had astonished the public by reaching the unthinkable height of ten stories, but in 1904, the city boasted no fewer than eighty skyscrapers, at least a dozen of which exceeded three hundred feet in height. "It is as if some mighty force were astir beneath the ground," commented *Harper's Weekly* in 1902, "hour by hour pushing up structures that a dozen years ago would have been inconceivable."

An equally extraordinary feature of the Empire City was wholly invisible that morning not only to McClellan but to all save the several thousand workers engaged in its construction. Begun four years earlier and now nearing completion, the "subway" was the largest municipal public works project ever undertaken in American history—larger than all but a handful of state and federal projects for that matter. Starting beneath McClellan's office at city hall, it ran to northern Manhattan, then under the Harlem River into the Bronx. Skeptical New Yorkers could scarcely believe the claims of IRT officials who predicted a fifteen-minute commute from Harlem to city hall (possible, they claimed, because of a brilliant mass transit innovation: a second set of tracks for express trains). Proof would come on opening day, sometime in late 1904.

Eventually the mayor's ferry *scrunch-thudded* its way into a V-shaped landing near the foot of Rector Street in lower Manhattan. As soon as the gangways touched the pier they were covered with hundreds of commuters scampering to work or to still another mode of transportation like a trolley or elevated train that would take them uptown. City hall was about one mile to the northeast, and McClellan, a man fond of walking several miles each morning from his home in Washington Square, welcomed the opportunity to stretch his legs. The first portion of the walk was anything but pleasant, as it took him from the reeking waterfront along narrow streets lined with tenements, warehouses, and factories. But within minutes he reached the cemetery of Trinity Church (wherein rested notables like Alexander Hamilton and Robert Fulton), turned left onto Broadway, and headed north to where two-thirds of a mile distant in the center of a small park stood city hall.

STORIES

O
utside McClellan's office, the area around city hall swirled with frenzied movement and sound. Thousands upon thousands of Gotham residents were on the move, walking briskly along sidewalks that lined traffic-choked streets. They bunched at corners, as if waiting until their collective numbers reached a critical mass, and then burst across the streets through small fissures in the long lines of trucks, wagons, cabs, streetcars, and carriages. None seemed to notice the cacophony of sounds—police whistles, streetcar bells, vendors' shouts, horses' hooves—coming at them from every angle. With serious expressions on their faces, they leaned forward and moved in a determined manner that made clear they were not out for a stroll.

It was, in short, an ordinary, sunny Tuesday morning in the middle of June. The area around city hall was a transportation hub, and every day hundreds of thousands of commuters passed this way. "The rush and turmoil of traffic here," announced a popular guidebook, "are indescribable."

For some it was simply a place to hurriedly transfer between ferries, elevated trains, streetcars, and hansom cabs. For others the city hall area was their destination, for in 1904 this was the city's central business district as well as its political center. Wall Street and the financial industry lay a few blocks to the south. To the east and west were the city's Hudson and East River waterfronts, flanked by countless factories and warehouses. To the north still more factories, shops, and office buildings. In every direction were restaurants, saloons, and newspaper stands. And right there in the immediate city hall area was Newspaper Row, the media capital of the nation.

Newspapers of every description and size emanated from the dozens of buildings that surrounded City Hall Park, but the heart of Newspaper Row consisted of an imposing assemblage of structures opposite the park's eastern edge along a street called Park Row. Despite their varied size and age, the signs adorning their facades let it be known that all were dedicated to the same enterprise. Just south of the ramp leading up to the Brooklyn Bridge stood the mighty *World* tower, the tallest in the world when completed in 1890. The paper was the great organ of Joseph Pulitzer and the city's top-selling newspaper. Adjoining it was a smaller, older building that held the offices of the *New York Sun*, a paper brought to literary and editorial prominence in the late nineteenth century by its editor and owner, Charles A. Dana. Towering over it was the *Tribune*, once the nation's paper of record under the direction of its founder Horace Greeley and still a major player in 1904. To the south across Spruce Street on the next block stood the new American Tract Society Building wherein evangelical Christian literature in every form was published. At the far east end of the block, set back from the formal Row, was the *Journal*, owned by William Randolph Hearst, publisher, reformer, congressman, and presidential hopeful. Next was the *Press*, followed by the *Evening Telegram* and the *Daily News*. Anchoring the far end of the lineup were the old men of Newspaper Row, the *Globe and Commercial Advertiser* and the *Post*, established in 1797 and 1801 respectively.

Change, however, was in the air in 1904. Soaring high above City Hall Park at the corner of Park Row and Spruce Street was the headquarters of the *Times*. Founded on this site in 1851, the once prominent paper teetered on the brink of bankruptcy in 1896 when it was saved by Adolph Ochs, a wealthy German Jew from Tennessee. Determined to make the

Times one of the nation's foremost papers, he decided to move the paper uptown to Longacre Square at 42nd and Broadway. To Ochs's delight, only eight weeks earlier the city had conferred its blessing on the bold move by renaming the location Times Square. That precedent had been set by media magnate James Gordon Bennett, Jr., who moved his *Herald* from Newspaper Row in 1894 to Herald Square uptown at 34th Street.

Despite these notable defections, the heart of the city's media empire in 1904 remained firmly entrenched in Newspaper Row, and every morning thousands of editors, reporters, photographers, typesetters, graphic artists, clerks, machinists, pressmen, truck drivers, and newsboys arrived to create yet another edition of their respective papers. With city hall just across the street and Wall Street only a few blocks away, most in the industry preferred it that way. Why move uptown when all the action was in Lower Manhattan?

Through the teeming multitude of New Yorkers near Newspaper Row came Martin Green. The bright sunshine and warm air on that beautiful spring morning seemed to take the edge off the hectic scramble on the streets and sidewalks. Green's destination shimmered before him in the early-morning sunshine like a beacon—the tall golden dome atop the *New York World* tower. He was minutes away from commencing another day as an assistant editor for the city's leading paper, one man among thousands involved in the intensely competitive business of big-city journalism. His job was to assign reporters to stories and edit the result while others set type, tended presses, sold advertising, crunched numbers, drove delivery trucks, and hawked papers. For those on the inside of the business, every day the goal was the same: to get the best stories, attract more readers, sell more advertising.

Green's readers certainly understood that journalism in New York was a business. But they also saw it as an essential service, nearly as important as the streetcar lines or the fire department. Americans of this era, noted historian Arthur Schlesinger, Sr., "had long since come to regard the newspaper as second only to the church and the school in importance."

Day in and day out, the city's two dozen daily papers helped New Yorkers—all 4 million of them—make sense of their often topsy-turvy surroundings. Every day readers picked up a paper—or two or three—and found their confusing and tumultuous urban world captured and distilled into neat and orderly columns spread out over eight to twenty pages. Moreover, the dailies organized it all into familiar and reassuring categories—politics, entertainment, fashion, sports, business, society, and local, national, and world news. Even as they related the details of the latest political scandal, murder, crime, or tragedy, the city's dailies provided New Yorkers with a reassurance that beneath all the chaos there was some order.

Tuesday, June 14, was no exception. As Green waded through the crowded sidewalks of Newspaper Row that morning, the fruits of his trade were everywhere on display. Every few feet groups of newsboys stood amid stacks of papers shouting out their names—"Get your *Herald* here!"—and announcing headlines to stories they hoped would entice buyers—"Poison Found in Popular Candies!" (*World*); "Legless Man Hired Cab to Go Begging" (*World*); "Ill Lion Attacks Physician" (*Herald*); "Automobile Held Up by Highwaymen" (*Herald*); "Nan Patterson Indicted for Murder of Young" (*Times*).

The latter story was the latest installment in what promised to be a major scandal. Nan Patterson, a Floradora showgirl, had been arrested several weeks earlier and charged with the murder of her lover, Caesar Young. A ne'er-do-well gambler and carouser who operated behind a veneer of respectability, Young was about to leave on a European vacation with his wife when he was found shot dead in a hansom cab. Patterson claimed he had committed suicide, but the police believed she shot him after he tried to break off their affair. It was a classic scandal story, one that Green and his fellow editors relied on to sell papers. With any luck this one would last through the summer doldrums into the fall and be capped by a sensational trial.

Martin Green read many of these headlines and no doubt many of the stories on his commute to Newspaper Row. Good newsmen, and he was widely considered one of the city's best, read all the papers to find new stories and keep abreast of the competition. But as a reporter for Pulitzer's *World*, he did so with an air of confidence that came from knowing that he worked for the city's leading paper. That morning's edition proudly proclaimed its supremacy in the exceedingly competitive newspaper business. The paper, its editors announced, sold an average of 556,304 papers every day, a circulation "much larger than that of any other daily morning newspaper in the United States." And lest any reader be swayed by the notoriously inflated claims of their rivals, they noted that the *World*'s numbers reflected the number of papers actually sold. All "returns, unpaid or free copies are deducted from The Morning World's stated city circulation."

Green had certainly come a long way in his thirty-three years. Born in Burlington, Iowa, in 1870, he managed to get a modest prairie education before dropping out to find work at the age of fifteen. After trying his hand at several jobs, he found success as an insurance agent. But when his company went bust still owing him five thousand dollars, Green took a job as a reporter for the *Burlington Gazette*. Four years later he moved to St. Louis to work for the *Star* and later its rival, the *Republic*. By 1896 his skillful reporting and reputation as an all-round newspaperman had caught the eye of William Randolph Hearst. The publisher offered Green a job at his latest acquisition, the *New York Journal*. Green took it and found New York to his liking. Five years later, in 1901, Green was lured away from the *Journal* by the *World*'s Charles E. Chapin, one of the most feared and respected city editors.

Most reporters detested Chapin. They called him "The Pirate," and he was known far and wide for his cruelty and autocratic manner. He seemed to enjoy humiliating reporters in public, and it was said he often waited until Christmas eve to fire them. Martin Green, however, got along with him just fine—no doubt because he was so good at his trade.

As Green and Chapin knew, the key to success in this city awash in newsprint was not simply to get the facts of a good story. Any idiot with a pencil and pad could do that, Chapin reminded his men every day. It was essential to be first, to get what Green and his fellow scribes called *the scoop*. Being the first to break a story about a new scandal, crime, or disaster was what pushed tomorrow's circulation figures higher than today's. It's what allowed for higher advertising rates and, who knew, maybe higher wages for reporters and editors.

For veteran newspapermen like Green, there was still one more level above the scoop. It easily surpassed the steady stream of sex, scandal, and sensation that fueled their industry, even if they did get the occasional scoop. It was the *big one*, the kind of story that stopped the city of perpetual motion in its tracks, if only temporarily. Such stories came along once every two years or so. Back in 1902 it was the New York Central Railroad tunnel cave-in that claimed the lives of fifteen men and injured scores more. Two years before that the city devoured edition after edition that told the horrific details of the great Hoboken pier fire in which nearly 400 workers and passengers on four steamships burned to death or drowned.

Green knew of even greater calamities from his days in St. Louis. Just before he left to join Hearst in New York, he experienced a big one the likes of which he doubted he'd ever see again. On May 27, 1896, a massive tornado struck St. Louis with winds in excess of 250 miles per hour. Hundreds of buildings, including the offices of Green's *Journal*, were destroyed and 255 people killed in what remains one of the most devastating tornados in U.S. history. Despite the loss of their office, Green and his colleagues still managed to generate small editions of the paper. "The rays of the rising sun disclosed to the view of the citizens of St. Louis yesterday morning scenes of desolation and woe unparalleled in the history of the city," read the lead story on May 29, "marking the path of the most extraordinary and destructive tornado of modern times." In the days that followed, Green churned out what in recent times has come to be called an "instant book" about the tragedy: *The Great Tornado at St. Louis, on the Evening of May 27th, 1896. A Story of Terror, Ruin and Desolation. Illustrated by 65 Photos Taken on the Morning after the Storm.* "Bruised and torn and bleeding," the book began, "staggering from the force of the blow, but still reliant and confident in her own strength, St. Louis to-day is . . . a beautiful picture even in her misery and pain." There are no records to indicate how many copies of the book were sold, but it may very well have been what caught the eye of Hearst and prompted him to bring Green to New York a few months later.

Most newsworthy calamities, from great fires to presidential assassinations, did not knock out newspaper offices as in the case of St. Louis.

Speed therefore was of the utmost when it came to reporting such stories. The first journalist on the scene of a scandal or calamity would be the first to get the story and pictures back to the newsroom, where the paper's army of workers could magically produce an "extra" in less than an hour. And as updates and new information came in, additional "extras" hit the streets until the editor deemed the story exhausted—at least until the morning when it might begin all over again.

Green knew, of course, that events such as these came without warning and at uneven intervals. There was no preparing for them, except to begin each day ready to engage should the opportunity arise. So as he approached the entrance to the great temple of Joseph Pulitzer that morning, he asked himself the familiar questions of great city editors: What stories would today bring? Would there be any big ones? Would his team of journalists get there first?

THE SHEPHERD

McClellan and Green, by virtue of their occupations, were constantly forced to see their city in all its vastness. The former was charged with governing the Empire City, the latter with telling its story. Most New Yorkers, however, lived in smaller worlds within the great metropolis. The familiar faces, family ties, and traditions found in neighborhoods provided them with an intimacy and stability that was alien to the wider urban society. They might venture out into the general chaos of the city each day, but always with the consoling knowledge that they were never very far away from their more manageable piece of it.

Reverend George Haas understood this reality more than most. As a prominent minister and several times president of the New York Ministerium of the Lutheran Church, his work frequently required him to travel to many parts of the city on official business. But his life was fundamentally grounded in his parish, St. Mark's Evangelical Lutheran Church on East Sixth Street in the Lower East Side neighborhood of Little Germany. As of 1904 he'd spent nearly half his life there and had come to love the neighborhood and its people, especially the members of his congregation.

Haas's congregation had in turn developed a deep respect and affection for him. They loved him for his gentle manner and congeniality. They valued him for his ceaseless energy and dedication to his parish. They revered him for his piety and sincerity. They marveled at his sharp mind and scholarly demeanor and wondered how they'd gotten so lucky. They loved their pastor for these reasons and still one more: he was a constant, a firm rock, a fixed point in an ever-changing urban world. For twenty-two years he'd served as pastor of St. Mark's and at age fifty showed no signs of slowing down—or worse, moving on to greener pastures.

Haas was born on May 5, 1854, in Philadelphia. His parents, John and Anna Haas, had emigrated from Germany during the great wave of German immigration in the 1830s and 1840s. John Haas was a music teacher by profession and managed to provide a modest yet comfortable home for his wife, three children, and his elderly mother. The Haases' Lutheran faith suffused their household and sustained them in their struggle to succeed in their adoptive America. It left a deep impression on the Haas children, as all three eventually found their home in the church. Young George, an eager and accomplished student, gained admission to the University of Pennsylvania in 1872 where he studied with an eye toward the Lutheran ministry. His younger brother John later followed in his footsteps, while Emma studied music and became a church organist.

Upon receiving his B.A. in 1876, George entered the Philadelphia Theological Seminary and graduated in 1880. The newly minted twenty-six-year-old minister came highly recommended and was hired right out of school to serve as an assistant to the Reverend Hermann Raegener, pastor at St. Mark's Evangelical Lutheran Church in New York City. It was a prestigious position and a measure of how impressive Haas was to those who met him, as St. Mark's was a major church in America's largest German neighborhood, known as *Kleindeutschland,* or Little Germany.

New York's Little Germany had its origins in the German emigration stampede that began in the 1830s. More than 10,000 Germans arrived in America in 1832 and nearly 25,000 in 1837. Still more came in the 1840s and 1850s, with more than half a million landing on the shores of America between 1852 and 1854 alone.

As more than one and a half million German immigrants poured into the United States in the 1840s and 1850s, some followed their dream to become landowners and farmers and headed for the agricultural frontier. Hundreds of thousands more flocked to cities like New York, Buffalo, Baltimore, Cincinnati, St. Louis, Chicago, Milwaukee, and New Orleans to ply their trades as tailors, cabinetmakers, stonemasons, brewers, and cobblers. Like the Irish who came in even greater numbers in this period, they clustered into ethnic enclaves by the thousands, seeking cultural refuge from the strange new world they had entered.

As early as 1840, New York emerged as the most German city in America, with a total German population rivaled only by Berlin and Vienna. The majority of these immigrants settled in a section on Manhattan's Lower East Side that came to be called Little Germany, or what the residents themselves called *Kleindeutschland*. By 1860 this neighborhood, comprised of the city's tenth, eleventh, thirteenth, and seventeenth wards, was home to half of the city's 120,000 Germans.

Like most immigrants, these Germans arrived with lots of ambition but little money. Thus Little Germany became not simply an ethnic enclave, but also a crowded slum with all its related problems. Tenements had no running water, and outdoor "privies" were the only means of disposing of human waste. That in combination with filth-ridden streets and poor diets provided breeding grounds for every form of deadly disease from cholera to tuberculosis. Added to these miseries were high rates of crime and violence. But as poor immigrants, the residents of Little Germany had no alternative but to live in such conditions.

Still, there were hopeful signs, especially when compared to the other major immigrant group arriving in the antebellum period, the Irish. Although German immigrants were poorer than their American-born counterparts, they arrived on the shores of America in far better financial shape than the Irish. In part this had more to do with the desperate condition of so many Irish famine refugees in the 1840s and early 1850s than with German prosperity. In any case, most Germans arrived with the two things that distinguished them from the Irish: capital and skills. This meant that many Germans found better housing and began earning decent livings in the skilled trades soon after arrival. By 1855 more than half the city's bakers, cabinetmakers, locksmiths, shoemakers, and tailors had been born in Germany. In contrast, only 9 percent of the city's unskilled and poorly paid laborers were German-born, compared with an astounding 86 percent Irish-born. Poverty figures provided an equally stark comparison—82 percent of immigrants admitted to the city almshouse were born in Ireland versus only 7 percent born in Germany.

With each passing year the German population rose still higher. In 1871, the year the German empire was established, New York's Little Germany would have been its fifth-largest city. Likewise it would have been America's fourth-largest city—bigger than Detroit and Milwaukee combined. This despite the fact that Little Germany constituted only half the city's German population.

Visitors to the area were stunned not only by the enclave's overcrowding and poverty, but also by how thoroughly German—and therefore utterly un-American—it appeared. Little Germany, wrote one observer in the 1850s, "has very little in common with the other parts of New York." He continued:

> Life in Kleindeutschland is almost the same as in the Old
> Country. . . . There is not a single business which is not run by
> Germans. Not only the shoemakers, tailors, barbers, physicians,
> grocers, and innkeepers are German, but the pastors and priests as
> well. There is even a German lending library where one can get all
> kinds of German books. The resident of Kleindeutschland need not
> even know English in order to make a living, which is a considerable
> attraction to the immigrant.

It was in this setting that St. Mark's was established in late 1847. Its first pastor, Rev. August H. M. Held, rented a new but unoccupied church building on East Sixth Street beginning in the summer of 1848. The congregation grew steadily in number, with Held baptizing 525 babies and marrying 300 couples in 1858 alone. The parish also opened a school and established a burial ground out in Queens. In 1857, as a sign of increased numbers and the rising prosperity of the German community, the congregation purchased the church for eight thousand dollars, making the last mortgage payment fourteen years later in 1871. In that same year, Rev. Hermann Raegener took over for Reverend Held. Under his leadership, St. Mark's grew to become one of the leading churches in Little Germany.

By 1880, with Raegener's health beginning to wane, the congregation agreed to hire Haas as its first assistant pastor. Haas adapted well to his new surroundings and responsibilities. At first he boarded at the house of Reverend Raegener and family at 110 East Seventh Street. But in 1882, only two years after his arrival and still rather young at twenty-eight years old, Haas was named pastor of St. Mark's. The promotion, and his subsequent marriage to Anna Hansen, an immigrant from Holland, prompted him to move one block east to 64 East Seventh Street. Eventually they were joined by Anna's mother, Elizabeth Hansen, and George's sister, Emma, an organist at St. Mark's. George and Anna had two children: George, born in 1888, and Gertrude, born in 1892.

Even before the arrival of Haas, St. Mark's had become far more than a mere gathering place for weekly religious services. Like most mid-nineteenth-century churches of all denominations, especially those servicing poor immigrant communities, St. Mark's developed into an all-purpose provider of programs and services for its members.

As pastor, Haas continued this effort and expanded it, a job made easier by the growing prosperity of Little Germany's residents. By the 1890s, St. Mark's was sponsoring religious societies like the Luther League, choral groups, Bible study classes for adults, and Sunday school for the children. The church also sponsored the Young Men's Beneficiary Association, commonly known as a "burial society," which collected monthly fees and provided members with death benefits and covered funeral expenses. The Ladies Aid Society, first established in 1868, raised money for the poor of the church and local community. The church's outreach efforts became so vast and multifaceted, it eventually established a newsletter called the *St. Mark's Monthly* to keep members apprised. Through it all, St. Mark's never lost sight of its religious mission. By the turn of the century it had been the scene of some 20,000 baptisms, 9,500 marriages, and 4,000 confirmations.

The congregation's rising prosperity also enabled it to upgrade their humble edifice. By the mid-1890s they'd raised $5,000 to add a council room to the church and install memorial windows, $2,500 to purchase an uptown church on East 71st Street in Yorkville, $22,000 for a parsonage, and $5,000 for a new organ. By the time of its jubilee celebration in 1897, St. Mark's was no longer a poor immigrant congregation, but rather a well-established German-American one. That it was more properly considered German-American rather than German was made clear in a telling decision in 1893 to offer services in English on Sunday evenings.

It was through this combined ministration to the spiritual, emotional, social, and practical needs of its members that Haas made St. Mark's a central fixture in the lives of his congregation. It bound people together through culture, faith, and experience and helped them negotiate the difficult adjustment from Old World to New and to withstand the stresses and strains of fast-paced urban life.

But the very prosperity that enabled St. Mark's to flourish financially and to offer more and more services to its congregation ultimately hurt the parish. Simply put, despite the emotional and cultural ties people had to Little Germany and St. Mark's, the lure of a better life uptown or in Brooklyn, one with steam heat and elevators, not to mention good schools and safer, cleaner streets, and shortened commutes, beckoned ceaselessly. It was a force akin to the one that had compelled them or their parents to leave Germany for the United States years earlier and involved a similar, bitter choice between leaving the familiar and traditional for the new and more comfortable. For many German families the choice was made easier by the fact that the emerging neighborhood of Yorkville on Manhattan's Upper East Side was nearly as German in character as Little Germany. The exodus of families that became noticeable in the 1880s quickened in the 1890s and showed no signs of abatement in 1904.

George Haas proved the ideal pastor for a church undergoing this slow hemorrhage of its membership in the midst of a disintegrating larger German enclave. He possessed all the administrative, spiritual, and oratorical skills necessary to sustain his parish in these difficult times. Yet the greatest thing he provided his people amid all this change was a vivid symbol of stability. Hass had arrived in 1880, at precisely the moment the exodus from Little Germany began; twenty-four years later he was still there. In fact, Haas had barely moved at all in his tenure at St. Mark's. His only two addresses since he moved to New York, 110 East Seventh Street and 64 East Seventh Street, were separated by less than a thousand yards. His sole place of work, St. Mark's, was but one block away at 323 East Sixth Street.

Haas's devotion and loyalty to his parish was not for lack of options. In fact, his reputation as a scholar, administrator, and eloquent homilist had brought him a constant flow of offers of higher salary and lighter duties from uptown churches, not to mention letters from seminaries and colleges seeking a professor of German and theology. Just days earlier, Haas had been offered a position on the faculty at Wagner College on Staten Island. But to this and many other offers Hass gave the same reply. No, thanks—he was quite happy just where he was. A dutiful shepherd, he refused to abandon his flock—at least until it abandoned him first. And who knew? There was always the possibility that German immigration might pick up once again, filling the old neighborhood and its churches with a new generation of German residents in need of experienced leadership and guidance. Reverend George C. F. Haas, it seemed, would stay so long as he was needed.

That Haas felt at home and content in his small ethnic parish was due not merely to his even temperament and strong faith. There was another, larger factor at work. For Americans of German ancestry had, by 1904, finally come to feel at home in America. For evidence, one needed only look to an event held the previous day.

Monday, June 13, had seen the streets of Little Germany filled with thousands of spectators on hand to observe the annual Schuetzen Bund parade. The Schuetzen Bund was a German-American shooting club that originated in Germany. In America it served as both a fraternal society and a club for shooting enthusiasts. They held local shooting contests (*schuetzenfests*) and social events throughout the year and frequently marched in Fourth of July parades and the like. But once a year in June the Schuetzen Bund held a weeklong national *schuetzenfest* that attracted marksmen from Schuetzen Bunds all over the nation. The actual shooting contests took place in Schuetzen Park in Union, New Jersey, but the grand parade was held in New York.

This year's Schuetzen Bund parade and *scheutzenfest* were certainly the most impressive yet. Some three thousand marksmen "in their many brilliant uniforms," according to one press account, marched in the parade from St. Mark's Place, through the streets in and around Little Germany, to Union Square. At their head was a force of mounted trumpeters and kettle drummers in traditional German costumes. It wasn't nearly as large an exhibition of ethnic pride as the annual St. Patrick's Day parade, but it nonetheless commanded the attention and respect of many New Yorkers beyond Little Germany, including Mayor McClellan, who sat on the reviewing stand at Union Square. Baron Speck von Sternburg, the German ambassador, was due to arrive on Thursday to observe the shooting contest for the grand prize.

That thousands of German immigrants and German-Americans could parade through the streets of New York bearing rifles and draw only crowds of admirers—including the mayor—indicated just how far Reverend Haas and his fellow Germans had come in America. Not many years earlier such displays of martial prowess and ethnic chauvinism would have been cause for alarm, for native-born Americans had long regarded Germans, as they did all immigrant groups, with suspicion and fear. Germans were denounced for, among other things, their refusal to learn English, their fondness for beer, and their devotion to socialism. But in 1904, Americans of German heritage enjoyed a rising tide of pro-German sentiment that seemed to portend the final eradication of centuries of anti-German prejudice.

Indeed, turn-of-the-century America was nothing short of infatuated with German culture. Most American colleges mandated the study of the German language, the literary works of Goethe, and the philosophical treatises of Kant, while orchestras across the country provided season after season of programs devoted to Beethoven, Brahms, Handel, Mozart, and Strauss. Upper-crust Americans were especially taken with the works of Wagner. The staging of his *Parsifal* at the Metropolitan Opera House in January 1904 brought sellout crowds and effusive praise from reviewers. "It is in every way," wrote the *Times*'s reviewer, "the most remarkable production that has ever been made upon the lyric stage in this country."

Having been born in 1854, the year of the anti-immigrant Know-Nothing insurgency, Reverend Haas was particularly aware of how far he and his fellow Germans had come in America. They had been coming to the shores of America for centuries, but now they could say they finally had *arrived*. After decades of struggle and uncertainty, they now enjoyed both prosperity and respect. Americans had come not just to tolerate German culture but to revere it. Nothing, it seemed, absolutely nothing, could set them back.

THE PROGRAM

Despite the pressures to leave Little Germany, the pull of the old neighborhood, especially St. Mark's, remained strong. Many former residents who'd moved to Brooklyn, Yorkville, or New Jersey jumped at every opportunity to come back, whether for a wedding, the *scheutzenfest*, or some other special occasion.

Without question, by 1904 one event loomed above all others as the single best excuse for returning to St. Mark's—the annual excursion held to celebrate the completion of the Sunday school year. Reverend Haas had originated the idea back in 1888 when he was still relatively new to his job as pastor. Like so many of his innovations, the idea of celebrating the close of the Sunday school year with a daylong outing proved immensely popular with his parishioners. At first the event was little more than a large picnic in a nearby park. But over time it developed into a substantial affair involving a chartered steamboat and an entire day at a recreation ground along the banks of Long Island or the Hudson River. As the excursion evolved from an innovation to a beloved tradition, it became for many participants a kind of annual celebration of St. Mark's and its resiliency over the decades. Not surprisingly, given the number of people who moved away each year, it also became a kind of annual reunion of St. Mark's families past and present.

This year's excursion—the seventeenth annual—would be the biggest ever. Mary Abendschein had seen to that. Like many an unmarried woman in her mid-thirties, Mary spent much of her free time involved in church activities. Back in early 1904 she'd been named chairwoman of the excursion committee, and she'd spent the better part of five months working tirelessly to ensure yet another successful event.

Apart from handling all manner of small details, Mary's ultimate responsibility was fundraising. Even if they sold every available seat on the steamboat, the revenue would not come close to covering all the expenses. So it fell to Mary to raise several hundred dollars in donations from local businesses to cover the difference between ticket receipts and the total cost of the excursion. To encourage donations, she produced a handsome program for the event that included the day's schedule of events and pages of advertisements from sponsoring businesses.

Some proprietors no doubt saw the opportunity to advertise in the excursion program as a way to reach potential customers. For most, however, it was an expression of support and thanks to St. Mark's and its pastor, Reverend Haas. In many ways it was a recognition of the fact that they shared a common destiny. So long as St. Mark's persisted, their shops and offices would continue to have customers and clients.

So beginning in April, as the weather began to warm up, Mary began her canvass of Little Germany. It was considerably smaller in 1904 compared to its heyday in the 1880s when Reverend Haas first arrived. A neighborhood that had once stretched from Division Street north to 14th Street and from the Bowery to the East River—an area of some four hundred blocks—had shrunk to a one-hundred-block area north-south from Houston to 14th Streets and east of Second Avenue to the East River. From a population high of 60,000 Germans in 1880, Little Germany now held fewer than 12,000. Crowding in on all sides were the newest immigrants, mainly Italians and Eastern European Jews.

This, of course, made Mary's job easier in that she had less ground to cover. More important, she had several things going for her when she approached each merchant. Unlike a typical door-to-door solicitor, most of them knew her from the neighborhood or church. Certainly they all knew Reverend Haas, the man whose parish she represented. Soliciting sponsors for the annual trip would be, in effect, a referendum on his leadership, and the results surprised no one.

In the weeks leading up to the actual outing, the indefatigable Mary Abendschein made the rounds, first securing commitments, then verifying ad copy, and finally collecting payment and going over final page proofs. By early June it was abundantly clear that her efforts had not been in vain. The program was the biggest yet, running twenty pages and including more than one hundred ads from saloon owner Peter J. Fickbohm at 91 Avenue D, to undertaker Philip Wagner on Second Avenue, to delicatessen owner Eugene Ansel of 103 East Fourth Street. Countless more businesses, unable to afford an ad in the program, did their part by purchasing tickets that they planned to hand out to favored customers, or perhaps to a family in the neighborhood unable to afford the cost.

By June 14, the seventeenth annual St. Mark's excursion was now fully planned and fully funded. The picnic grounds of Locust Grove on Long Island Sound were reserved as well as the "commodious steamer," according to the program, *General Slocum*, chartered at a cost of $350. Professor George Maurer and his band had been hired and a program of German and American favorites agreed upon. All the necessary supplies of food and drink had been ordered and volunteers found to deliver them to the steamer the evening before the event. Two off-duty New York City policemen had been hired to accompany the throng to ensure everyone's safety.

Only one worry remained. What if it rained? That would be a disaster.

ESCAPE

Mary Abendschein's success in selling ads and more than fifteen hundred tickets for the St. Mark's excursion reflected not only the devotion of the congregants to their parish, but also their desire to get away. For as long as anyone could remember, New Yorkers were of two minds when it came to their city. On the one hand, they loved it as a place of splendor, wonder, and optimism. Immigrants thousands of miles away heard its siren call and sacrificed everything to get there. Entrepreneurs came from the hinterland and abroad to tap into its phenomenal business opportunities. Entertainers flocked to its stages with the understanding that success in New York meant fame and fortune. Still others were attracted by its fast pace, openness, and cosmopolitan culture. New York left such an impression on its residents that many could hardly imagine living anywhere else.

Yet those very same qualities that made the city so appealing also had the power to repulse on occasion. The incessant competition, from the struggle for customers in the marketplace to the fight to secure a seat on the trolley, left them weary. So too did the pollution, the noise, the jostle. Above all, there was the rapid pace of life. Everything in the city seemed to move faster in 1904, and not just those things propelled by steam. The trade-mark rapid-fire conversational style of New Yorkers, noted by visitors as early as the mid–eighteenth century, got faster. It also covered more ground thanks to the rapid spread of the telephone. "Telephone before making sales calls," advised an advertisement in that morning's issue of the *Sun*. "You may save an hour or a half day. You know the value of your time."

The hurried pace of Gotham's pedestrians likewise sped up, facilitated by newly paved streets and stone sidewalks. So too did popular music, es-pecially the type called "ragtime" that shocked the prim and proper with its rollicking animal beat and racy words. Recreation increased in velocity as an ever-growing number of enthusiasts took to bicycles and competed with evening strollers for the pathways in parks. Even the use of tobacco sped up with the growing popularity of the cigarette. At the turn of the cen-tury, while the rest of the nation stuck to their cigars, snuff, and plug to-bacco, New Yorkers consumed upward of a quarter of all the "coffin nails" sold in America. Soon, an article that morning in the *Globe and Commer-cial Advertiser* predicted, voting would be sped up. A new voting machine recently perfected promised to "usher in an era of quick voting when re-sults of elections will be known at once instead of sometimes days after-ward."

This high-speed lifestyle of turn-of-the-century New York was most noticeable to the newcomer. "One must keep moving," wrote one shocked Hungarian visitor, "rest is not understood. . . . The impulses toward mo-tion govern every one; so much so that if they sit down their chairs must have rockers." For the countless new immigrants then settling in the city, the speed of modern life was not a mere curiosity, but a new reality they had to adjust to if they hoped to succeed. "I came to understand that it was not the land of fun," remembered Michael Gold of his immigrant upbringing in turn-of-the-century New York. "It was a Land of Hurry-Up."

This accelerated way of life carried a price, of course. Nervous debility, or what doctors and pseudodoctors of that era called *neurasthenia* and those in our era call chronic fatigue syndrome, had emerged in recent years as an epidemic born of the modern lifestyle raised to such extremes in Gotham. As the rhythms of industrial life grew faster and more frenetic at the turn of the century, more and more men and women complained of insomnia, nervousness, and exhaustion. How could this be? many asked. The people most prone to the affliction worked at desks, not plows—why, then, were they so exhausted? Not surprisingly, it had been a New York physician named Dr. George M. Beard who coined the term and pioneered in its study. Still, neither he nor his colleagues had a true medical explanation for such symptoms and certainly no cure beyond changes in diet and extra rest. Men like Theodore Roosevelt attributed it to a lack of vitality on the part of a generation grown soft and urged men to pursue the "strenuous life," a lifestyle that included retreats from the office and urban environment to the restorative challenges of hiking, camping, and climbing.

So no matter how infatuated with their city, virtually every New Yorker in June 1904 entertained thoughts of escape from the crowded spaces, jarring commutes, and above all, the stifling summer heat. It set in during the first weeks of June, rose to dreadful, deadly heights in July and August, then slowly began to recede through September. There was no escaping it. The heat radiated from the hard dusty ground and off the faces of buildings, making even shady spots unbearable. Horses dropped dead in their harnesses and corseted women fainted on the sidewalks. In the tenement districts, where the heat mixed with the putrid smells of overflowing privies and filthy streets, the effect was beyond description.

Nightfall brought only limited relief, especially during the breathless days of a heat wave. "It is quite the thing in the evenings," wrote one observer in 1901, "when the stored up heat of the day begins to ooze out of the brick walls and mushy asphalt to take the wife and family from the crowded stoop to the pier. There one escapes the sullen discomfort of reflected heat, but not the crowd." When they returned to their tenements later in the night, tens of thousands pulled mattresses onto rooftops and fire escapes in the hope of finding some relief, and every year dozens died from falls.

Electric fans were a luxury enjoyed only by the rich. The same was true of ice, though charity organizations occasionally distributed it for free during heat waves. Air-conditioning, despite the recent success two years earlier by an enterprising Brooklyn engineer named Willis Haviland Carrier in designing an "apparatus for treating air," was still a long way off.

For the first three centuries of settlement in New York, most city residents had few options for dealing with the heat. The very rich, of course, enjoyed the country air while reclining in their summer homes in upper Manhattan or out on Long Island. The rest stayed behind, lacking the money, time, and means to get away. But by the end of the nineteenth century, with the emergence of a large middle class, not to mention new modes of transit and a new ethos of leisure time, far greater numbers of New Yorkers looked forward to escaping what one writer called "the seething, sweating city" for at least part of the summer.

Increased leisure time was becoming the norm at the turn of the century for Americans of all classes. The wealthy enjoyed extended stays at resorts and spas on both sides of the Atlantic, not to mention cruises aboard luxury liners. For middle-class Americans, choices were more modest—a week's vacation, perhaps even two, to the mountains, the country, or the seashore. That summer vacations had become mainstream was indicated by the explosion of ads for renting houses by the shore and hotels on the lake in the newspapers starting in early May. Nearly all the editions for Sunday, June 12, had special sections devoted to vacation options. "Wood, Stream and Field Invite the Summer Guest," read the section's headline in the *New York Times*, "Vacation Crowds Have Already Begun to Throng Resort Hotels and a Brilliant Season is in Prospect." Page after page spread before New Yorkers a thousand choices. There were lakeside cabins in the Catskills, resort hotels in the Poconos, campsites in the Adirondacks, and cottages by the Jersey Shore, the latter being the choice of Mayor McClellan. All promised plenty of fresh, cool air and activities galore from fishing and boating to tennis and dancing. "The number of summer resorts that seek the patronage of New Yorkers," observed one guidebook, "is legion."

Some curmudgeonous types like financial titan Russell Sage decried the increased popularity of vacations. "During the eighty-eight years of my career," asserted the crusty octogenarian in "The Injustice of Vacations," which appeared in the June issue of *The Independent*, "I have not once taken a vacation." He went on to decry the practice as an unjustified and expensive inconvenience to employers.

But Sage represented a fast-disappearing sentiment. At the turn of the century the annual vacation—some as long as *two whole weeks*—had become a standard feature of middle-class life. It indicated not merely one's economic status but also one's values. In the age of Roosevelt, vacations were necessary departures from the "effeminizing" tendencies of modern life, a chance to reconnect with nature and family in a healthful, vigorous setting. "Nowadays the grownup is no less cognizant of the importance of a period each year devoted to recreation and amusement," asserted one writer, "when business cares may be forgot, and the glories of wood and stream and field enjoyed to the utmost." Even the city's hard-nosed financial newspaper, the *Globe and Commercial Advertiser*, was moved to mock Sage's extreme stance on vacations. That morning it ran a large cartoon, "Russell Sage's Idea of a Joyous and Rollicking Vacation," depicting a young clerk chained to his desk on a hot summer's day working his way through a massive stack of papers labeled "WORK."

For working-class New Yorkers, their choice to take a vacation or not was dictated by financial, not philosophical, considerations. Most lacked the money and job security to hope for any more than a few day trips to the shore during the hot summer months. A vacation properly understood was simply out of the question. For them the coming of the summer months meant endless days and nights of stifling heat with little or no opportunity for escape. Certainly some families would manage to get a day, perhaps two, at a nearby beach. They might also enjoy a few picnics in the park. Some of the more adventurous poor, those who possessed time but not money, headed for Rockaway Beach to live by the shore in rented tents costing as little as $4.75 a week. "Just as soon as the thermometer begins to climb upward," observed the *Times* in early June, "whole families migrate there from Harlem flats and from cities which are never swept by sea breezes." But most remained trapped in the city, trying to make do while dreaming of October.

In recent years their plight had gained the attention of Progressive Era reformers who decried the lack of recreational space in the slums. On the Lower East Side, where the population density of more than 250,000 people per square mile was greater than anywhere else on earth, there were only a handful of small parks. Back in 1811, when a group of forward-thinking merchants and lawyers had devised Manhattan's legendary street grid as a way to promote rapid, orderly urban growth and commercial development, they set aside less than 1 percent of the island's land for parks. "It may, to many, be a matter of surprise," wrote the planners in anticipation of some criticism, "that so few vacant spaces have been left . . . for the benefit of fresh air, and consequent preservation of health." There was no need to, they explained, for "those two large arms of the sea which embrace Manhattan Island [i.e., the Hudson and East Rivers] render its situation, in regard to health and pleasure . . . peculiarly felicitous." Clearly they had misjudged the degree to which the commerce they wished to unleash would utterly dominate and befoul the rivers and their banks.

So in 1904, most children simply took to the streets and back alleys for play—often far from the moral supervision of parents, teachers, and clergy. Some of the more adventurous boys swam off the piers along the East River, seemingly unaware of either the filth in the water or the danger posed by boats and currents.

To counter this problem, reformers pushed the city government to build new public parks in working-class neighborhoods. One such park, Seward Park, had just opened on the Lower East Side at Essex Street and East Broadway. It stood as a monument to Progressive Era ideals, for it required the city to seize the land by eminent domain and demolish dozens of privately owned tenements to make way for the park.

Reformers also led successful campaigns to build public swimming pools—actually floating barges fitted out as pools—along the Hudson and East River waterfronts. Demand was so high—some 6 million swims were counted in 1903—that children were only allowed to swim in fifteen-minute shifts, but some relief was better than none at all. In the winter of 1904, Mayor McClellan signed a bill authorizing construction of ten new "floating baths" for deployment, and in June the first six were nearing completion.

One place that drew growing numbers of New York's working class was Coney Island. First established as a seaside entertainment spot for the upper class in the 1860s, it gradually came to cater to the multitudes. By the 1880s, Coney Island was drawing thousands of visitors to its hotels, beaches, restaurants, amusements, and outdoor concerts. Located in Brooklyn just eight and a half miles from the southern tip of Manhattan, Coney Island was easy to reach by some combination of streetcar, elevated train, and ferry. By the 1890s, writers commented on the astonishing scenes on weekends when tens of thousands descended upon the place to find relief from the unrelenting heat and din of the city. It is, wrote one admirer in 1896, "our homeopathic sanitarium, our sun-bath and ice-box combined, our extra lung, our private, gigantic fan."

The rise of Coney Island was not greeted by everyone with such glee. For it was a well-known fact that much of the activity there was decidedly immoral. Dozens of saloons along the waterfront and on side streets slaked the thirsts of working-class men, while nearby an equal number of brothels and gambling houses catered to other needs and wants. This aspect of Coney reflected the attitude of the ruthless local chieftain who dominated it, John Y. McKane. What struck many observers as especially outrageous was the fact that such activity went on in broad daylight without the slightest attempt to conceal it. "Coney Island, our popular summer resort, has been a suburb of Sodom," railed Rev. A. C. Dixon. "Indeed, Sodom bore no comparison to this place for vileness." To critics like Dixon, McKane offered no apology. "This ain't no Sunday school," he once quipped.

In 1895, after McKane was packed off to jail for election fraud, Coney Island passed into the hands of a new generation of entertainment entrepreneurs. They looked at Coney Island and envisioned something even larger. They would take Coney's original concept of seaside escape and expand it beyond anyone's comprehension. If tens of thousands came on a typical summer day, why not hundreds of thousands? If the public craved amusement, why not build them an entire city of rides, sights, fantasies, and exhibitions? Indeed, why not build several of these cities?

The one impediment to this vision was Coney Island's unsavory reputation. So long as drinking, whoring, and gambling remained at the top of the list of amusements at Coney Island, untold numbers of people—and their money—would stay away. Simply put, they recognized, in the words of one contemporary, that "vice does not pay as well as decency." Coney Island was thus reformed. By the turn of the century one could still find a shot of whiskey, a hooker, and a game of faro at Coney, but only on the periphery and in places far more discreet.

Most important was not what the new Coney entrepreneurs did away with, but what they built in its place. In 1895, Capt. Paul Boyton constructed Sea Lion Park, the first of several enormous amusement parks at Coney Island. Two years later George Tilyou, a local entrepreneur, opened Steeplechase Park. As these parks and their vast array of rides and amusements drew larger and larger crowds each year, still more visionaries entered the fray. In 1903, Frederic Thompson and Skip Dundy bought out Boyton and transformed his park into the spectacular Luna Park, which opened in May 1904. That same year William H. Reynolds opened his $3 million park, Dreamland, across the street.

Opening night on May 14, 1904, was an event that drew nationwide attention. "There were more dazzling, wriggling, spectacular amusements offered than had ever before been collected together at any one place at any time," gushed one reporter. Luna offered the Trip to the Moon, Twenty Thousand Leagues Under the Sea, and Whirl-the-Whirl, not to mention boxing horses and snake charmers. At Dreamland, a city drenched in a sea of dazzling electric lights, patrons could choose from dozens of attractions, including Dwarf City, home to one thousand midget residents going about their daily lives in shops, schools, firehouses, and farms. If that were not enough, there was the Incubator Building full of tiny premature babies being nursed to health. All this and more for a pocketful of nickels.

Later that evening, as patrons left Luna Park, they were handed copies of the first issue of the park's very own daily paper, the *Evening Star*. It included an interview with Police Commissioner William McAdoo, who pronounced the new and improved Coney Island "clean, moral, and magnificent." Tilyou, Reynolds, Thompson, and Dundy could scarcely have hoped for a more ringing endorsement of their effort to remake Coney into a wholesome entertainment mecca. The next day the *New York Times* confirmed it. "Coney Island is regenerated," read a front-page story, "and almost every trace of Old Coney is wiped out."

Still, Coney's reputation as a "Sodom-by-the-Sea" lingered in 1904, especially among families concerned about the wayward tendencies of youth in an era of plummeting moral standards. They might not be able to shelter their children from the many moral pitfalls of contemporary American life, but they were not about to invite an encounter with a destination described by one outraged reformer as "a place where humanity sheds its civilization and becomes half child, half savage." So when the committee at St. Mark's charged with organizing the seventeenth annual Sunday school outing sat down to discuss their many options, Coney Island was not one of them. Their fellow parishioners could go there on their own—many had—but they would not go with the blessing of the church, its council, or pastor. Not when more refined options, like the many picnic grounds that dotted the shores of Long Island Sound, beckoned.

SAFELY HOME

A t about 5:00 P.M. the mayor pushed his chair away from his desk and stood up. He'd worked all day, with an hour off for his ritual lunch at his specially reserved table at the Hardware lunch club, and still his desk was full of papers related to matters demanding his attention. Nonetheless, it was time to go, for his commute to the cottage at Long Branch would take at least ninety minutes if the ferries were running on schedule. After conferring with his secretary John O'Brien, he left city hall and walked southwest toward the river. It was a beautiful evening and the sight of the ferry—his means of escape from the stress and strain of the job—lifted his spirits. In a few minutes, as the ferry pushed across the Hudson toward the setting sun, he would see the city slowly grow smaller and less overwhelming, if only for twelve hours or so.

The ambitious mayor had a lot on his mind these days, especially the matter of the presidential nomination. When he took office six months earlier, he thought himself wiser and stronger than the man who put him there, Charles Francis Murphy. Over the boss's objections, McClellan ignored Tammany loyalists and instead appointed men of his own choosing to key departments, including the police. He then instructed the latter to begin a major effort to root out graft and corruption—vital sources of Tammany's power.

Initially the mayor's show of independence seemed to have the desired effect. In February, talk of McClellan for president had been commented upon favorably by several major newspapers. In keeping with his gentlemanly bearing, McClellan pooh-poohed such talk and protested that he wasn't the least bit interested. "I have been paying no attention to matters political," he declared, "and have steadfastly declined to discuss politics since I took my present office." Privately, however, he confided to friends that he wanted the nomination badly.

But soon his troubles began. Within a few months of his inauguration he came to realize that he'd greatly underestimated Murphy's strength and resourcefulness. By the early spring, rumors abounded that Murphy, annoyed by McClellan's unwillingness to be bossed on crucial matters such as appointments and by his police commissioner's zealous enforcement of the liquor laws, was considering dumping the mayor at the nearest possible opportunity. The presidential nomination seemed to be slipping from his grip.

To make matters worse, even if McClellan suffered for his resistance to Murphy's demands, he continued to get slammed by the Republican press for being a slave to Murphy's whims. "Whatever pretense of devotion to the public welfare Mr. McClellan may make," went a snippy *Tribune* editorial that morning, "it is evident that he has no courage to resist any demand, however outrageous, that Charles F. Murphy may be disposed to make." Somehow he'd managed to alienate both the machine and the reformers. He couldn't win.

Still, as the young mayor stood on the ferry that evening, there was room for a shred of optimism. In the days before political conventions were slick, prepackaged coronation spectacles, they occasionally produced unexpected nominees. McClellan could still hope he might emerge as a "dark horse" candidate. Only a week and a half earlier the *Times* carried an encouraging article about a meeting in the city of high-ranking Democrats who opposed the nomination of the front-runner, Judge Alton B. Parker of upstate New York. "Say Guffy Is Out For McClellan Now," blared the front-page headline, referring to Democratic national chairman James M. Guffy of Pennsylvania. And just that very morning the *Sun* carried an encouraging story of continued interest in a McClellan-for-president boon. "The undercurrent of sentiment in favor of Mayor George B. McClellan of New York," one Indiana delegate was quoted as saying, "is becoming perceptively stronger."

McClellan clung to this thin possibility as the ferry put more and more distance between him and his city hall prison. But in his heart of hearts he feared it was too late. He was trapped in a job he did not want, held captive by a man he detested. No amount of tranquillity at his Long Branch cottage on the Jersey Shore could offset the disturbing thought that dominated his mind: the man who would be president was going nowhere.

An hour or so later, after McClellan landed in New Jersey, a shrill blast from a steam horn on the *General Slocum* announced that it was time to head home. As soon as its cargo of a thousand exhausted and sunburned revelers was aboard, Capt. William Van Schaick gave the signal and the steamer pulled away from the pier to begin its journey back to Manhattan. The day had gone off without incident, and now all that remained was the fairly routine matter of piloting the boat home safely. It was a journey the captain and his pilots had made more times than they could count and one they could probably accomplish blindfolded. Except for one five-minute portion of the journey: the passage through Hell Gate.

Hell Gate was the narrow, rocky choke point where Long Island Sound met the northern end of the East River. A two-hour differential between the tide in the sound and New York harbor created a massive imbalance of water that resolved itself all day long through Hell Gate. Twice daily the outgoing tide sent water pent up on the sound side exploding through the narrow passage. Twice daily the incoming tide returned the favor. The result was an endless procession of perilous whirlpool churns, riptides, and crosscurrents—features dangerous even on clear days with no wind.

New York had no shortage of colorful and dramatic names for its neighborhoods—The Tenderloin, The Swamp, Millionaire Mile, Hell's Kitchen. But these were suggestive appellations. Hell Gate was between-the-eyes blunt, no interpretation needed. It was one of the most dangerous passes on the East Coast and the graveyard of hundreds of shipwrecks. The most famous was the British frigate *Hussar*. It went down in 1780 carrying an enormous quantity of gold and silver coin intended for the pockets of British officers and soldiers then trying to quell the American rebellion. Divers and salvage teams foolish enough to risk it have been looking for the wreck and its cargo ever since.

Truth be told, Hell Gate had been partly defanged a few decades earlier. Fed up with the never-ending stream of shipwrecks, the city pleaded with Washington for help. The Army Corps of Engineers arrived in 1876 and cleared away tons of jagged rock with a series of spectacular dynamite charges. This made Hell Gate safer, but hardly safe. Or as East River pilots liked to say, it went from suicidal to merely treacherous.

This evening, piloted by experienced hands, the *Slocum* passed through Hell Gate without incident and pressed on toward its destination. For Van Schaick it was just another day in a long and successful career of moving people by steamer from one point to another along coastal waterways. He considered himself the best captain in the business, and his peers surely agreed. Only the year before he'd been honored with an award by the Masters, Mates and Pilots Association for transporting some 30 million passengers without a fatality. In his mind he possessed the three things that mattered most when it came to running a safe steamboat: knowledge, intuition, and experience. No amount of government regulation could replace it.

His employer of the last thirteen seasons, the Knickerbocker Steamboat Company, agreed and paid him well for his services. He was a worthwhile investment, as was the new coat of white paint put on the *Slocum* a few weeks earlier. The company's president, Frank A. Barnaby, was a tight-fisted businessman loath to part with his money. But he recognized that his company sold not merely transportation, but a leisure experience that began with the boat's appearance. The classier it looked, the more bookings and profit he could count on.

Barnaby, as Van Schaick knew only too well, cared far less about the things his customers could not see. In fact, he cared very little for the steamboat business at all, for he considered himself a real estate man first and foremost. The safety regulations regarding passenger steamers as stipulated by the United States Steamboat Inspection Service (USSIS) mandated that specific numbers of life preservers and lifeboats be carried on each boat. They also required that fire hoses and standpipes be placed throughout the boat and that crews be trained and drilled regularly in their use. Pipes connected to the boiler were mandated in all holds so that a blast of steam could be used to extinguish a fire.

Barnaby, like many of his fellow steamboat operators, viewed such regulations as annoying and expensive. What made them costly was not compliance, however, but defiance. Every spring the USSIS would send out inspectors to conduct safety inspections on steamboats, and every year brought the same result. Through incompetence, corruption, or both, inspectors routinely gave a boat a quick once-over and granted a passing grade. Only on the rarest of occasions did they actually test a boat's life preservers and fire hoses. If they indicated an interest in doing so, it usually meant they were angling for a larger bribe to look the other way. But Barnaby's troubles did not end with a ten-dollar bill clasped into the hand of a departing inspector, for many—out of either honesty or an attempt to avoid suspicion—still filed reports indicating violations and recommending fines as high as two thousand dollars. This then necessitated furious lobbying before USSIS officials in Washington to reduce or eliminate the fines. In recent years Barnaby and his competitors succeeded nearly every time.

Veteran captains like Van Schaick resented the annual inspection nearly as much as Barnaby, for it called into question his competence and opened him up to criticism from Barnaby and possible dismissal if any fines were levied. This year's inspection had occurred just five weeks earlier. On the morning of May 5, USSIS inspectors Henry Lundberg and John W. Fleming arrived at the pier, clipboards in hand. Fleming, the assistant inspector of boilers for the New York region, had a very specific task and disappeared into the hold to examine the boiler and engine. Lundberg, on the other hand, was an assistant inspector of hulls, which meant he was charged with examining everything but the boiler and engine, from the condition of the hull to the number of lifeboats. He was the one they watched.

That Lundberg was a novice—only five months on the job and still in his probationary period—was obvious. This might work to Van Schaick's advantage in that his lack of experience—his "training" consisted of following five veteran inspectors on their rounds for three weeks—likely meant that many potential violations would go unnoticed. It might also prove disastrous if Lundberg turned out to be one of those eager reformer-minded crusaders fresh from his civil service exam. Fortunately for Van Schaick, his fears were quickly laid to rest, for Lundberg gave every evidence that he'd been given a thorough old-school training and proved an eager learner. He'd clearly learned that the successful completion of his probationary period and passage to the coveted status of civil service "untouchable" depended not on making trouble, but rather on playing by the unwritten rules of a system of mutual cooperation between the inspector and the inspected.

Lundberg, accompanied by a mate and engineer, look a brief tour of the steamer, pausing here and there to ask a few questions and scribble a few remarks on the USSIS Forms 922 and 923 held tightly in his clipboard. With a stick he poked at the life preservers held in overhead racks, most of them bearing the faded boast "Kahnweiler's Never-Sink Life Preservers," and asked the mate to take a few down for closer inspection. The latter purposely showed him some relatively new life preservers in a transparent charade to gain a passing mark for the remaining twenty-five hundred life preservers on board. Had the inspector actually been looking for violations, it would have been obvious—starting with "Passed June 18, 1891" (the year of the boat's launching) stenciled neatly on their faded canvas coverings—that nearly all of the life preservers on board the *Slocum* were old and very likely defective. Had he handled one of the decrepit things, he surely would have noticed that the once-solid chunks of cork in them had been reduced to useless dust, with the buoyancy of dirt. But Lundberg had been schooled by experienced inspectors in the fine art of looking the other way. With the stroke of his pencil the twenty-five hundred life preservers scattered about the *Slocum* were judged "up to date and of good quality."

Lundberg showed similar skill in assessing the steamer's fire hoses and standpipes. The latter were located in several places throughout the boat's main deck. Neatly coiled above them were fire hoses. Together they gave every appearance that in the event of a fire, the crew could attach the hoses to the standpipes in a matter of seconds. That appearance was all that mattered to Lundberg. He was not at all concerned when his symbolic turning of a few standpipe valves produced no water. That, he was assured, was due to the fact that the boat's pump was not turned on at that moment. He did not ask them to demonstrate the hoses and pumps, for inspectors were paid on the basis of how many inspections they conducted (i.e., one hundred inspections equaled $1,200, five hundred or more equaled $3,000), and wasted time was wasted income. He'd save additional time by ignoring the many lines on the USSIS form painstakingly prepared by some earnest bureaucrat. Where it asked for specific information about the boat's fire hoses, such as length and pressure per square inch, Lundberg simply scrawled "in good condition."

On the *Slocum*'s upper deck, Lundberg again displayed the skill of a USSIS veteran. There he found the steamer's six lifeboats in an utterly unusable state. By all appearances they'd never been moved since the *Slocum* was launched thirteen years earlier. Thick layers of paint had literally glued the boats to their V-shaped chocks on the deck, while wire had been wound through the pulleys on the overhanging davits that were used to launch them in an emergency. No expert eye was needed to see that these boats were more or less permanently attached to the boat. But Lundberg had learned that efficiency, not exactitude, was the mark of a successful USSIS inspector. He dutifully measured each boat, and recorded the information on USSIS Form 923. He also marked all six boats as "swung under davits"—that is, held aloft and ready to be launched at the first sign of danger.

Lastly, Lundberg went belowdecks to inspect the boat's bulkheads and hull—for what, it was not clear, since he had absolutely no knowledge of steamboat design or potential hazards short of an obvious leak or wood rot. If he were especially diligent, or at least if he sought to convey that image, Lundberg might have poked his head into one of the *Slocum*'s forward compartments where the boat's electricity generator and steering machinery were located. Had he done so, he would have noticed that this "lamp room," as the crew called it, was filled—in violation of USSIS codes—with cans of lamp oil, brass polish, sheets of canvas, oily rags, and many more highly flammable objects. But based on later testimony, it appears that Lundberg avoided this problematic situation altogether.

A few final demonstrative jottings on his forms and Lundberg, along with Fleming, was on his way. Whether the two did so a few dollars richer we'll never know. But given the permissive culture of the USSIS and the pervasive influence of Tammany Hall corruption, they'd certainly have been judged fools by their fellow inspectors if they hadn't.

From the perspective of his boss, Van Schaick had done his job and done it well. The *General Slocum* was cleared to operate for its fourteenth season. At $350 per day to charter it, plus receipts from its daily runs to Rockaway, Barnaby could count on grossing something close to $40,000 by Columbus Day.

As a captain, however, Van Schaick knew he had another standard to answer to, that of his profession. His ultimate responsibility was to ensure the safety of his passengers. This duty was enshrined not merely in the tradition of the sea that called for the captain to be the last man off his vessel, but also in federal laws governing steamboats passed in 1871 and still operative in 1904:

Every captain, engineer, pilot, or other person employed on any
steamboat or vessel, by whose misconduct, negligence, or inattention to
his duties on such vessel, the life of any person is destroyed, and every
owner, inspector, or other public officer, through whose fraud,
connivance, misconduct, or violation of law, the life of any person is
destroyed, shall be deemed guilty of manslaughter, and, upon
conviction thereof before any circuit court of the United States, shall be
sentenced to confinement at hard labor for a period of not more than
ten years.

But Van Schaick had begun his career in a different era. In the 1860s, Americans accepted the inevitability of accidents (trains, factories) and the powerlessness of the government to do anything about it. What mattered most to men of his generation was knowledge, intuition, and experience. That was what got you through storms, collisions, and fires, not some silly rule dreamed up by some landlubber USSIS official riding a desk in Washington, D.C. And with fifty years under his belt, Van Schaick was perhaps the most experienced and highly regarded captain in the area.

This did not mean that the captain had never had his moments. In one week during the *Slocum*'s first season, Van Schaick ran aground on a sandbar near Rockaway and a few days later slammed into another steamer. Three years later, in 1894, he collided with a tugboat and ran aground four times, on one occasion causing serious structural damage to the *Slocum*. A more serious collision occurred in July 1898 when the *Slocum* struck a lighter off the Battery and received a gash in her bow. More groundings, accidents, and breakdowns occurred in the seasons that followed, but no more than usual for a busy steamer plying the waterways of the busiest port in the Western Hemisphere. On average there were more than 154 accidents and groundings in the New York district each year.

Scrapes like these, however, were expected in the career of any captain. The true measure of one's worth was not how many accidents they got into, but the ultimate results of them. Van Schaick had the two statistics that mattered most: no lost boats and no lost passengers. By 1904 he was famous for it. Who could possibly presume to tell him how to run a safe boat?

So while Barnaby refused to buy new life preservers and fire hoses and install steam pipes in the hold, Van Schaick refused to conduct fire drills or tests of the equipment. Barnaby saved his precious pennies, Van Schaick his self-respect and pride.

Van Schaick's self-assuredness regarding the safety of his steamboat was no doubt strengthened by the fact that accidents involving steamboats—other steamboats—happened all the time. Indeed, as if to underscore this perception, later that evening an errant barge forced the steamboat *Chester Chapin* hard onto the rocks in Hell Gate. Fortunately no one was hurt and the vessel was soon pulled free.

Of course, Van Schaick and the passengers aboard the *Chester Chapin* knew that sometimes steamboat accidents could be disastrous. Indeed, everyone in America knew this because for decades steamboat horrors on the high seas and inland waterways happened all the time. "Accidents involving destruction of life and property have become so frequent upon the Western rivers," wrote one observer in 1840, "that we look as regularly, when we open a newspaper, for a steamboat disaster, as for the foreign news." The same was true of oceangoing steamers. Steam engine explosions were the forerunners of modern-day catastrophic airliner crashes. Just as a jet airliner is utterly vulnerable to the smallest of technological glitches when in flight, so too were steamboats at sea or on rivers and lakes. In the case of the former, a single hairline crack in a plane's rudder can cause the pilot to lose control of his jet and send it hurtling to the ground, killing everyone on board. Similarly, a fire on board a ship, even one close to shore, often spelled doom for all hands.

Given the large number of steamboats operating out of New York harbor, the city saw its share of steamboat calamities. One of the worst involved the steamboat *Henry Clay* in 1852. Just minutes after getting under way on a trip up the Hudson River, a fire broke out in the boiler room. What happened next was described in excruciating detail by a local minister in a sermon delivered shortly after the tragedy. "We take a position on the eastern shore of the Hudson," began Rev. D. M. Seward, ". . . on a bland and beautiful day in summer. A steamer passes along, her flags gaily streaming in the wind, bearing on her side the eminently suggestive name of a recently deceased statesman." Aboard one could see crowds of jolly passengers enjoying the trip, "none of them dreaming that this hour of sunshine and gladness brings with it the last moments of their early life." But suddenly there is dense smoke pouring from the steamer, which turns toward the shore at full speed.

It is a moment of awful suspense. The burning steamer rushes onward with fearful momentum and thrusts her prow, fast and deep into the sand! Oh, what a scene of dismay, of distress, of inexpressible agony succeeds. Scores and scores are imprisoned by the flames; between them and the shore intervene, here the raging fire, and there a depth of water, which it requires a swimmer's skill to pass. Helpless women, trembling between two deaths, draw back from the water with a shudder, and cling to the burning vessel, until the unpitying flames, marching up to their last refuge, cruelly force them off. Timid, lovely children left protectorless, in the wild dismay of the moment, strive to clamber over the deck, and cry piteously for help, until the fierce flame wraps them about as a winding sheet, and their stifled sobs are hushed in death. Many leap overboard at once in frantic desperation, and in their wild and violent struggles force one another down to an instant grave. Stout and brave swimmers are there; they bring some safe to shore, and return again on their heroic errand, but now they are drawn beneath the surface by the desperate grasp of the drowning, and are seen no more.

Hearken! What wails of anguish and terror pierce the skies. Mothers in heart-rending tones crying for the children that have been torn from their grasp; sisters and daughters vainly struggling in the waters, imploring assistance in the final notes of terror and despair; husbands frantically calling upon wives, and fathers upon children.

A moment longer, and those dying cries and struggles are over. The
dreadful work of death is finished . . . transpiring under the very
shadow of our homes. . . .

In all, sixty people perished that afternoon aboard the *Henry Clay.*
Thirty-seven days later the *Reindeer* exploded near Albany, killing thirty-
one.

More and more, as steam replaced sail, the number of accidents and
resulting deaths rose. That steamer technology grew safer did little to diminish the toll, simply because the number of steamers in service rose
dramatically, as did their size and passenger capacity. Almost every year
in the 1850s and 1860s a steamboat exploded and burned. None was
greater than the explosion of the *Sultana* in May 1865 on the Mississippi
River, a disaster that claimed as many as two thousand Union soldiers.
Indeed, the steamboat accident was so commonplace in this era that
when in 1871 future secretary of state John Hay published a poem about
a heroic riverboat captain, Jim Bludso, who died saving all his passengers
after his vessel caught fire, it became a classic recited for decades to
come.

And, sure's you're born, they all got off
Afore the smokestacks fell,—
And Bludso's ghost went up alone
In the smoke of the Prairie Belle.

Such was not the case in New York on July 30, 1871, when the
steam-powered Staten Island ferry *Westfield* exploded, killing 104. A
subsequent investigation revealed that the boat's boilers had been seriously compromised by corrosion. Despite howls of protest and demands
for stricter safety measures in the wake of the *Westfield* tragedy, little was
done to improve safety beyond passage of a new set of rarely enforced
regulations. This was made abundantly clear only nine years later in New
York when the paddle steamer *Seawanhaka* suffered an engine explosion

while plying the always treacherous waters of Hell Gate. Captain Charles
D. Smith chose to beach his wounded craft immediately in shallows just
beyond Hell Gate known as Sunken Meadow. His quick thinking, not to
mention heroic rescues by nearby boats, saved most of his three hundred
passengers, including such notables as *New York Sun* editor Charles A.
Dana, millionaire merchant and future mayor W. A. Grace, and publishing magnate James W. Harper. But sixty-two perished, including Captain
Smith.

Once again tragedy aboard a steamer produced cries of outrage and
charges of negligence followed by an investigation and pledges by public
officials to raise safety standards and strengthen enforcement. Yet, as before, the changes were minimal and steamboats continued to explode and
catch fire. But because the number of fatalities was low, public pressure to
reform the steamboat inspection service never persisted. Late-nineteenth-
century Americans, moreover, were more accepting of accidents and the
deaths and injuries that resulted. Charges of negligence were often levied
in the wake of train wrecks, hotel fires, and ferry sinkings, but uttered
more as cries of despair and anger rather than the openings of major legal
actions seeking punitive and compensatory damages. Lawsuits for negligence in this era rarely succeeded, because the law and legal establishment
reflected Victorian America's perception of risk and accident. Life, they
understood, was full of perils, and there was only so much one could do—
or expect others to do—to minimize risk to life and limb. Their Christian
faith, no matter what denomination, supported this worldview, and in the
editorials, sermons, and pitiful testimonials that followed catastrophes
they often alternated between scathing indictments of those deemed responsible and plaintive questions about the inscrutable nature of God's
will and purpose.

The most recent waterfront calamity had taken place just four years
earlier. On June 30, 1900, a fire broke out among some cargo piled on the
Hoboken waterfront. Fanned by a stiff breeze and fueled by ample
amounts of cotton and oil, it quickly raged out of control and jumped to
nearby steamships of the German Lloyd Line. Four massive vessels

caught fire, many loaded with passengers, crew, and sightseers. Fireboats, tugs, and other boats converged on the harrowing scene, but there was little they could do. The *Kaiser Wilhelm der Gross* fared best. Although afire, the ship pulled away from the pier and all aboard were rescued. The *Saale* and *Bremen* likewise cast off, but not before the fires aboard them roared out of control. Rescuers watched in horror as victims trapped belowdecks tried desperately to wriggle through small portholes of ships that had been turned into floating crematoriums. The *Main* burned and sank at its pier. By the time the fires were extinguished, four hundred were dead. "Nobody who saw it ever forgot the Hudson on that summer night," wrote New York fire chief John Kenlon years later, "four great liners vomiting flame and smoke, surrounded by puffing tugs and busy fireboats, while perhaps two dozen smaller craft floated hither and thither in the most congested waterway in the world, aflame from stem to stern."

Certainly Captain Van Schaick had not forgotten it. How could he? It was one of the most spectacular maritime disasters in American history, surpassed only by scenes of naval warfare. Still, it was not the kind of event that veteran pilots dwelt upon. It was a freak accident, gruesome to be sure, but one nonetheless beyond the control of mere mortals and their safety measures. Such a scene of horror and destruction might make old salts like Van Schaick shudder, but it had no impact on their approach to their job. Nor did more recent news that three weeks earlier, on May 26, 1904, the steam-powered towboat *Fred Wilson* had exploded near West Louisville, Kentucky, killing eleven.

By the turn of the century, new technology and increased safety standards rendered boiler explosions rare events. In fact, Americans in 1904 had grown accustomed to the idea of loading thousands of people on a small vessel and heading out to sea—across the Atlantic and along the coast. They believed steamers to be more or less safe, especially for travel across short distances. The truly dangerous way to travel was widely understood to be the railroad. Between July 1, 1902, and June 30, 1903, for example, 9,840 Americans were killed on the railroads (1 for every

70,620 passengers) versus 1,303 lives lost on steamers (1 for every 422,102).

Most Americans would have agreed with the USSIS Annual Report for 1904 when it asserted that "transportation by water is . . . the safest of the many methods of transportation." Certainly Captain Van Schaick did—and he had the record to prove it.

PERILS REAL
AND IMAGINED

They began to fill with passengers that evening even before the *Slocum* tied up at its pier. At various locations along the city's two rivers, steamers bound for Coney Island took on thousands of New Yorkers. Passengers took their seats and talked excitedly about the evening that lay ahead—the hours of rides, games, food, and exhibitions made all the more sensational by the great shower of white light that bathed the three great parks. Since no one could possibly experience all that Coney Island had to offer in one night, especially with the addition that year of Luna and Dreamland Parks, many debated what to see and in what order. Without a doubt, many planned to see one of several offerings in a new and immensely popular entertainment genre: the disaster spectacle.

All spring, crowds packed a massive theater at Dreamland done up to look like a Roman temple to witness the Fall of Pompeii. Audiences found themselves both terrified and thrilled by the most modern special effects known to the industry, including a pyrotechnic Vesuvius eruption that routinely sent dozens bolting for the exits before the show was over. Equally spectacular and popular was the reenactment of recent disasters like the Johnstown Flood, which in 1889 saw 3,000 people swept away after a dam burst and inundated the town. Likewise the reenactment of the Galveston Flood of 1900 drew huge crowds to see the bustling city of Galveston, Texas, put under fifteen feet of raging sea by a monumental hurricane, an event that claimed some 8,000 lives. Both tragedies still loomed large in the popular memory and every day drew thousands of eager viewers.

Why these spectacles of death and disaster appealed to so many people is not hard to discern. To some extent, people came to marvel at the ability of Coney's engineers and designers to pull off such astonishing epics. More important, they were drawn by the prospect of "seeing" the disaster they had read and heard so much about. In an age before film began to capture for the masses scenes of war and disaster, the public hungered for a chance to view scenes of mass destruction. Still photography, beginning with the Civil War photographs of Mathew Brady, had satisfied an earlier generation seeking more than the dry details of battles and fires provided by newspapers. Now, at the turn of the twentieth century, audiences wanted more and the entrepreneurs at Coney Island were prepared to give it to them.

But the crowds that flocked to see the Fall of Pompeii and the Galveston Flood were after something more than mere spectacle. For out of all these tales of human tragedy there were always stories of courage, heroism, and sacrifice. Audiences gasped, cheered, and cried as rescuers risked their lives to pluck the innocent from the jaws of death and parents sacrificed theirs to save their children. If New York's highbrow set found their inspiration in performances of Shakespeare and the Greek tragedies, the city's great unwashed found it at Coney Island.

There was also something oddly comforting about these disaster spectacles. For every day city dwellers faced a wide array of very real perils that seemed only one errant step, one unsuspecting moment away. Every day New Yorkers picked up the newspaper to read stories of calamities big and small. It all added up to an annual total of nearly eight thousand New Yorkers perishing for reasons other than natural causes—accidents, murder, epidemics, and more. To outsiders, death in the big city seemed utterly random and unpredictable. The residents of poorer districts like the Lower East Side, of course, knew differently. Death was a more frequent visitor in their neighborhoods than in Gramercy Park or on Fifth Avenue.

Danger lurked at every intersection. Each year hundreds of New Yorkers were killed or maimed by careening streetcars, runaway horses, or out-of-control automobilists. Just that afternoon two little girls out picking flowers had been killed by a speeding trolley. Worse were the perils encountered in the workplace, the result of lax safety standards and intense competition that led many a building contractor and factory owner to cut costs by scrimping on safety. Even the home offered only partial refuge. Each year gas leaks alone killed hundreds, while others were done in by building collapses, falls from open windows, and tumbles down flights of stairs. The home also afforded no defense against the greatest killer of all, disease, the invisible force that constantly ravaged the city, especially the poorest sections like the Lower East Side. Diseases like diphtheria, typhoid fever, tuberculosis, and pneumonia struck hard in the hot summer months and took their greatest toll among the very old and the very young. In the case of the latter, there were additional threats, particularly infantile paralysis.

Given these perils of everyday urban life, a trip to one of Coney Island's disaster spectacles allowed the public to count their blessings. These disasters were the problems of *other* people and they dwarfed anything the audience had experienced. The more horrific the destruction and the greater the loss of life, the safer they felt.

B ut the popularity of the Johnstown Flood and the Fall of Pompeii was dwarfed by a different kind of disaster spectacle that opened in the spring of 1904. Luna Park's Fire and Flames exhibit was not based on any specific catastrophe, but rather on everyday life in the crowded tenement districts of New York City. When the curtain was raised, there stood on-stage several full-sized tenements aligned to resemble a portion of a typical Lower East Side block. The "street" in the foreground teemed with hundreds of passersby, pushcart peddlers selling their wares, and children playing hide-and-go-seek.

Suddenly this tranquil urban scene erupted in chaos. First smoke and then flames began pouring from an upper tenement window. Onlookers shouted "Fire!" and ran about in panic. Women and children began screaming from windows near the flames—"Help! We're trapped! Help!"

Just when all seemed lost, the loud clang of a fire bell proclaimed to all that help was on the way. A moment later several fire engines arrived. Dozens of burly men, many of them real firemen moonlighting for extra cash, leapt from the rig and proceeded to save the day. Several ran into the building with axes while others unfurled hoses and began pouring streams of real water into the flaming windows. Another group stretched out a tarp and caught the women and children as they jumped from the windows. In a few minutes it was all over. Heroic manhood had saved innocent lives and property, and everyone could return to their everyday lives.

The creators of Fire and Flames recognized that in 1904 nothing so frightened the public like fire. This was not because fires claimed the most lives each year. Far from it. In 1903 fires swept away just nineteen people, far fewer than those taken by disease or traffic accidents. What made fire so terrifying was its unique nature. In the list of worrisome possibilities, fire stood in a category all its own. There was nothing else quite like it.

Unlike the annual summer epidemics, fire had no season. It struck every day of the week, every month of the year. There was no opportunity to psychologically steel one's nerves, no preparing for it by purchasing medicines (no matter how useless) or keeping the children indoors, as was the case with summer epidemics. Fire came suddenly and without warning, the result of a spark from a match or cigarette, an accidentally overturned lamp or a simple stove fire. It moved with lightning speed, accomplishing its task in minutes. A typical tenement fire might leave behind a smoke-filled apartment and several people with frazzled nerves, or the corpses of a dozen innocents caught in its path.

People groped for words to accurately describe fires. Press accounts of conflagrations typically referred to fire as if it were an animate force. Fires "raged" out of control, "leapt" from building to building, "raced swiftly" through an apartment, and "devoured" property and lives. Accounts similarly attributed physical features to fire, frequently describing "tongues" of flame that "licked" at victims hanging out windows. Others wrote of "ravenous" blazes that "roared" and "clawed" their way through a building.

These same writers likewise employed sinister language to characterize fires as evil forces, often calling them "fiendish," "monstrous," "murderous," and "rapacious." Currier and Ives titled one of their many lithographs of heroic firemen "Facing the Enemy." One of the most common terms employed embodied all these animate and otherworldly characteristics: a fire was "a demon." Such perceptions of fire likewise led to descriptions of firemen "smothering" and "drowning" flames. Indeed, one of the more popular models of fire extinguishers in the mid–nineteenth century was called Phillips' Fire Annihilator.

Fire was especially unnerving because people knew they were powerless against it. Fire-prevention technology and laws lagged far behind the realities of urban life. Fire escapes were mandated by law, but a lack of enforcement allowed many landlords to avoid them altogether, or to comply with the letter of the law by affixing a pathetic ladder or set of wooden stairs to their building's rear facade. Few buildings had fire alarms and only a handful, mainly new ones catering to upscale renters, possessed sprinklers or fire hoses. In 1904, fire still had the upper hand.

Perhaps the truest measure of the level of fear inspired by fire can be found in the many instances of deadly panics it sparked. On September 19, 1902, for example, some two thousand African-Americans crowded into the Shiloh Baptist Church in Birmingham, Alabama, to listen to an address by Booker T. Washington. Just as the evening's events were about to get under way, there came cries from an adjacent room of what sounded like "Fire!" In seconds the orderly crowd disintegrated into a crazed mob frantically making for the exits. Church leaders appealed for calm but to no avail, and when it was all over more than one hundred people lay crushed to death. And the fire? There was none. Someone had mistaken shouts of "Fight" emanating from a fracas between some youths. It was with these kinds of horrors in mind that Oliver Wendell Holmes would later declare that free speech did not permit a person to shout "Fire!" in a crowded theater.

There was an additional aspect to fire that made it so worrisome to so many—they couldn't live without it. Tens of thousands of years since the first humans managed to capture and manipulate it for their own ends, modern man's reliance on fire had only grown more acute. Fire heated and illuminated the homes of 4 million New Yorkers. Fire cooked their food, propelled their trains and steamboats, and drove the factory machinery. Fire also provided the sleepless city with light each night via tens of thousands of gas lamps. Fire meant life—a fact made abundantly clear a few years later in Jack London's famous short story, "To Build a Fire."

It was an irony from which there seemed no escape. New Yorkers were utterly dependent upon and surrounded by the very thing they dreaded most. Fire, according to an ancient truism, was "a good servant, but a bad master." Few in 1904 New York City would disagree. All they had to do was look in the daily papers to find a regular column entitled "Yesterday's Fires" listing the address, time, and amount of damage for each fire as if it were a box score.

The year 1904 had begun with people talking about fire and its destructive powers, for in December 1903 a fire tore through Chicago's Iroquois Theater, claiming 602 lives. The scale of the horror in Chicago was so great that many cities, including New York, toughened their fire codes at public venues like theaters. By then two additional catastrophic fires had come and gone. On February 7, fire destroyed twenty-five hundred businesses in Baltimore's central business district. A few weeks later, on February 26, fire broke out in downtown Rochester, New York, and reduced dozens of buildings to smoldering heaps.

The creators of Luna Park's Fire and Flames show, however, knew that when it came to fire, the other side of fear was fascination. Nothing drew a crowd quicker than a fire. As George Templeton Strong, the indefatigable diarist and chronicler of mid-nineteenth-century New York, wrote one evening, "They consider fires a sort of grand exhibition (admission gratis) which they have a perfect right to look at from any point they like and choose the best seats to see the performance." In the nineteenth-century city, fires were the closest thing to a modern spectator sport.

New Yorkers not only found fires uniquely entertaining, they also came to revere the men who put them out. This was what Strong meant when he referred to the performance. Beginning early in the nineteenth century, men began forming neighborhood volunteer fire companies. They were neighborhood fraternal clubs as much as they were firefighting forces, and by the 1850s, New York City had several thousand of these "fire laddies" organized into dozens of neighborhood companies with evocative names like the Black Joke, Dry Bones, and Big Six. They donned brightly colored uniforms, pulled gaudily decorated pumpers, and in an age before professional sports heroes, engaged in conspicuous acts of bravery in saving lives and extinguishing fires. So intense was the competition between rival companies that brawls—to see which company would earn the honor of extinguishing the blaze—frequently erupted when two arrived at a fire simultaneously.

That other fixture of nineteenth-century urban America, the beat cop, could not compete with the fireman for the public's affection. To be sure, policemen enjoyed a certain degree of respect for their bravery and service, but they also suffered for their association with patronage, corruption, extortion, and violence. Despite the grumblings of a few elitist malcontents over their occasional brawls, firemen were loved by nearly everyone. Only the American soldier, and perhaps not even him, was a more revered figure among Americans, especially young boys. "They play fire-engine vigorously with a piece of string and restive snorting boy-horses," wrote one visitor to the East Side, "a real fire sets them wild."

Firemen were lionized for their bravery and strength in short stories, dramas, popular songs, and most especially the series of color prints produced by an enterprising duo named Nathaniel Currier and James Merritt Ives and called "The Life of the Fireman." With scenes depicting heroic firemen at work putting out fires and carrying victims to safety, the series sold hundreds of thousands of copies to an infatuated American public.

New Yorkers' love affair with fire laddies eventually led to the development of an urban superhero named "The Mose" to take his place alongside cowboy king Pecos Bill, lumberjack Paul Bunyan, riverboat legend Mike Fink, and railroad worker John Henry. A creation of the Bowery stage, the Mose stood eight feet tall and possessed the strength of ten men. When he wasn't rescuing women and children from burning buildings, he brawled with rival firemen or ne'er-do-wells who preyed upon the weak. In less stressful moments he swam across the Hudson in just two strokes or leaped the East River in a single bound. To slake his mighty thirst he carried a fifty-gallon keg of beer on his belt. Long after the Mose had departed from the Bowery stage and the city of New York abolished the volunteer system in favor of a professional force, the fireman endured as a heroic figure in the city's popular culture. They starred in countless dime novels, adorned everything from sugar bowls to weather vanes, and even the first feature film with a discernible plot was about them, Edwin S. Porter's 1903 *The Life of an American Fireman*. One of the hit songs of 1900 was "The Midnight Fire Alarm March and Two-Step."

Fire and Flames was surely a brilliant idea, given the public's obsession with fire and firemen, but it was also quite risky. What if, after expending many thousands of dollars to build the set and hire the hundreds of performers, the crowds failed to come? What if they found Fire and Flames a little too close for comfort, a little too real and scary?

Any fears the promoters harbored were immediately squelched within a week of the show's opening. Almost overnight it was clear that Thompson and Dundy had hit upon a brilliant idea. By mid-June, Fire and Flames had become Luna Park's biggest draw and the only show mentioned in its advertising—THE ORIGINAL OF ALL SUMMER SHOWS—UNEQUALLED BY THE WORLD OF IMMITATORS—ASK YOUR NEIGHBOR. There was no need to, for the show was the talk of the city. Every performance sold out as thousands plunked down their dimes to see for themselves what their neighbors had been talking about. The show's believability was such that dozens of patrons routinely fainted as the fire reached its crescendo while others got caught up in the frenzy and joined the actors in shouting for somebody to save the poor unfortunates.

That evening as the steamers returned to Manhattan, many of their exhausted passengers doubtless replayed the scenes of Fire and Flames in their minds. By choosing so familiar, so real a theme, Thompson and Dundy had taken the disaster genre to a new level. Fire and Flames was not a disaster spectacle viewed at a safe distance of time and space. Rather it was an event that audiences immediately recognized and plunged into as though they were part of the storyline. And why not? They did it nearly every day in their neighborhoods. Only this time Thompson and Dundy provided them with what they craved: a guaranteed happy ending. They allowed New Yorkers to join their firemen heroes in vanquishing a tenement fire—their single greatest day-to-day fear.

And the best part? It only cost a dime.

PERFECT DAY

From the moment she awoke the next morning, Mary Abendschein knew her prayers had been answered. Bright sunshine streamed in through the windows of her apartment, filling it with the warmth and glow of a magnificent spring morning. As the one in charge of organizing the St. Mark's seventeenth annual Sunday school outing, she had done everything to ensure that the day would go off without a hitch. Still, there remained one thing she could not control, one thing that could make or break the event: the weather. Now as she looked out the window into a cloudless sky and felt the caress of a gentle breeze on her cheek, the last of her fears melted away. Today would be perfect.

Across town at its Hudson River pier, the crew of the *General Slocum* scurried about performing routine tasks in preparation for the day ahead. Some brought the requisite supplies aboard while others cleaned and hosed down the vessel until it sparkled in the early-morning sun. Still others attended to specific jobs related to their rank and position.

Walter Payne, an African-American porter whose responsibility it was to fill the boat's lamps each morning, arrived in the lamp room at 6:30 A.M. Already the windowless storage room located belowdecks just forward of the pilothouse was partially illuminated by an open torch held by Elbert J. Gaffga, the *Slocum*'s oiler. He was hard at work making sure the steamer's vital steering machinery was in working order. Payne stepped into the room, removed a lamp from a hook on the wall, and placed it on the large table in the center of the room.

The small compartment seemed even smaller this morning because the previous evening three large barrels filled with glassware for the picnic had been brought aboard and stored there. Payne could tell that someone had already removed the glasses, because the hay in which they were packed lay all over the floor. He struck a match, lit the lamp, and, as was his custom, threw the match on the bench. A few minutes later the room was again in darkness as both men left to attend to other duties. The ritual was identical to that performed every morning aboard the *Slocum*, but with one exception. One of them had unwittingly left something behind.

Throughout Little Germany on the morning of June 15, 1904, family after family was awakening to the same delightful realization as Mary Abendschein. Many children—and as a result their parents—had slept poorly the night before, too filled with eager anticipation to fall asleep. But all signs of grogginess dissipated within minutes of awakening as excitement filled the air. The long-awaited event—a whole day by the waters of Locust Grove—had finally arrived and the weather was simply gorgeous.

The Zipse household was no exception as it buzzed with joyful enthusiasm. Sophie Zipse and her seven children scurried about their little apartment at 335 East 21st Street, getting dressed and packing the last of their blankets, towels, games, and, of course, good things to eat. The younger children could hardly contain their excitement, but the three oldest Zipse children, Mary and Sophia, twins age seventeen, and William, age fifteen, looked forward to a day of flirting and dancing with other teens. For William the day held special significance. Although only fifteen, he was a successful sales representative for a die company and a part-time student. A driven young man determined to succeed, he rarely took time off from school and work. The annual St. Mark's outing to Locust Grove, however, was one occasion when he made an exception. Besides, he told himself, all would not be fun and games. With his father staying behind, unable to take time off from his job at a bottling factory, William would fill the role of man of the family. It was a responsibility the mature and ambitious teen welcomed, even as he fully expected to have his share of fun.

Oscar Piening was of a different mind. Ten years earlier as a young boy he'd accompanied his father on a boat excursion that ended in disaster. He was saved but his father was killed. Ever since that day Oscar vowed he'd never set foot on another boat as long as he lived. His mother and sister, however, had not been on the fateful trip and were thus of a different mind when it came to the St. Mark's outing. That morning Oscar watched with an uneasy feeling in his gut as they prepared to go. They would be five in all, since his sister was bringing her three children.

For nineteen-year-old Lillie Pfeifer, this year's trip would be different from all the others she'd attended in the past. In previous years she'd gone as a child, even into her late teens. This year, however, she'd go as a woman, for only a few months ago she'd married Charles Pfeifer, a policeman. As much as she might want to frolic and dance with the other teenagers on the boat that day, she knew that custom and propriety dictated that she spend the day in the company of ladies—the married women, mothers, grandmothers, spinsters, and widows of the parish. This was especially so in her case, because her husband would not be along for the trip. The difference between last year and this would be enormous. She'd dress, speak, and carry herself differently. It was an experience that many a young woman in her situation eagerly looked forward to, an affirmation of her passage from childhood to adulthood. As a young newlywed, she also could expect to be fawned over by the other women. And with no children she'd have no responsibilities other than to make conversation and partake of the food and drink. It promised to be a thoroughly enjoyable day—certainly better than a day all alone as a childless housewife.

Not everyone in Little Germany greeted June 15 with a smile and a skip in their step. Modest as the ticket price was, many families simply could not afford the trip, especially if it meant taking a day off from work. Others chose not to go out of fear. For people not accustomed to traveling the waters on steamboats, the trip to Locust Grove appeared too risky. They read of steamboat accidents all the time in the newspapers and feared the prospect of a boiler explosion or sinking. The father of sixteen-year-old Wilhelmina Rauch held this view. A veteran of the New York City Police Department, he had seen his share of accidents and death and wanted no part of it for his family. He knew the unsafe condition of many of the city's steamboats, and despite weeks of tears and protest he had adamantly refused to let her go on the trip. She hated him for his stubbornness and dreaded the coming days when all she'd hear were stories of the glorious day at Locust Grove.

Similar grumblings emanated from the home of the Knell family. None of the family's six children were allowed to go on the trip because one of them, George, was still recovering from serious injuries suffered when he was struck by a trolley over a year before. The accident cost him a foot and several fingers and his recovery was slow in coming. By early June it became clear that he would not be strong enough to attend the St. Mark's outing. That meant no one could go, because their father could not take the day off from work, and their mother needed to remain at home to attend to their brother. No, despite the endless pleas, they could not go without their parents as some of the neighborhood children would. Having suffered the trauma of nearly losing one child, their parents were leery of letting any of them venture too far from home, no matter what the occasion. So while the sun shone brightly outside, the atmosphere in the Knell household that morning was decidedly chilly.

Another young boy named George—George Oellrich—had nearly done the same thing to his siblings. Just the day before he'd fallen ill and would not be allowed to go on the excursion. But his parents decided the other Oellrich children—Frederick, age six, Wilhelmina, age five, Elizabeth, age three, and Helen, age eighteen months—would not be deprived of a day at Locust Grove. The Oellrichs, simply put, were better off than the Knells and could thus manage to have George stay home with his father while his mother took the rest on the trip. William Oellrich owned a prosperous poultry business in Brooklyn and had no trouble taking the day off to look after his ailing son. Besides, for a man like Oellrich, being able to send his family back to Little Germany—the old neighborhood—was an opportunity to keep in touch with old friends, but more important, to exhibit his success. The only disappointment was that he would not be able to accompany his beautiful family in their holiday finery and personally receive the praise of his former neighbors.

For the family of Paul and Anna Liebenow, the St. Mark's excursion likewise marked a return to the old neighborhood, albeit a more modest one compared to the Oellrichs', for Paul was a bartender. Several years previous, he'd moved his family to Harlem, then the city's fastest-growing neighborhood, to be closer to his place of work at the fashionable Pabst Harlem, a restaurant and entertainment venue at 256–8 West 125th Street. Like most who left Little Germany, the Liebenows did so with mixed emotions. Moving to Harlem, then considered one of the most desirable white middle- and upper-class neighborhoods in the city, was a step up for the working-class family. It also meant that Paul could walk to work from their apartment at 133 East 125th Street, a luxury not to be scoffed at in 1904. Still, they missed the familiar faces and institutions of St. Mark's parish and the surrounding German enclave. Today was a welcome chance to return to the fold. To mark the occasion, the day before Paul had stopped in at Palmer's haberdashery just a few doors down East 125th Street for a new fifteen-dollar suit and a one-dollar hat—nearly a week's wages. Even a humble bartender wanted to look his best on the excursion, accompanied by his young wife and their three daughters, Helen, age six, Anna, age three, and the baby Adella, just six months.

Joining the Liebenows were Paul's two sisters. Annie Weber lived with her husband Frank and two children, Emma (age eleven) and Frank, Jr. (age seven), at 404 East Fifth Street, just one block south of St. Mark's Church. Martha Liebenow was Annie and Paul's unmarried younger sister. The two families, plus Aunt Martha, had planned to spend the day together—just as they had so often when the Liebenows lived in Little Germany. Both Paul and Frank considered themselves fortunate to have the day off.

The ten Webers and Liebenows were hardly the only extended families planning on a day at Locust Grove. Indeed, for many in the neighborhood the annual St. Mark's excursion served as a kind of family reunion—especially in recent years with so many families having moved uptown to Yorkville or across the rivers to Brooklyn or New Jersey. Three generations of the Kassenbaum, Torniport, and Schnude families, eighteen in all, were scheduled to meet at the pier. The party of relatives from the Muth, Schnitzler, and Hessel families totaled fourteen. Ten members and three generations of the Weis family, including Tillie Weis, her seven children, daughter-in-law, and first grandchild, were assembling down the block at 532 East Fifth Street.

While some husbands and fathers like Frank Weber and Paul Liebenow managed to take a rare weekday off, most families were under the care of women. Mary Prawdzicki had her hands full preparing her brood of five children in their small apartment at 85 East Third Street. Emilia Justh, wife of cabinetmaker Joseph Justh, would have her four daughters and one son to look after. Louisa Hartung, wife of tailor Magnus Hartung, had a similar number of children, but perhaps an easier day ahead of her since her five girls were older. Maria Fickbohm and Frances Iden, mothers of three and five children respectively, had them all beat—for both would bring a servant to help them look after the children. As these women bid their husbands good-bye, they reminded them to be at the pier that evening to welcome them home and help carry their belongings and very likely a slumbering child.

Amelia Richter could not count on any such help, at least not from her husband. He had died several years earlier, leaving her a widow mother of seven young children. Determined to keep her family together, Amelia worked up to twenty hours a day, often seven days a week, at cleaning offices, doing laundry, and taking in piecework. "Her hands were hard," one neighbor remembered, "but her children were always clean." Things had begun to lighten up somewhat for the beleaguered Amelia in the past two years, as her oldest three children left school for work to support the family. Today, perhaps to recognize her accomplishment, Amelia would take the day off and head for Locust Grove. So too would all her children, except her oldest boy, fifteen-year-old William, who dared not risk his promising job at a downtown commission house. He would join the other men of the house at the pier that evening to help get everyone home.

By 7:30 A.M., hundreds upon hundreds of residents of Little Germany and surrounding neighborhoods began filling the streets for their formal walk to the pier at the end of East Third Street, where they expected to find the steamboat *General Slocum*. They could be seen gathered in front of tenements waiting for stragglers, standing at prearranged rendezvous points for other families to join, crowded in front of groceries picking up last-minute items.

Some were already at the Third Street pier—the habitually early, the impatient, and the experienced who knew the benefits of snaring the best seats on the upper hurricane deck. Among them was Mary Abendschein, the organizational genius behind the whole event. True to form, she was there early, just in case there were any last-minute problems. She also had the honor of handing out the *Journal for the Seventeenth Annual Excursion of St. Mark's Evan. Lutheran Church*, the program she'd labored so long and hard to produce for the event. In it revelers found, in German and English, everything they needed to know, including the musical program to be provided by Professor George Maurer and his band, the menu and prices (clam chowder 20¢; beer, and ice cream, 5¢), a schedule of services and programs at St. Mark's, a few jokes, and nearly one hundred sponsoring advertisements purchased by local businesses.

For Mary, thirty-four and as yet unmarried, her work on behalf of the church filled a major void in her life. Unable to prove her worth according to the highest standards of the day—as a wife and mother—she threw herself into volunteer work at St. Mark's. Today was one of those days when such selfless effort was rewarded, when a single woman considered perilously close to spinsterhood could shine, handing to each family as they boarded the *General Slocum* the tangible evidence of her great labors and dedication to the parish.

It was also a day to shine for Pastor Haas, who likewise had arrived early to greet personally each family as they boarded the boat. Although others, especially Mary Abendschein, had worked to make the excursion possible, he would be seen as the host and receive the heartiest congratulations and good wishes. It was a moment he'd come to savor, an annual reminder now for seventeen years of why he drew so much satisfaction from his job at St. Mark's and why he consistently turned down attractive offers from prestigious uptown churches, seminaries, and colleges. Haas was one of those men, rare in any age, with the strength of character and knowledge of his own heart to truly know where he belonged. This insight produced a self-confidence and sense of purpose that allowed him to withstand the temptations born of innate ambition and a society fixated on upward mobility to leave St. Mark's for some elusive promised land. On this morning, this shepherd, seeing the beaming smiles of his flock and receiving their warm greetings and appreciative words, wouldn't trade places with anyone.

By now a grand procession was taking form along the avenues and side streets of Little Germany to the pier at East Third Street. On any given Wednesday in the month of June, the streets of Little Germany teemed with activity. Storekeepers threw up their shutters and brought merchandise out onto the sidewalk. Pushcart peddlers hawked their wares and newsboys cried out the headlines. Commuters headed off to their places of work and children to school. But on this day it was evident that something else was happening. Whole families, often several blended together, moved with purpose toward a common destination.

They were easily picked out from the crowds that normally dominated the streets and sidewalks each morning. Dressed in their holiday finery, they evoked images of churchgoing families normally seen on Sundays. To the modern mind, the idea of men donning dark suits and women high-collared dresses and fancy hats for a day by the shore seems absurd. But in early-twentieth century America, it was the order of the day regardless of social class—especially for a church-sponsored outing. Respectability went before comfort and pragmatism. Men might remove their hats and jackets and loosen their ties during a baseball game, and the little ones would inevitably end up cuffing their pants and hiking their dresses to splash in the shallow water. But that was the extent of the concessions made to leisure and recreation. The days of swimsuits, shorts, T-shirts, and bare limbs and feet were another generation off. The group photographs so often taken on these outings always captured the same scene of manner and morals, propriety and sobriety. In 1904, even as seaside recreation boomed in popularity, Americans rich and poor went to the beach and the park as if dressed for a wedding, or perhaps a funeral.

Observers of the growing procession could also tell who was going to the shore that morning by the things they carried. Over their shoulders, under their arms, and in their hands they lugged the items necessary for a day of playing, dancing, sitting, and eating at Locust Grove. Experienced excursionists knew what to bring—blankets for sitting and napping, toys and games to keep the children occupied, extra clothes and towels, and, of course, food and drink. For those concerned about getting too much sun—in 1904 fair skin was still a sign of middle- or upper-class status—they brought parasols and broad-brimmed hats. Children carried dolls, toy boats, fishing poles, kites, and baseball gloves and bats. More than a few of these children of the city brought with them empty jars in the hope that they might be so lucky as to bring home some token of their day in the country—a firefly, robin's egg, or frog.

Although such scenes of conspicuous recreation normally took place on Sundays, no one who witnessed the procession through the streets of Little Germany that Wednesday morning thought it the least bit odd. For weeks the St. Mark's excursion had been the talk of the neighborhood. Even those who had no intention of going knew about it. Mary Abendschein had seen to that, canvassing hundreds of the neighborhood's businesses seeking sponsoring advertisements for the event program. Gossip and stories of past trips flew about the neighborhood as anticipation mounted. By the morning of June 15 there was scarcely a soul in Little Germany who did not know about the event.

So as the delighted crowd moved methodically to the steamboat, they were greeted by those who would remain in the neighborhood. Shopkeepers shook hands and shouted well-wishes to customers and friends. Older residents, for whom a long day in the sun held no appeal, waved from stoops and windows. Men on their way to work—some of whose wives and children were already on their way to board the *Slocum*—ribbed the few husbands who did manage to get the day off. Long-faced children heading off to school at P.S. 25 on Fifth Street and First Avenue looked on with envy while teachers smiled at the prospect of a day of half-empty classrooms.

Mothers urged their broods on, mindful of the 8:45 departure time, not to mention the desire to claim some of the choice seats aboard the *Slocum*. At the same time, they struggled to keep everyone together, especially at street crossings, lest one of the small ones get run down by a charging teamster or automobile. They also wanted everyone to keep as clean as possible—no easy task in the filth-ridden streets of New York in 1904.

M oving through the crowd was bandleader George Maurer. For him the day held a dual purpose. First and foremost it was a workday, and he was on the lookout for his six fellow musicians. Maurer and his band had been hired by the church to provide music on board the *Slocum* and at Locust Grove. But this was a booking unlike almost any other he could expect to get that year, for he lived in Little Germany and knew many of the people on the trip. So for at least part of the day, the fifty-two-year-old Maurer could count on enjoying himself with friends and family—with him that morning was his wife Margaret and three daughters. August Schneider, one of his musicians, also brought his wife, Dora, and their three daughters. Unlike their usual engagements in crowded, smoky wedding halls and concert saloons, today promised to be comfortable, light-hearted, and fun.

Two other men there at the pier had similar thoughts. Police officers Albert T. Van Tassel and Charles Kelk of the city's River and Harbor Squad had been hired by St. Mark's to accompany the excursion and make sure everyone was kept safe and sound. Compared to their regular days stalking the wharves and alleys of the city's gang-infested waterfront, or patrolling the waters in leaky rowboats and launches, a sunny day at Locust Grove with a church group was a positively cushy assignment. They might have to fish a child or two out of the water or restrain an inebriated adult, but the odds favored a quiet day sipping lemonade and eating untold amounts of good German fare. And since they were moonlighting, they'd walk away at the end of the day with a nice piece of change in their pockets.

Perhaps the happiest person in the crowd of excursionists that morning was eleven-year-old Catherine Gallagher. She'd begun her day much like Wilhelmina Rauch, filled with gloom and despair over the fact that she could not go on the trip. Since the family could afford only three tickets, her mother, Veronica, planned on taking Catherine's two younger siblings, nine-year-old Walter and nine-month-old Agnes. Catherine was barely out of bed that morning when her mother pressed a few coins in her hand and sent her to the corner store for a few last-minute items.

It was so unfair, she thought, as she headed down three flights of stairs. By the time she reached the store, tears were streaming down her red cheeks.

"What's the matter, Catherine?" asked the woman who owned the store.

"Everyone's going on the St. Mark's trip but me," she sobbed. "I haven't got a ticket."

Nonsense, said the kindly woman, as she reached into a drawer and pulled out a ticket. Like many local businesses, she'd bought a handful of tickets as a gesture of support for the church and handed them out to friends and customers.

"You have a good time," she said, smiling, as she handed a disbelieving

Catherine the coveted ticket. Clutching the ticket and groceries in her hands, Catherine bolted home to get ready for the trip, her first ever on a boat. Less than an hour later she was standing at the East Third Street pier waiting to board the *Slocum*, still astonished at her good fortune.

It was a miracle, she thought. "I must be the luckiest girl in the world."

ALL ABOARD

Sometime after 8:00 A.M., the *Slocum* had rounded the Battery and tied up at the East Third Street recreation pier to await the members of St. Mark's parish. With the scheduled departure time of 8:45 less than thirty minutes off, several hundred people were already waiting. Their collective chattering and laughing filled the air, drowning out the incessant creak and groan of a vessel lashed to a pier. Many families had arranged to rendezvous at the pier, and the scenes of joy attending their meeting gave added emphasis to the morning's holiday atmosphere.

To them and the families that soon followed, the steamer instantly caught their eyes as they approached. From its tall, majestic smokestacks, thick plumes of black coal smoke wafted up and over the vessel. It was the perfect combination of grace and might, and loomed before them as a white chariot set to take them away from their obligations and worries, if only for a day.

At 8:30 A.M., Captain Van Schaick gave the signal to First Mate Ed Flanagan to begin boarding. First up the gangplank were policemen

Van Tassel and Kelk, followed by Reverend Haas and his special guest, Rev. George Schultze from Erie, Pennsylvania. The latter took up positions to the left and right of the gangway to allow them to personally greet and welcome each passenger as they boarded.

Next to them sat deckhand John Coakley gripping a mechanical counter in his hand. By law the *Slocum* was required to count each passenger as they boarded to ensure that no more than the legal maximum— 2,500 in the case of the *Slocum*—went aboard. But as with everything regarding the steamboat industry and the law, passenger "counting" in practice left plenty of room for interpretation. Coakley, a green deckhand with only eighteen days' experience on the job, counted according to the standard operating procedure aboard the *Slocum*: one click for every adult and one for every two children fourteen years old or younger. As a result, the precise number of passengers aboard the *General Slocum* on its last voyage will forever remain a mystery. Coakley recorded 982, but a far more accurate estimate compiled by the city many months later put it at 1,331, a number that included 800 females and 531 males, of whom more than 500 were younger than twenty years of age.

Up the gangplank they came, faces beaming and eyes wide in search of the best seats. "There was never a happier party than we were when we boarded the boat," remembered Annie Weber, whose family came aboard with their relatives the Liebenows. "[W]e went on board laughing and talking, the children romping ahead with my sister." They greeted Pastor Haas and Pastor Schultze and headed for seats on the forward middle deck. Hundreds more families followed in much the same manner.

The bulk of the passengers filled the *Slocum* in no time, but families and individuals kept coming right up to the posted departure time of 8:45 A.M. and beyond. Then the pleading began. Passengers still waiting for friends and family to arrive prevailed on Pastor Haas to hold the steamer just a few minutes longer. The good-natured minister inevitably gave in— several times over—delaying the departure by nearly an hour. The last to board was a young girl and her brother who came flying down the pier just before the gangplank was hauled up.

Watching this scene from the main deck was Mrs. Philip Straub. Moments earlier she had hustled her family onto the *Slocum*. Now as deck-hands prepared to haul up the gangplank, she questioned her decision. Dark premonitions of some terrible, unknown disaster had haunted her mind all night. Her husband had dismissed her worries and said they were proof she needed a day off.

But she wasn't so sure. Impulsively she turned to a man next to her, a stranger, and told him of her fear. Without saying a word, he grabbed his wife and five children and raced for the gangplank, shouting to the deck-hands to wait. Hard on his heels was Straub with her children in tow. In less than a minute, eight bewildered children and three disbelieving adults stood gasping for breath on the pier. Before any could speak or cry, the gangplank disappeared and the crew began to cast off. Shouts went up to the pilothouse and the twin paddle wheels began to turn.

Passengers on the steamboat hung over the railings and waved to the people still standing on the pier, just as they had seen it done in vaudeville shows and in nickelodeons. As they waved, those on the port side couldn't help but gaze in wonder at the frightened group still standing on the pier. Who in their right mind would pass up a trip like this?

UNDER WAY

S he's away, sir," called pilot Ed Weaver through the window as the *Slocum* separated from the pier. Van Schaick nodded and instructed his pilots to bring the boat downriver a quarter mile to the Williamsburg Bridge. There, with sufficient momentum, they would swing the vessel about 180 degrees and proceed upriver toward Long Island Sound.

A bell clanged above the thunder in the boiler room, calling Chief Engineer Ben Conklin's attention to a light indicating additional steam. With two turns of a valve the thunder emanating from the W. & A. Fletcher Company engine grew louder, sending a low vibration through the boat's superstructure and into the wooden deck planks. For a brief moment, as the vessel's speed reached that of the breeze off its bow, the air seemed perfectly still. A few seconds later a slight wind kicked up, ruffling the whiskers of Van Schaick's wiry gray mustache.

The seventeenth annual St. Mark's Church Sunday school outing was under way.

Captain Van Schaick stood on the foredeck just ahead of the pilothouse. After more than five decades in the business of moving people and cargo on the water, under every conceivable set of circumstances, this was the sort of day he looked forward to. A gorgeous sun-drenched morning was unfolding beneath a cloudless sky. A soft meandering breeze out of the south luffed the flag atop the pilothouse and promised to take the edge off the above-normal temperature. And on board was a church group of mostly women and children—the easiest of all groups to handle.

In the pilothouse, First Pilot Edward Van Wart stood at the wheel and guided the boat assisted by Second Pilot Edwin Weaver, who kept a close watch on the river already jammed with traffic. Tugs, lighters, barges, tankers, launches, and steamers moved at varied speeds in every conceivable direction. Each presented its own unique hazard—big lighters piloted by captains who thought they owned the water, lumbering ferries that cut across the main traffic lanes, powerless barges towed by tugs that swayed at the end of their cables.

That was on the water's surface. Hidden from view were countless maritime perils. Jagged outcroppings of Manhattan schist were everywhere, though experienced pilots like Weaver and Van Wart knew them all. Worse were the telephone-pole-sized semiwaterlogged pieces of wood, remnants of long-abandoned piers. Floating just beneath the waves, they often ripped huge holes in the sides of wooden-hulled steamboats like the *Slocum*. Up ahead lay Hell Gate. With more than thirty years' experience guiding steamboats, Van Wart knew that the captain trusted him implicitly. He also knew that he'd be in the pilothouse standing next to him as they passed through it.

Elsewhere aboard the *Slocum*, the crew and staff concerned themselves with far more mundane tasks. First Mate Ed Flanagan, in charge of the deckhands and kitchen staff and bar, made his rounds. Steward Michael McGrann sat at a table and counted nearly a thousand dollars in change, mostly coins, for use as change at the bar and concessions. Deckhand John J. Coakley gave a tour of the boat to the two policemen hired to accompany the group. Others answered questions, directed passengers, and kept an eye out for wayward children. Down in the boiler room, firemen shoveled coal into the boilers while in the engine room Chief Engineer Ben Conklin and his assistant Everett Brandow monitored the pressure gauges and responded to signals from the pilothouse.

Most members of the *Slocum* crew took solace in the fact that their long hours and low pay were offset by frequent stretches of downtime and the chance to work in the open air. Coakley was the sort always on the lookout for opportunities to kick back. Feeling a touch parched, as he often did at this time of day, he dropped into the bar. Hired by the Knickerbocker Steamboat Company only eighteen days earlier, he had already learned that it was customary on group outings for bartenders to treat the crew. In fact, earlier that morning Captain Van Schaick had warned the bartender, "Don't give my men too much to drink today." But as this was Coakley's first trip to the bar, the bartender did not hesitate to draw a glass of beer and plunk it down in front of him. It was a ritual Coakley planned to repeat several times that day.

Not all those working aboard the steamboat enjoyed such freedom. In the galley, the cook, Henry Canfield, was slicing and dicing his way through a small mountain of vegetables destined for the large chowder kettle on the stove. Over in the corner sat Edwin Robinson, a nineteen-year-old novice doing what nineteen-year-old novices did: peel potatoes. Canfield and Robinson were among eight African-American members of the thirty-five-member crew, and theirs would be a day of incessant toil. On this and every other trip, they worked nonstop in a setting like any restaurant in Manhattan, only smaller. They earned half what white crew members did and rarely got the chance to set foot on deck. Then there were the indignities suffered at the hands of white crewmen and passengers. But who were they to complain? In turn-of-the-century New York, they were lucky to have work at all and they knew it.

The passengers began enjoying themselves from the moment the trip got under way. Groups of parents and grandparents chatted avidly while packs of excited children scurried from rail to rail, not looking for anything in particular but not wanting to miss anything either. Here and there adults stood among them pointing out landmarks and identifying the many classes of vessels plying the waters around them. Already the picnic baskets were open and the first of many treats handed out. Several children played at games like bean ball and jacks.

Adding to the festive atmosphere was the music of Professor George Maurer's German band. Gathered on the main afterdeck, they began playing a long list of favorite songs, which set dozens of girls and boys to dancing while their parents tapped their feet. Sixteen-year-old Frieda Gardner was among them and was having the time of her life. It was almost too good to believe—a whole day with her friends far from the overprotective eyes of her parents. Still, she felt a bit ill at ease even as she twirled about the dance floor. Her mother had forbidden her to attend. Would someone tell? She hoped not. If Mother finds out, she thought, I'm dead.

Many of the passengers aboard the *Slocum* that morning had never been on a boat before today and were still a little nervous. They were chided by other, more experienced excursionists who pointed to the countless life preservers suspended above the decks with wire netting and six steel lifeboats and four rafts on the top deck. There was nothing to worry about and, besides, their trip covered only inland waterways. They would never be out of sight of land. And if that were not reassuring enough, Maurer's band soon struck up the popular hymn *"Eine Feste Burg Ist Unser Gott"* ("A Mighty Fortress Is Our God"), prompting passengers young and old to join in the singing. A song about God's love and protection through hardship and toil, it offered comfort in its rhythmic lines:

> *A mighty fortress is our God*
> *Our helper He amid the Flood*

Also reassuring was the sight of Reverend Haas making his way from group to group throughout the crowded steamer. Tall, handsome, and at ease in such social situations, the fifty-year-old minister moved effortlessly through the throng. Others had done most of the planning and fretting over the trip, but he was the host. He greeted parents, complimented them on their children, agreed that the weather was especially fine (praise God), and issued mock warnings about eating too much. They in turn extended their congratulations to the pastor for yet another perfect outing.

Another St. Mark's fixture receiving congratulations and good wishes from nearly everyone was John Holthusen. He had been the head of St. Mark's Sunday school for twenty-seven years—longer than Haas had been pastor—and had just announced his retirement. That made the seventeenth annual excursion all the more special, for it was in a way being held in his honor. All thirty-one students from his last class were aboard for the special occasion, as were his two daughters.

Even as they chatted amiably with friends and family, passengers kept an eye on the passing panorama. Traveling up the East River on a clear morning provided a unique view of the wider city in which they lived. They could see it all—the beauty and filth, the wealth and poverty, the new and old—and it was hard not to stare. Viewing the city in this manner was part of the charm and entertainment value of a steamboat excursion, but it also provided passengers a unique perspective on their lives and aspirations. The Empire City offered limitless possibilities to the intelligent and ambitious, but also many pitfalls and perils. Signs of success were everywhere, but so too was the grim evidence of failure. This duality was visible in their own neighborhoods every day, but this morning offered a chance to see it writ large—and better still, from a distance. Amid the countless thoughts and emotions conjured up by the passing urban panorama, most passengers aboard the *Slocum* had one in common: the thrill of knowing that for this one day they could suspend their struggles and worries and enjoy a day by the water.

Many passengers also delighted in the knowledge that they were being watched. They knew this because they themselves had often stared in envy at passing steamboats filled with revelers bound for a day at the shore. They knew it also because people on the shore and on passing boats waved to them while countless workers along the shore looked up from their workbenches and leaned on their shovels for a moment or two. A few captains even let fly a blast from their horns to the delight of the children. They were a spectacle of joy that morning, or what one journalist later called "a freight of human happiness."

One worker who paused from his morning routine was John Ronan. "Look at the *Slocum*," said the freight handler along the Astoria waterfront, summing up the opinion of many. "Don't it make you hate to work when you see a crowd having as good a time as that?"

Part Two

HORROR

A little fire is quickly trodden out,
Which, being suffered, rivers cannot quench.
—WILLIAM SHAKESPEARE, *HENRY VI, PART III*

They shall go out from one fire, and
another fire shall devour them.
—EZEKIEL 15:7

THE DEMON

Its exact origin will never be known. Most likely it originated with a match or cigarette carelessly tossed by a crewman, but it may have come from a lamp accidentally overturned by the roll of the vessel, or a spark from an overhead wire. In the end, all that mattered was that somewhere in the lamp room below the main deck of the *General Slocum*, a particle of fire had found a home.

The room was dark but very warm and filled with a great menu of flammable material. Stacked in one corner were cans of kerosene for the boat's lanterns and jars of polish for its brass fixtures. Along the walls on pegs, hooks, and nails hung clothing. Scraps of wood lay in a pile against a wall beneath a shelf loaded with oil-based paint. Just inside the door were three sacks of charcoal. And near the middle of the room were the barrels used to transport dozens of glasses for use during the picnic. Dry hay, used to separate the glasses, filled the barrels and lay about the floor.

Nestled somewhere in this hospitable environment—by all later accounts probably in the hay—the tiny ember lay glowing. Most scattered particles of fire like this one, like the millions of eggs spawned by an Atlantic codfish, die quickly. They simply consume the fuel they brought with them—a tobacco fragment, a few molecules of wire casing, a match splinter—and die.

Pyrologists, the people who study fire behavior, note that a tiny ember of fire can stay alive in what they term an *incipient phase* for hours, days, even weeks under certain conditions. That's why modern firefighters remain at a fire scene hours after the fire has been extinguished, pulling down ceilings and poking holes in walls looking for hidden embers. The ideal conditions for an incipient phase fire include a warm, dry location with ample oxygen and fuel—precisely those found in the forward storage room on the *Slocum*.

Such conditions, however, merely extend a fire's incipient phase. To reach Phase 2, or the *emergent smoldering* phase, a fire must progress from its original source (a match) to an ordinary combustible such as paper, wood, or cloth. As it does so, the evidence of fire—smoke and smell—grows, but there are still no flames. Most people who smoke in bed experience lots of near misses before the day arrives when they finally go up in flames. They simply wake up with singed sheets before the fire progresses to Phase 3. Or it simply burns out. In some settings, like the *Slocum*'s lamp room with its door closed, the odds are overwhelming that a Phase 2 fire will self-extinguish by steadily consuming all available oxygen or immediate fuel.

For the tiny Phase 2 fire burning quietly and imperceptibly in the *Slocum*'s forward lamp room, three scenarios were possible. It might evolve into a fire beyond anyone's control and result in unthinkable catastrophe. It might flourish briefly before being brought under control by the crew, resulting in only some short-term panic and perhaps a canceled day trip. Or it might simply self-extinguish and be discovered long after the danger had passed.

So long as it remained a Phase 2 fire in a stable environment, the surrounding combustibles—hay, wood, paper, oil, cloth, charcoal—were almost irrelevant. But if something radically altered the room's environment and introduced a sudden rush of oxygen, the fire would jump to Phase 3 or *free burning*. At that point the wooden-hulled boat would be in grave danger. That would only happen, of course, if someone opened the door.

Deckhand John Coakley stood at the bar just a few minutes before 10:00 A.M. enjoying his midmorning glass of lager. Droplets of condensation on the outside of the glass announced the coolness of its contents. The beer's foamy head rocked back and forth with the rhythm of the deck as the boat cleared the northern end of Blackwells Island (later renamed Roosevelt Island) at about 86th Street. The only thought on Coakley's mind was how long he could stretch this break out before a visit by the first mate or captain sent him bolting back to work.

The serenity of the moment was broken by an unfamiliar voice. "Mister, there's smoke coming up one of the stairways." He turned around to find a small, excited little boy. Perturbed, he put his glass down and went to investigate. Probably a puff of steam, ran an irritated thought across his mind. Passengers, especially boys with Tom Sawyer–sized imaginations, were forever mistaking steam for smoke and needlessly riling passengers and distracting deckhands from their duties. His glance to the bartender said, Back in a minute.

A dozen reluctant steps out the door brought Coakley to the top of a set of stairs. Smoke, *real* smoke, not steam, flowed upward. Still, nothing to panic over, thought Coakley. Probably just a burst exhaust pipe leading from the boiler. Even if it was a real fire, the small amount of smoke suggested it was nothing serious.

He glanced at the speaking tube, or "blower" in sailor parlance, protruding from the wall. Should he alert the captain in the pilothouse? Not for something this trifling. Although green, Coakley had already learned several of the unwritten laws by which all deckhands operated, chief among them being, Don't draw attention to yourself, especially from the officers.

Coakley cleared the cloud of smoke with a wave of his hand and disappeared down the stairs to investigate. At the bottom he came to the heavy door of the forward storage cabin. A thin thrust of smoke emanated from the slight gap between the bottom of the door and the deck.

Had he been trained in fire safety and procedure, Coakley would have known not to blindly open the door. But since the *Slocum*, like most steamboats of its kind, had not held a fire drill in anyone's memory, he put his hand on the lever and jerked the door open. In seconds the fire leaped from the emergent smoldering to the free-burning stage. Engorged with a sudden resupply of oxygen, the silent, smoldering embers in the hay spit out the first tongues of orange flame. In less than a second the flames began to expand at a temperature surging past 1000 degrees. Dry hay, as it turns out, is a superb fire accelerant. Being of low density, it has a very high heat release ratio (HRR). That is, it generates heat very quickly, and heat is what determines the speed at which a fire moves and grows. Remarkably, a barrel of dry hay or a brittle Christmas tree has a higher HRR (500–650 kilowatts) than a pool of gasoline (400 kilowatts).

Coakley, unaware of what he'd set in motion, simply saw a small fire that needed putting out. Looking about the vast tangle of things in the room, he spied a piece of canvas. Perfect, he thought, a couple of whaps with that and no more fire.

Except that the canvas was tied to the floor. Coakley, now sweating, pulled violently but couldn't free it. The *snap crackle* of the burning hay along with the rapidly rising heat told Coakley he'd better do something quick. By the door he found a sack of charcoal and dropped it on the flames. For a moment, the fire disappeared from view. He turned and bolted to find First Mate Flanagan. *This* was a situation for involving the higher-ups.

Coakley's decision to throw charcoal on the fire might appear to be the fateful action that ensured the coming catastrophe. Actually, it was his failure to close the lamp room door. The fire, its growth only temporarily slowed by the charcoal, quickly resumed its progress in the free burning phase. Oddly enough, the lamp room would serve merely as the inferno's launch pad and would itself sustain remarkably little damage despite its array of inflammables. The open doorway allowed oxygen to pour into the lamp room through its four air vents, fanning the flames and pushing them up the stairwell-soon-turned-chimney to an unlimited supply of oxygen and wood.

At that moment the *General Slocum* and its passengers were in grave danger. They still might be saved. If anyone knew how.

ALARM

While Coakley raced to find Flanagan, Captain Van strode into the pilothouse to oversee the passage through Hell Gate. For a brief moment the open door let in the joyful sounds of Professor Maurer's German band, but it did little to lighten the mood inside. The steamer was just short of Hell Gate, and already the current had the full attention of pilots Van Wart and Weaver. They knew it had been only twelve hours since the *Chester Chapin* had landed on the rocks just ahead.

The key to a safe passage through Hell Gate was steady speed and anticipation. Speed was essential for maintaining maneuverability. A boat suddenly downthrottled by a spooked pilot could be swept onto the shore in an instant. Anticipating the movement of currents and other boats was likewise vital. Failure to foresee a looming crosscurrent or discern another vessel's course could also spell disaster. Van Schaick immediately began issuing instructions.

Just then a sharp voice broke Van Schaick's concentration. "Hey, mister!" On the deck below stood twelve-year-old Frank Prawdzicky. Having seen the flames and smoke in the stairwell, he'd come to sound the alarm. "Hey, mister," the breathless boy repeated, "the ship's on fire!"

Van Schaick glared at the young messenger. He'd heard it a thousand times before and it still enraged him just the same. Practical jokes and boys, he knew, went hand in hand. But pranks on steamboats involving the words fire, sinking, or overboard were not funny. They caused panic and endangered the lives of the crew.

"Get the hell out of here and mind your own business," boomed the irritated skipper before returning to the pressing business of navigation. In less than a minute they'd be through Hell Gate and out of harm's way—if the damn kids didn't kill him first.

Coakley raced up the stairs in search of Flanagan, once again passing the blower he might have used to alert the captain in the pilothouse. At the top of the stairs a few passengers peppered him with questions about the smoke. Not wanting to cause any panic and desperate to find Flanagan, he pushed his way through without saying a word. The smoke from the stairway grew darker and started to billow.

He ran everywhere about the main deck, through the saloon and along the port and starboard passageways, but found no one but passengers. At last he came upon Flanagan and Second Mate James Corcoran supervising some deckhands. Coakley did his best to compose himself and pulled Flanagan aside. "Mate, the ship's afire forward, and it's making pretty good headway."

Normally a first mate put little stock in the judgments of his deckhands, especially those with only eighteen days' experience. But Coakley had just spoken one of the most dreaded words in the business—fire. Flanagan wheeled and led the men on a dead run past the main deck cabin, where Coakley's beer still sat on the bar. Smoke from the stairwell beyond had begun to fill the room, and by now a crowd of several dozen milled about with panic etched across their faces.

Is the boat burning? Is the fire under control? Are we in danger? Does the captain know? How many lifeboats are on board? Where are the life preservers? What should we do?

Flanagan offered no answers and instead spun about to consider his options. He'd seen a few fires on steamboats and knew instinctively that this one was different. Although he was normally loath to do so, never wanting to arouse the ire of Captain Van, he ran to the blower that led to the pilothouse and shouted, "The ship's on fire!" Then, without waiting for a reply, he sprinted aft to the engine room in search of Chief Engineer Conklin.

At that moment Conklin and his assistant, Everett Brandow, were chatting amiably about the exceptional performance of the Fletcher engine while a small group of boys and mothers stood nearby watching it in operation. Flanagan raised his voice in order to be heard above the roar of the engine, but not so loud as to reach the ears of the nearby passengers. "Chief," he blurted out in a voice laced with the very fear he desperately wanted to conceal, "the ship's afire forward." Stunned, the veteran Conklin listened as the first mate issued instructions. "Get to the pump," Flanagan said, referring to the steam pump that provided water to the boat's fire hoses. As Conklin leaped to his feet, Flanagan ran to the fire hose station about thirty feet away. Neither the boys nor their mothers heard a thing above the sound of the engine and assumed Flanagan was just giving routine orders.

As Conklin headed for the pump, it occurred to him that in his thirteen years on the *Slocum* he'd never seen anyone send water through the fire hoses, not even to test it. This better work, he thought, as he twisted the valve several times to get water for the fire hoses. The immediate swoosh of water surging through the pump and into the standpipe leading to the fire hose eased his mind a bit.

The *Slocum* had two fire stations, one at either end of the steamer's starboard side. Each consisted of a standpipe with a wheel valve and a coupling designed to accommodate a fire hose. Suspended above was a coil of fifty feet of hose. Theoretically this arrangement, along with two hand-operated fire pumps, provided the *Slocum* with total coverage in the event of a fire.

The nearest fire station was thirty feet forward of the blazing lamp room. Flanagan reached it moments after notifying Conklin and pulled the gray fire hose down with a musty *thump*. He quickly attached the hose's coupling to the standpipe while Tom Collins, a deckhand hired only four days earlier, grabbed the nozzle and made for the fire ten yards aft. As he ran, the hose twisted and kinked every couple of feet.

Flanagan then spun round the wheel valve to open the flow of water into the fire hose. At first everything seemed to work flawlessly. Water surged through the pipe and the pressure jolted the hose to life.

Then it all went awry. Collins shouted that he had only a trickle of water, and the reason immediately became obvious to Flanagan and the other deckhands. The creases and kinks in the hastily unfurled hose became choke points, allowing only a fraction of the water through. Several men jumped to straighten the hose out, but it was too late. What was cheap unlined linen hose in 1891 was by 1904 utterly useless. Rotten and weak, the never-tested hose was incapable of handling the high water pressure caused by the kinking and it burst in five or more places, sending streams of water everywhere but out the nozzle. A second later and the pressure tore the hose from its coupling. As water rushed out across the deck, Flanagan and several deckhands looked up to see that the flames had now reached the top of the stairs and were moving in their direction.

Just then Walter Payne, the African-American porter, rushed in with a rubber hose. Surely, they thought, this one would withstand the water pressure. Frantically, Flanagan and his men tried to attach it to the standpipe, but to their astonishment it would not fit. In their excited state they had failed to notice that the coupling from the torn fire hose was still attached to the standpipe, thus preventing the attachment of the rubber hose. "I saw then," recalled William Ortman, who watched the struggle from the ice cream stand, "that the boat was doomed."

Flanagan, now nearly out of his mind with panic, decided there was nothing left to do. "Get to the boats," he shouted, and everyone scattered. No further effort to fight the flames would be made by the crew, not even to slow its progress. This became one of several factors, along with rotten life preservers, that transformed the crisis into a catastrophe. Ortman was right

about the *Slocum*. There was no saving it. The only uncertainty remaining
was the fate of her thirteen hundred passengers.

Up in the pilothouse, Van Schaick and his pilots had just begun to re-
lax, for they had just guided the *Slocum* through Hell Gate without
incident. The steamboat was now just passing a shallow called Sunken
Meadow, approximately even with East 110th Street. Suddenly at 10:06
A.M., seven minutes after Coakley discovered the fire and three minutes after he notified Flanagan, word of the unfolding disaster finally reached the
pilothouse. "The ship's on fire!" boomed Flanagan's terror-stricken voice
through the blower.

Calm, Van Schaick thought to himself, project calm. In five decades on
the water, through all manner of scrapes, he'd learned the value of keeping
his head. Crewmen, both good and bad, instinctively adopted the demeanor of their captain in crisis situations. Keep cool and the crew listens
and follows orders; panic and the situation dissolves into chaos. "I'll go
down and see about it," he said coolly to his pilots, instructing them
matter-of-factly to hold the boat's course and increase speed to full power.

Opening the pilothouse door once again brought no rollicking sounds
of Maurer's band, for it had stopped playing. Instead, above the engine's
drone, the captain detected sounds of commotion. But he had no time to
discern what it was about, for no sooner had his foot touched the deck outside than a torrent of flame exploded out of the steamer's lower port side,
reaching upward to the decks above. It seemed, he later testified, "like a
volcano." Suddenly he could hear what the commotion was about—it was
the chilling sound of women and children screaming.

Instinctively, Van Schaick moved quickly to the stairs to get a closer
look. This was worse than any fire he'd experienced on one of his steamboats, and he needed to know its extent and speed in order to decide upon
a plan of action. With his men manning the fire hoses—surely, he thought,
they must have at least one good stream of water on it by now—it might be
contained long enough for them to get to safety. He hit the stairs and
started down when he met the fire dashing upward. "I got part of the way

down," he recalled, "and the fire drove me back. It was sweeping up from below like a tornado."

This is it, he thought, as he sprinted back to the pilothouse. I've lost her. It was the moment all captains spend their careers not thinking about—the loss of their vessel. He'd seen all manner of maritime disasters in the course of his fifty years—deadly collisions, boiler explosions, founderings in storm, sudden sinkings, and uncontrollable fires. But these had always been other captains' tragedies. He'd had his share of near misses—who didn't—and he knew that the longer he kept at it, the greater the likelihood his turn would come. As the poem about Jim Bludso and his *Prairie Belle* stated so matter-of-factly,

> *All boats has their day on the Mississip,*
> *And her day come at last,—*

Running toward the pilothouse away from the flames, Van Schaick knew in an instant that the *Slocum*'s day had come. After half a century on the water, he'd lost his first boat. What he did not know—or refused at that moment to even consider—was that unlike the great Jim Bludso, he would not get all his passengers to shore.

GOD HELP US

Pastor Haas had just completed his tour to the steamboat's three decks, a ritual he performed at the outset of every excursion. Walking about the three decks allowed him to mingle with his flock and play the role of host. Equally important, it enabled him to make sure everything was in order aboard the boat. This year's choice to charter the *Slocum* had made the latter task a mere formality, for it appeared to him to be in tip-top shape. Striding along the shiny varnished floorboards of the promenade deck with the warm spring breeze tussling his dark hair, he smiled at the passengers and looked for his family.

The pleasure of the moment was broken by a most unexpected sight. Haas saw smoke coming up a narrow stairway leading down to the main deck. No need to panic, he thought, it must be coming from the galley. He'd just passed that way a few minutes earlier and saw the cooks preparing the chowder. He stood there calmly for a minute, hoping the smoke would soon abate. A few passengers took notice and drew near to him, fixing an anxious, expectant gaze in him that asked, Is everything all right?

The answer came quick enough. Instead of diminishing, the smoke intensified and grew darker. Worse, it smelled of burning wood, not food, and carried with it the muffled sounds of commotion and confusion down below. Immediately, Haas knew this was serious. A real fire had broken out below and it was growing stronger. He, like Van Schaick, also knew that his chief responsibility was to prevent panic. No matter how this dangerous situation was resolved, it was absolutely essential that everyone remain calm. To do this, he understood, he'd have to lie. Under these circumstances, God would surely forgive him.

"It's just the coffee burning in the galley," he lied to the group of anxious onlookers. Nothing to worry about, he assured them. But as a precaution, he suggested they move to the stern of the boat. Then with an exaggerated slowness designed to obscure the storm then roiling within him, he strolled away to find his wife and daughter. Out of respect, his listeners played along, waiting until he was a reasonable distance away before bolting to spread the alarm and find their loved ones.

The fear of fire that lay dormant deep within them all had, just like the fire itself, suddenly come to life.

Just below Haas on the main deck, the fire was about to pounce on its first victims. Ten minutes earlier the word had gone out along the decks that ice cream would be served down on the main deck. Martha Liebenow, the unmarried sister of Paul Liebenow and Annie Weber, swept up her three-year-old niece Anna and took six-year-old Helen by the hand. She would take them, along with their older cousins Emma and Frank, she explained to their parents, downstairs for the ice cream. We'll be right back, Aunt Martha assured the adults, who smiled at the prospect of a few minutes of peace without the children.

They moved quickly, for they could see that scores of other children had the same idea. "Children were falling all over each other," one boy later recalled, "in an effort to get to the tables which held the refreshments."

Just a few feet away in the engine room was the group of young boys and their mothers who had gathered to watch the mighty Fletcher engine in action. A few minutes earlier they'd seen Flanagan burst into the engine room, but they had not heard him tell Conklin of the fire. While the boys watched in hypnotic wonder the thumping rods and pounding piston, their indulgent mothers covered their ears and fanned themselves in the hot and cacophonous room.

"Suddenly and without the least warning," recounted thirteen-year-old John Ell, "there was a burst of flames from the furnace-room that rushed up through the engine room and flashed out about us." Terrified and disoriented, the boys and mothers came shrieking into the room where the ice cream was being served, their clothes and hair on fire. "There was a most terrible panic," he remembered, as everyone struggled to get to the side of the boat. Ell tried to run with his mother and brother, whose clothes were ablaze, but he fell and the crowd swept them away. Martha Liebenow, her nieces, and nephew were doubtless caught up in this mad rush to get away from the fire. If they managed to get out of the room—and many did not—they were swept along with the crowd and pinned to the railing, which soon gave way. Even if they hung on at this point, they had little time left, for the fire had by now swept past, leaving them surrounded by a rapidly closing circle of flame.

On the deck above, the Webers and Liebenows did not hear the panic that was now consuming their children and sister, but someone did notice the black smoke wafting upward. "It was a big puff," remembered Annie Weber, "and it startled everyone." But when someone said it must be the chowder boiling over in the galley, "we all laughed at our fears." Such reactive denial of real peril, say psychologists who study responses to disasters, is very common. People are either too engrossed in an activity to allow the sight of danger to register or, as was the case with the Webers and Liebenows, they are too terrified to acknowledge it. In either case this denial is always short-lived. On the promenade deck of the *Slocum* it lasted less than five seconds. "The laughing changed to a cry of horror," said Annie, "when a sheet of flame followed the smoke."

Suddenly above the strains of music, they could hear the sounds of commotion below. In an instant, pandemonium broke out as people rushed to the railings to see for themselves. They could see people scurrying about and hear them shouting about a fire. Almost immediately, recounted one survivor, "there was a loud roar as though a cannon had been shot off, and the entire bow of the boat was a sheet of flames." Adding to the terror of the moment was the sudden realization that some passengers were already leaping over the railings into the river.

Paul and Anna Liebenow had the same reaction as every parent on board—*where are the children!* The last they had seen of them they were descending the stairs with their Aunt Martha—the same stairwell now belching smoke and flame. Stay here and wait for us, Liebenow and his brother-in-law Frank Weber told their wives. They would find the children. Anna Liebenow clutched her six-month-old Adella to her chest as she watched the two men head aft and disappear into the veil of smoke.

By now smoke was visible on the hurricane deck. One of the first to notice was a six-year-old girl named Lillie Manheimer. While the adults in her group chattered away and bounced to the sounds of Professor Maurer's band, her wandering eyes caught sight of a steady stream of smoke emanating from below. It took her a minute or so to summon the temerity to intrude upon the conversation and say, "I think the boat is on fire, auntie. See all the smoke?" Her Aunt Millie yanked her aside and scolded. "Hush!" she said. "You must not talk so; you may create a panic." She was right—the fear of fire was so great that the mere mention of it frequently touched off deadly panics.

The crowd on the main afterdeck were among the last to know of the fire. The seven members of Professor George Maurer's band were filling the air with the sounds of festive music, obscuring temporarily the shouts of panic and alarm breaking out amidships and above. But in that brief moment of silence between the strains of the last note and the start of the audience's applause, a piercing shriek could be heard coming from the forward part of the vessel. Everyone, including the musicians, froze in terror—an instinctual response to sudden fright found in virtually all mammals—and listened. Many thought someone, most likely a child, had fallen overboard, but most sensed that something worse was transpiring.

Maurer, still at the center of attention, hesitated a moment, not sure what to do. He looked over to his wife and three daughters seated nearby and read the pleading look of terror in their eyes. This would not be a scene anticipating the famed decision of the band aboard the *Titanic* to continue playing as the liner went down. There simply wasn't any time (the *Titanic* took two hours and forty minutes to sink). Looking forward, Maurer saw billows of black smoke heading in his direction and heard the unmistakable cries of "Fire!" This was a matter of seconds, he thought, minutes at best.

He dropped his baton, an unspoken signal to the musicians and crowd alike that it was time to act. Bedlam broke out in an instant as dozens of passengers snapped out of their momentary catatonic state and began running. In scenes now being played out all over the boat, some ran for children and other loved ones, others made for the racks of life preservers, while a handful pleaded for calm.

Not everyone panicked at this moment. In every situation of extreme stress and chaos, there are those who possess a unique ability to remain calm, think clearly, and formulate a wise plan of action. It is a capacity as vital to a commander's success on the field of battle as it is to a person caught in an unfolding disaster. Kate Kassenbaum was just such a person. "I realized that we were in the gravest peril," she remembered, "and that if we expected to escape with our lives some of us at least must keep cool heads." She called her ten family members together at the railing and in a calm and quiet manner explained that they must stick together and help each other out.

Mary Hartman was made of the same stuff. She held the hands of her two daughters, twelve-year-old Clara and fifteen-year-old Margaret, and pulled them to her side. We must stick together, she told them, until the steamer docks or we can clamber aboard a rescue boat. The firmness of her voice gave the girls hope that they would be saved. But as all three looked toward the bow of the *Slocum*, a chill of terror went through them. Bearing down upon them, the Kassenbaums, and everyone else were two destructive forces moving at roughly the same speed—a huge mob of panic-stricken passengers followed by a wall of orange fire.

"God help us!" Clara Hartman remembered her mother saying. "God help us!"

PANIC

Pastor Haas was one of the fortunate ones, for only a minute after leaving the smoking stairwell, he found his wife and daughter. Quietly, so as to prevent panic, he whispered to them to follow him to the stern of the boat. It became very clear almost immediately, however, that panic—that unquantifiable, deadly force—had begun to spread. Haas quickly realized that his calm pronouncements that people should begin moving to the stern were as unnecessary as they were unheard. Everyone, excepting those in search of missing family members, was scurrying aft.

Just as soon as Haas had guided his family to the stern railing of the promenade deck, he left them and ventured forward through the stream of terrified passengers. If ever his flock needed a shepherd it was now, and Haas did not flinch. "Stay calm!" he urged in a tone loud enough to project authority while avoiding any hint of fear. "Stay calm!" John Holthusen, the Sunday school principal, later remembered the scene with awe. "Pastor Haas seemed to be everywhere—calm and collected, striving to stay the panic."

Psychologists and sociologists who study crowd behavior note that groups typically disintegrate into panic and chaos in situations where there is no leader to offer direction and reassurance. The history of disasters and

near disasters, not to mention warfare, is full of stories where the timely assertion of leadership averts a panic. On board the *Slocum* that morning
were three potential leaders: the steamboat's officers, police officers Van
Tassel and Kelk, and Haas. While the first proved utterly incapable of ex-
erting any kind of meaningful leadership, the policemen and Haas acted in
exemplary fashion, urging calm and giving direction.

But the fire aboard the *Slocum* was no ordinary situation of terror. Unlike a theater fire, where the crowd at least knows that safety lies just
beyond the building's walls, the fire aboard the *Slocum* presented an un-
thinkable scenario—a fire from which there was virtually no escape. They
were surrounded by water, something the passengers considered only
slightly less terrifying than fire—even with life preservers strapped on. In
this unique setting, no amount of leadership could stem the rising tide of
panic.

In 1904 people were just beginning to understand the dynamics of
what turns a crowd into a panicked mob. Only recently (1897) French psychologist and sociologist Gustave Le Bon had given a name—"conta-
gion"—to the process by which emotions, including panic, spread through
a crowd. But precisely *how* panics become contagious would not come to
light for decades. Today most sociologists and psychologists see panic as
developing in a series of escalating stages. First, in a large group faced with
a situation of extreme stress and fear, a small number of people succumb to
their feelings of terror and begin acting in an antisocial and individualistic
manner. They refuse to take direction and begin to see the people around
them as mere obstacles to their frantic quest to escape. They push and
claw, for example, their way to an exit. Second, as Le Bon observed, such
behavior becomes *contagious*, spreading quickly through the rest of the
crowd. As panic spreads, it gains momentum and intensity. Feeding off one
another's fear, people become ever more focused on self-preservation, and
as a result, more violent. Finally, the crowd reaches a stage sociologists term
"demoralization," where individuals shed any remaining social constraints
and descend into an atavistic struggle for survival. In this "kill or be killed"
state of mind, normally peaceable and moral people will bite, pummel, or
trample anyone who gets in their way.

Given the unique setting and the speed with which the flames moved, it took almost no time for a full-scale panic to develop aboard the *Slocum*. "There was a rush away from the spot from which the smoke came," recalled John Holthusen. "Screams of women and cries of children rent the air. Men began to shout and there were cries of 'keep cool,' 'where are the lifeboats?' 'don't crowd,' etc., but I doubt if many heard them."

They didn't. No amount of leadership and pleading, not even from Haas, a man so many loved, trusted, and respected, could stop the crowd's descent toward demoralization. "A panic that has seized on a few sheep," wrote Le Bon, "will soon extend to the whole flock." So it was on the *Slocum* that morning—and the shepherd was powerless to stop it.

Haas pressed on through the retreating crowd like a salmon swimming upstream, refusing to surrender hope that the disaster could be averted. Up ahead just beyond the crowd he could see the flames now, moving with astonishing speed through the main cabin of the promenade deck. If he could close the large side-by-side doors of the cabin, it would slow the fire's progress and shield the mass of passengers crammed on the stern until the captain brought the boat to shore. Haas struggled forward through the retreating crowd, still preaching calm, until he reached the doors. They were hot to the touch and the fire was only feet away. Smoke stung his eyes and throat as he quickly closed the right-hand door. The left-hand door, however, jammed—probably due to the heat, which swelled the wood and turned to glue its several coats of paint and varnish. As the fire ate into his fingers and sparks singed his face, Haas poured every ounce of strength he had into it, but still the door refused to budge. He shook and kicked it. Please God, he prayed, give me the strength. But it was no use.

Standing a few feet away, John Holthusen watched in amazement. His friend was, he recalled, "surrounded by flames" and still struggling with the door. And when he lost sight of him a few seconds later in a cloud of smoke, he felt certain Haas had died.

Haas, as it turned out, was badly burned but still alive. Unable to withstand the flames, he reluctantly retreated to the railing in search of his family. He found them pinned to the railing amid a scene of sheer terror and panic. A steady flow of frantic passengers pressed toward the boat's stern. "Women were shrieking and clasping their children in their arms," Haas remembered. We need to get on the other side of the railing, he told his wife and daughter, otherwise we'll be crushed to death. One by one he helped them over, and then he followed. There was nothing left for him to do but pray and wait—for what he did not know.

Order rapidly broke down throughout the vessel as panic spread to every quarter. Some passengers, as is common in panic situations, stood paralyzed by fear, frozen in one place, shouting for their spouses, children, and relatives. Fourteen-year-old William McGaffney came across a girl about his age in this catatonic state. She made no attempt to save herself and stood silently, twisting the ends of her necktie. McGaffney picked her up and threw her onto an approaching tugboat.

Most, however, recalled Bernard Miller, "acted as though they had lost their minds." Panic quickly reached the demoralization stage and packs of fear-crazed passengers raced from one side of the steamer to find loved ones and refuge. Seeking order and safety, they created chaos and hazard. And as Kate Kassenbaum and others in the minority who remained level-headed discovered, they were at the mercy of the panicked majority. Kassenbaum had kept her cool when the panic started and managed to gather her family of ten along a railing. Hang on for as long as possible, she quietly urged them, and stick together. "But my words of warning were not more than out of my mouth," she recalled, "when there came such a rush of panic-stricken and frenzied people to the stern of the boat that no human being could have stood up against it." She closed her eyes and hung on as they crashed into them. When she opened her eyes she was all alone. "Not one of my family was to be seen anywhere. They had been whisked away from me in the mad rush."

Kassenbaum could at least cling to the hope that she'd find them again. But many other passengers suffered a far worse fate at the hands of the mob. Demoralized by panic and propelled by collective momentum, it stampeded anything in its path. Fainting women, slow-moving grandparents, and scores of small children were simply crushed to death. Many survivors would be forever haunted by the memory of having trampled, however unwillingly, innocent people caught underfoot. Most never noticed.

Although warped by fear, their minds were nonetheless fixated on a clear and rational goal: to get away from the flames and into a life preserver or lifeboat. Most of the passengers—like the great majority of Americans in 1904—did not know how to swim. They were city people, and were too busy and too poor to learn. Even if they had the time and money, where would they go to swim? The city had only a handful of public pools, and the crowds they attracted limited swims to a mere fifteen minutes a day. Up until this very moment, swimming had seemed about as necessary as piano lessons.

Paul Liebenow, unable to find his children and now separated from his brother-in-law, decided to return to their wives with a few life preservers. That way at least they and the baby would have a chance to survive. There were some twenty-five hundred life preservers on board, stowed throughout the boat in clusters suspended from the ceiling by wire mesh. Many hung more than eight feet above the deck. Liebenow saw crowds gathered beneath them, their arms stretched upward reaching like Tantalus, grasping futilely for their only hope of survival. Young boys shimmied up pipes and men boosted each other upward to jerk the wire mesh loose. Liebenow found a cluster he could reach, but to his horror discovered that the wire holding them in place refused to give. The rusted wire sliced into his fingers as he fought to free them. Finally, with blood running down his arms, he yanked once more and the life preservers fell to the deck with a thud.

In most cases the lifejackets cascaded down upon the desperate people below, touching off a frenzied, Darwinian struggle among the thoroughly demoralized crowd. Gone, it seemed, were the good Christian people of St. Mark's parish, Sunday school teachers, church sextants and ushers, members of the choir and Luther League. In their place were savage individuals capable of unspeakable acts of violence and cruelty. "Mothers who had

started side by side with an endless fund of sympathy for domestic diffi-
culties," wrote one journalist, "were fighting like wild beasts." Many had
their babies torn from their arms in the struggle. Frieda Gardner, still terrified that her mother would discover that she'd gone on the trip against her
wishes, was pounced upon by a woman who ripped her life preserver off.
Similarly, men with an equally vast fund of sympathy for late-Victorian
ideals of chivalry and manliness, punched and kicked women and children.
One man desperate for a place along the railing sunk his teeth into a
woman's hand until she jumped.

The agony of the bitter struggles for life preservers was quickly compounded when the passengers found, much to their horror, that most of the
life preservers were worthless. Their canvas coverings long since deterio-
rated over thirteen seasons of sun, salt, and sea, they ripped open like paper sacks. "As fast as anyone tried to use them they would burst open,"
recalled William Vassner, "or the straps would come off."

Out of the tattered life preservers spilled useless gray matter—once-
solid chunks of cork that had long since disintegrated into fine dust. It
blinded many as it cascaded down from the racks above and littered the
decks below. Some of it poured over the sides of the boat into the water, or
ended up there when the defective life preservers burst on impact. "The
powdered cork from the life preservers was so thick [in the water]," related
one survivor, "that some of us were nearly choked by the stuff."

Some passengers took off in the hope that usable lifejackets could be
found somewhere else. Others simply dropped the tattered remains and
jumped. "I tried all six life preservers, and they were all rotten," remembered one boy. "So I had to jump overboard just as I was." Fortunately for
him, he knew how to swim.

In those sections of the steamer where lifejackets were not clawed to
pieces or where their flaws were not obvious to the naked eye, passengers
dutifully put them on and jumped. Few of them, absorbed as they were
with the task of securing lifejackets about themselves and their children,
seemed to notice that almost no one who entered the water wearing one
ever resurfaced.

With three children to handle, Elizabeth Kircher didn't notice. She and her two oldest children could swim, but her youngest, seven-year-old Elsie, could not. Thank God, she thought, as she found one of Kahn-weiler's Never-Sink Life Preservers and strapped it on her. She then helped her over the side and waited for her to resurface. She never did. "She had sunk as though a stone were tied to her," her father bitterly remarked after-ward. "The only one lost was the one who wore a life preserver." The same grim truth applied to the Ottingers. Kate Ottinger herded her four children to the railing and began putting life preservers on them. Her oldest, Willie, refused one, insisting he could swim and urging her to quickly put it on his younger brother. "With that she said something like a prayer," he remem-bered, "and then pushed me in the water." Witnesses later told him his mother and siblings entered the water wearing life preservers and sank like stones.

Over and over the same dreadful scenario was played out. Splash, noth-ing . . . Splash, nothing . . . Splash, nothing.

Only in the aftermath of the disaster did the survivors reach the un-thinkable but inescapable conclusion that the rotten lifejackets had actually *dragged* many straight to the bottom. Unlike solid cork, cork dust has the buoyancy of dirt. Absorbing water on impact, each lifejacket instantly be-came twenty or more pounds of deadweight—a burden difficult even for an accomplished swimmer to bear for more than a few minutes.

Some of the terrified passengers placed their hopes in the six steel lifeboats and four life rafts on the *Slocum*'s hurricane deck. The lifeboats were good size—22 feet long by 6 feet wide—and capable of holding twenty or more passengers. Frank Weber found himself in a crowd of men and boys working frantically to free them. Despite their vigorous pulling, the boats barely budged. Realizing that the boats were tied down, some drew out penknives and tried to cut them free. They managed to cut the ropes, but to everyone's shock and dismay, they discovered they were also held with wire and were immovable. Long ago, it seems, someone had grown tired of the boats rattling about in rough weather and had them meticulously wired in place. In desperation the crowd grabbed the gun-wales and tried to rock the boats free. Nothing worked, and with the flames coming at them from all angles, Weber and the rest left the lifeboats and re-treated.

Throughout the mounting fury of the fire, many passengers looked to the steamboat's crew for help and direction. Many of the passengers had never been on a steamboat before today, but they knew to expect assistance from the crew in an emergency. As George Heins later put it, they looked to the crewmen to take control and tell people to remain calm, "the way they do in books."

But as the fiasco with the fire hoses clearly indicated, the crew of the *Slocum* was not up to the task. Indeed, almost from the moment the fire broke out they had been part of the panicked masses, distinguishable only by their uniforms. Flanagan and Coakley would later tell grand stories of heroism and self-sacrifice, but witness after witness related a different story. "The deck-hands and crew of the boat were absolutely of no aid in saving lives," charged Frank Weber. Another offered an even harsher assessment. "The men acted as if they were crazy. They were worse than the women." At first they refused to offer assistance to the pleading passengers. Then, when confronted by angry crowds, they reluctantly pulled down a few dozen life preservers before disappearing.

One member of the crew who executed his duties flawlessly was Michael McGrann, and he paid the ultimate price as a result. As the boat's steward, he was in charge of the money, some one thousand dollars in coins and small bills. When word of a fire reached his ears, he knew just what to do. A seasoned veteran, he knew that panic and chaos presented a superb opportunity for a criminal to make some easy money—so much so that criminals in the city often staged fights or shouted fire to allow for easy pocket picking. If he allowed that to happen here, the Knickerbocker Steamboat Company would fire him in a heartbeat—not the sort of thing welcomed by a man with a wife and five young children to support. So he quickly filled a bag with the coins and bills—at least twenty pounds—and donned a life preserver handed to him by a fellow crewman.

Minutes later, now aware that this was no false alarm, McGrann went to the railing, swung his legs over, and jumped. A good swimmer, he probably felt he had little to worry about. But freighted with the Knickerbocker's precious lucre and no doubt wearing a defective life preserver, he broke the water's surface like a torpedo, surfaced briefly and called for help, and then disappeared. When in the aftermath of the tragedy the Knickerbocker Steamboat Company was accused of practicing a deadly "criminal economy," the irony of McGrann's drowning under the weight of the company's money would be lost on no one.

Equally dedicated to the end were the engineers down below in the engine room. "The part of the boat where I stood was filled with a dense black smoke," Conklin later testified. "I was obliged to cover my mouth with my arm in order to breathe." Conditions were worse where Brandow stood, yet both men remained at their posts until the bitter end. Conklin, not aware that Flanagan and his men had abandoned the fight against the blaze almost as soon as it began, stayed at the steam engine pump to ensure that it was sending water into the standpipe. Brandow manned the steamer's engine, responding to signals from the pilothouse regarding speed and direction. One tugboat captain, who could tell that at least one engineer was still at his post when the boat hit, told his men he was certain the engineers were lost. Miraculously, both would manage to escape.

The fire, propelled by the forward progress of the steamboat, charged from the forward sections of the vessel toward the stern, filling the decks, stairwells, and interior rooms with thick choking smoke now laced with the sickening smell of burning flesh and hair. Disoriented and unable to see, passengers tumbled down stairs or over railings into the river. Everywhere terrified children ran crying, desperate to find a parent. Sparks and burning embers fell everywhere, setting people on fire. The roar of the fire and crackle of burning wood grew louder, as did the pitiful screams and cries for help. "There are no letters in any language to spell such sounds," wrote one journalist. "Once heard they are seared upon the memory as with a white-hot iron."

Cornered by fire or crushed by the crowd, passengers jumped from every corner of the boat. "Twenty would jump at once," Willie Keppler recounted, "and right on top of 'em twenty more would jump."

From many places, countless abandoned children were simply thrown overboard. It was a ghastly task made possible only by a rough weighing of cruel probabilities. Those doing the hurling knew that most of the children they put over the railings would drown, but that was better than the alternative. "I would rather see you drown," one man told a little girl as he put her over the railing, "than burn to death." And, they told themselves, some might be saved by other passengers in the water or by the many boats now trailing the steamer. So over they went, shrieking for their mothers and clutching the air as they fell into the cold dark water below.

The fate of young children still with their mothers was scarcely better. Desperate mothers, wrote one reporter, "fought like trapped animals to reach the edge of the crowded decks in order that they might give their little ones the more merciful death of drowning." As they pushed through the crowds clutching their infants and toddlers, they cried out, Can you swim? Please save my baby! Help me I beg you!

A few found saviors, often in the form of young boys and girls who knew how to swim. In some cases, little ones were passed over the heads of the crowd to the railing and handed to a waiting boy or girl, who then jumped. For fourteen-year-old Arthur Link, it happened spontaneously at the railing when he noticed a woman about to jump with her baby. "If you can't swim," he shouted, "give me that baby." She did and promptly jumped to her death. Link followed and swam the baby to a nearby boat. Twelve-year-old Louise Gailing knew the baby handed to her. She'd come along with the Erklins of Hoboken, New Jersey, as a nanny to care for their young baby. Just before the family jumped, the mother, aware that Louise could swim, handed her the baby. She plunged in with the infant clutched to her chest and then swam with one arm to a nearby boat.

Most mothers, however, found no guardian angels. Or they could not bear the thought of handing their own flesh and blood to a stranger. Some jumped in clutching them to their breasts; others threw them out as far as they could to avoid the paddle wheels and dove in after them. Many mothers put life preservers on their children even when it meant they would have none. "My mother gave me a life preserver, that's how I got saved," recounted little Walter Mueller from his hospital bed. "I guess she didn't have none herself, because they can't find her."

Many terrified victims, adults and children, never had to make the choice of when and where to jump. They were simply forced overboard by the crush at the rails. Albertina Lembach was fortunate enough to collect her five children in the chaos and find a space at the rail near Pastor Haas and his family. Mrs. Haas urged her to stay with the boat as long as they could, but that quickly proved impossible. "There was a fearful rush," she remembered. "People ran shrieking to the rail and it gave way, letting most of them fall into the water. In the rush three of my children were swept away." Lena De Luccia told a similar story. "I was close to the rail," she tearfully recalled, "when a wave of frenzied women and children forced us overboard." She immediately lost sight of her four children. Nearly all were swallowed, one eyewitness later wrote, by "the hungry jaws of the devouring tide."

THE DECISION

C hased back to the pilothouse by the flames, Van Schaick rapidly explained the situation to his two stunned pilots. There's a huge fire raging belowdecks and the passengers have begun to panic. We don't have much time and need to . . . to do what? Land the steamer, yes, but where?

Van Schaick wasn't sure. They had just then passed through the manic waters of Hell Gate, but were hardly free of jagged shoals and whirling currents. In a nearly identical situation twenty-four years earlier, the captain of the *Seawanhaka* had immediately beached his burning steamboat on the Sunken Meadow just beyond Hell Gate. Some 62 passengers perished in the fire and water, but more than 200 were saved by his quick thinking. Most jumped into the shallow water, where they waded ashore or climbed aboard rescue boats. But Van Schaick ruled that option out, for in his judgment they were too far past the Sunken Meadow and could not risk trying to bring the steamboat around in the unpredictable currents. If it hit a rock and lost power or steering it might never reach shore and instead simply burn in the open water, taking everyone on board with it. Even if they pulled it off without incident, he reasoned, the maneuver might take three minutes.

Yet other factors argued in favor of an attempted beaching at Sunken Meadow, or somewhere close to it. Bringing the *Slocum* around would have the added benefit, as any captain knew, of putting the fire at the bow downwind of the remaining half of the boat. The *Slocum* would surely be lost, but not as quickly as with the vessel charging into the wind and fanning the flames from bow to stern. And then there were the dozens of boats in pursuit of the distressed steamer—wouldn't they be able to off-load most if not all of the passengers even if the *Slocum* hit a shoal?

If he considered these factors at all, Van Schaick quickly rejected them. That left two possibilities. The first, and the one that seems obvious to any landlubber gazing at a map of the East River, was to put the vessel hard over to port and make for the docks along the Bronx waterfront, or hard over to starboard and head for the Queens shore. Indeed, that's what the great Bludso had done—

And quick as a flash she turned, and made
For that willer-bank on the right

And it's what the captain of the ill-fated steamer *Henry Clay* did when it caught fire on the Hudson in 1852. "The boat suddenly changes her course," remembered the minister in his description, "with unslacked speed she approaches the shore."

But again the specter of the river's treacherous shoals and fierce currents dominated Van Schaick's mind and he rejected that option as too risky. What he wanted was a safe and familiar place where he could bring the flaming boat to a stop. He knew every inch of the river, and in a flash it came to him. There was a small island off the Bronx shore. On its western side, if he remembered correctly, the water ran deep and there was a sandy beach—ideal for bringing a large steamer as close to shore as possible.

There was only one problem. It lay nearly a mile upriver—at least three precious minutes away. A full-speed sprint for it would surely feed the flames and push them to the stern. But that known risk was one Van

Schaick was prepared to accept, and once he'd latched on to the plan there was no changing his mind. Psychologists who study leadership and decision-making note that in situations of extreme stress, normally rational people will choose a course of action (often the riskiest option, it turns out) and refuse to deviate from it despite mounting evidence that it's the wrong one. Often the more hopeless the situation becomes, the more determined they are to carry out their original plan.

Such a fixated mind-set can and often does produce positive results. During the Civil War, for example, Adm. David Farragut became a national hero when during the Battle of Mobile Bay he shouted, "Damn the torpedoes and full steam ahead!" and breached the Confederate hold on the lower Mississippi. But it is just as likely, as was the case with Pickett's Charge at the Battle of Gettysburg, to bring disastrous results.

His mind made up, Van Schaick shouted to his pilot Van Wart, "Put her on North Brother Island!" The veteran pilot, trained to carry out orders and not question them, signaled to the engine room for more steam and opened up the throttle.

The race—to safety and rescue, Van Schaick hoped—was on.

MURDEROUS INTENSITY

B y now the fire was spreading rapidly belowdecks. The steamboat, made entirely of wood, provided an enormous quantity of fuel. But there were other factors at work in this and nearly every fire aboard a wooden vessel that made it burn far faster than an ordinary house fire. A boat's wood, constantly exposed to wind, sun, and salt, will rapidly dry out and become brittle unless measures are taken to prevent it. At the turn of the century, steamers like the *Slocum* had their wood planking routinely "slushed down" with a warm mixture of linseed oil and turpentine. It penetrated deep into the wood fiber and thus kept it flexible, strong, and water-resistant. It also progressively turned the wood into something akin to a Duraflame log. Annual coats of oil-based varnish likewise protected the wood, but also added to its unusual inflammability. As Jonathan Klopman, a Massachusetts-based marine surveyor, puts it, once a fire on such a vessel gets out of control, it goes "Kawoosh!"

Klopman also points out that the key factor in a fire's progression on a boat is not the availability of wood, but rather oxygen. Every child in modern America is told to "stop, drop, and roll" if ever on fire. Running, they are taught, fans the flames and only makes the fire worse. Captains then and now are similarly instructed to swing their vessel around so the wind blows the flames away from the passengers and crew until help arrives. Captain Van Schaick's decision to "run" for North Brother Island at full speed into the wind had the perverse effect of speeding the boat's demise by feeding the fire. As the steamer moved ahead, the large air ducts placed throughout its forward sections swallowed air and forced it belowdecks into interior rooms. Under normal conditions this kept the *Slocum* and its boilers supplied with abundant fresh air. On June 15, 1904, it turned a minor storage room fire into a catastrophic inferno.

By the time the first passengers actually saw the flames, the fire had long since achieved what one journalist so aptly termed "its murderous intensity." But fires are greedy in nature. They are never satisfied with their immediate surroundings, no matter how rich in oxygen and fuel. So using the raging hold as a launching pad, the fire aboard the *Slocum* raced upward, as is characteristic of ship fires. "The flames kept sweeping up in puffs," testified one survivor, "each one growing higher and spreading." It left virtually untouched most of the *Slocum*'s lower regions and instead headed in the direction where oxygen was most plentiful. Like a giant octopus it sent out tentacles of flame that probed for openings—not just large ones like stairs and air vents, but invisible ones like gaps in planking and seams between walls. It found aboard the *Slocum*, a floating tinderbox of a boat, an endless supply of highly flammable pathways through which it could extend its reach. Additional supplies of oxygen discovered in this way only fueled the fire's insatiable desire for still more.

Onward it surged, filling in the gaps between the probing lines of fire until it burst through the upper decks and the hit the mother lode—the inexhaustible supply of oxygen surrounding the boat. With its upward progress now complete, the fire engorged itself with oxygen and began moving outward in all directions. In less than a minute it stretched from the starboard to port rail on the main deck, cutting off the bow section from the rest of the vessel. From here it proceeded to move simultaneously forward to the bow and aft to the stern in a relentless effort to envelop and consume every particle of fuel on the entire vessel. "The flames were sweeping back as the boat raced on," remembered Annie Weber, "and it was like the breath of a red-hot furnace."

Nearly every passenger who later described the fire expressed astonishment at the lightning speed with which it moved. "The boat went up in five minutes," declared porter Walter Payne. "Poof! Just like a powder keg." Reverend Haas thought it moved even faster. "In three minutes from the time the fire started," he remembered, "all the decks were ablaze." Victims huddled in seeming places of refuge were scattered when tentacles of fire exploded through windows or floorboards. "The flames spread in bursts," asserted fourteen-year-old John Ell, "that soon had the entire deck enveloped."

To many the fire seemed more than just fast, it appeared to actually chase them like a tiger loose at a circus. "When I ran back to look for my children," Frank Weber told a reporter, "the flames seemed to follow me." Cornered and out of options, some parents turned the tables on the pursuing fire and "rushed like maniacs into the very heart of the flames in the vain search for their little ones."

Some of the pursued, perhaps because they were too frightened to jump, never made it into the water. One by one or in groups the fire found and devoured them in scenes never forgotten by those who witnessed them. "No brain can imagine the fullness of that horror, no pen can write it," wrote one reporter nonetheless determined to try. "Feeble mothers covered their babies with their bodies, presenting a living barrier of flesh and blood to the flames that leaped toward their darlings." But these selfless acts of maternal love only delayed the inevitable. "Helpless, screaming and praying for mercy, they were shriveled before the fiery breath of the flames."

Some surrendered to their fate in silence, as witnessed by seventeen-year-old George Heins. During his frantic attempt to free one of the boat's lifeboats, he turned to check the progress of the advancing flames. His eye caught the figure of a small girl kneeling in prayer about fifty feet away. He ran to grab her, but she disappeared without a whimper in the advancing wall of flame.

Despite its best efforts, the fire left behind—temporarily, of course—a few pockets of refuge here and there throughout the vessel. Clusters of passengers huddled in them, either too scared to jump or determined to wait for the boat to hit land. As the flames moved in, they hung on the outside of the railing, desperate to stay on the steamer until the last possible moment. Heat in excess of 2,000 degrees Fahrenheit burned their flesh, though many were so panic-stricken they barely noticed.

Anna Frese was one of them. The fifteen-year-old hung outside the railing near the bow of the steamer. Her father kept telling her to hold on just a little longer and to jump only on his word. Just as the *Slocum* beached on North Brother Island, he told her to jump. To her astonishment, she was unable to let go. Without her realizing it, the intense heat had seared her right hand to the melted railing paint. With all her might she tore herself free and jumped, leaving behind a large patch of skin and her dreams of one day becoming a concert pianist.

A FAINT RAY
OF HOPE

To those standing onshore or on the decks of nearby rescue vessels, the sight of the *Slocum* as it steamed at full throttle upriver almost defied description. "No artist," wrote a journalist in the aftermath, "unless he dipped his brush in the colors of hell, could portray the awful scene of a majestic vessel, wrapped in great sheets of devouring flames. . . ."

Superintendent Grafeling of the gas works at Casino Beach near Astoria noticed smoke coming from near the port bow of the steamboat. He grabbed his field glasses and trained them on the strange spectacle. Immediately he saw bright orange shards of flame shooting out from the clouds of smoke. He knew then the boat was on fire, but wondered why the band continued to play.

William Halloway, an engineer on a dredge at work just off the Astoria shore, saw the burning vessel and let fly four loud blasts from his steam whistle as a signal to other boats that the *Slocum* was in trouble. He then set off in hot pursuit. He was followed by Captain McGovern of the launch *Mosquito,* who was employed on the same project, and countless others, including eleven members of the Bronx Yacht Club who put out in three small launches.

On the Bronx side, Officer John A. Scheuing of the 34th Precinct was walking his beat along 138th Street near the water when he heard someone shouting about a steamer on fire. Looking down a side street that led to the river, he saw the *Slocum* coming upriver covered in flames. He bolted across the street to where a soda wagon stood and ordered the driver to take him to the river's edge. With a crack of his whip they were off, scattering pedestrians and other vehicles that lay in their path. At the water's edge, Scheuing jumped from the wagon and ran for the pier. Up ahead he could see several small boats, and beyond them the burning wreck of the *Slocum* as it approached North Brother Island. He jumped in a small rowboat and rowed as fast as he could to the scene of the disaster.

Scheuing was followed almost immediately by several other policemen, who likewise put out in boats. Officer James A. Collins was at the East River near 134th Street when he saw "a solid mass of flames" moving upriver. He ran to a nearby call box and got word to the fire department. Then he sprinted two blocks to a dock at 136th Street and with another policeman, Officer Hubert C. Farrell, commandeered a nineteen-foot boat and instructed its mate to make for North Brother Island.

Moments after they cast off, Engine Company No. 60 and Ladder No. 17 roared to the river's edge, expecting to find the *Slocum* at one of the nearby piers. In frustration they watched the burning boat moving away from them and knew there was nothing they could do. Nearby, however, one piece of firefighting apparatus was heading off in pursuit, the fireboat *Zophar Mills*.

Out on Rikers Island, where the city maintained a prison workhouse, two inmates saw the *Slocum* pass and ran for a boat. John Merther and Dan Casey knew they were taking a big risk, for their actions might easily be taken for an escape attempt, but there was no time to seek permission. Fortunately, when they reached the small skiff, they were met by one of the workhouse doctors, who joined them.

Some who saw the *Slocum* that morning were in a better position than others to offer assistance. One of them was John L. "Jack" Wade, a tough harbor rat of a tugboat captain. Somewhat slight of build, he nonetheless exuded strength and self-assuredness. His tug, named *John Wade* in honor of his father, was a workhorse of a boat—not much to look at, but capable of performing all manner of jobs on the New York waterways. While many of his fellow captains piloted a tug for one of the big towing companies like Moran or for one of the railroads, Wade was an independent operator. He owned the *John Wade* outright and earned his living working job to job along the busy waterfront, "in the manner of a cruising cabman on land," according to one description.

He was working on North Brother Island when he spied the *Slocum* charging upriver, a mass of smoke and flame. Some captains in his position that morning hesitated and some looked the other way, certain that others would come to the steamer's aid. They had in mind men like Jack Wade, tug captains who acted on instinct when sighting a boat in distress. It did not matter if he knew the vessel or the captain—though in this case he certainly knew both—for among men of his breed there was a code of honor that demanded only one response: to offer immediate assistance. This was not a job but an obligation.

It took Jack Wade only a second or two to act. From a distance the steamer—the *Slocum* by all appearances—looked to be in bad shape and getting worse by the second. But Wade had seen a lot of ship fires in his day, including that day four years earlier when the four German Lloyd liners caught fire in Hoboken. Wade and his men had been in the thick of it that day on the Hudson and witnessed truly horrifying scenes of death and destruction—scenes not soon forgotten, even by a hardened tug captain. This situation looked bad, but obviously a far cry from the day when nearly four hundred perished on these waters. Or so it seemed.

Wade rushed into the pilothouse and shouted to his pilot, Capt. Robert Fitzgerald, to go full throttle for the burning steamboat. Half a minute later the grimy, soot-covered tug was picking up steam, plodding out into the channel to meet the oncoming *Slocum*. Suddenly the blazing vessel, thundering along at top speed, passed before the intrepid tug. Wade and his men could scarcely believe their eyes. Two-thirds of the steamboat was engulfed in a fire sending sheets of flame thirty feet into the air. Women and children could be seen racing about the decks on fire, while others cascaded over the sides into the dark water below. Here was all the horror of the Hoboken fire now concentrated on a single wooden steamboat.

Fitzgerald instinctively swung the *Wade* into the wake of the passing *Slocum* and began following the stricken vessel. Where was Van Schaick going? Wade and Fitzgerald wondered. They'd seen the old man and his pilots struggling in the pilothouse as the ship passed. He'd better stop soon, they agreed, or he'll have no boat left to land.

As the tug began its pursuit of the *Slocum,* Wade realized he was not alone. For a dozen or more captains had had the same reaction. The moment they saw the *Slocum* on fire, they put on steam and gave chase. The tug *Walter Tracey* was heading upriver not far behind the *Slocum* when its captain realized what was happening and called to his fireman and engineer for top speed. Moments later the tugs *Arnot* and *Wheeler* turned and joined the race, followed by the *Sumner, Margaret,* and *Goldenrod.* Several of them were towing barges and sloops that they simply cut loose in order to catch the *Slocum.*

Some passengers, their vision obscured by panic or smoke, never noticed the armada of rescue boats in pursuit of the *Slocum.* Most, however, did see the boats putting out from shore or changing course in midstream to give chase, and it encouraged them to hang on a bit longer. Haas later remembered that when he and his family saw the boats as they clung to the railing at the far end of the promenade deck, "a faint ray of hope came to us." They just might be saved after all—if the boats could only catch the steamer.

Wade and his fellow tugmen had the same goal in mind: to pull alongside the burning vessel and take off as many passengers as possible. This desire grew more urgent as the growing number of bodies floating in the wake indicated that people had begun to jump—or fall. "To see the faces of those little ones, who drifted by struggling against death, but just out of our reach," recalled one pursuer, "was agony to every one of us." Some captains, unable to bear the agony and seeing no sign that the *Slocum* was about to slow down or stop, gave up the chase and began plucking victims dead and alive from the water.

The rest pressed on, but few boats could match the *Slocum* for speed. "She went like the wind," noted Captain Hillery of the *Goldenrod*. Only one managed to get alongside long enough to rescue some passengers. Captain Flannery of the *Walter Tracey* drew his tug alongside the burning steamboat, and in an instant a shower of children spilled across his deck from above. Some jumped; others were simply thrown by parents and by-standers. Catherine Gallagher, the eleven-year-old who received a last-minute ticket for the excursion, remembered that a man appeared out of nowhere and dropped her over the rail onto the tug. A few seconds later, the dauntless rescuers pulled away, fearful of setting the *Walter Tracey* on fire or getting blown to bits should the *Slocum*'s boilers explode. In his heart and head, Captain Flannery knew he'd done all he could to save dozens, but the decision to retreat did not come easily, nor would it be one easily forgotten. "Until my dying day," he later told reporters, "I will hear the anguished cry that went up as I cut loose the burning boat."

CRUEL WATERS

Passengers fortunate enough to jump without one of the *Slocum*'s deadly life preservers, or who managed to wrench themselves free from one in the water, were scarcely out of danger even if they could swim. Thundering toward them were the massive thirty-one-foot paddle wheels mounted on either side of the boat. Those still aboard watched in horror as people disappeared beneath the churning paddles. Only bubbling water and foam appeared on the other side, as if the unlucky had been ground to dust.

A second peril to those in the water came from above. While a good many passengers jumped from the *Slocum* as individuals or, as one eyewitness described it, "in pitiful little clusters of three, four and five at a time," huge numbers poured over the sides in a tangled mass of terrified humanity. Only the last to go over stood any chance of surviving the fall, as the first were knocked unconscious by those who landed upon them. Such was the fate of bandleader George Maurer. After he abandoned hope of finding a decent life preserver, he brought his family to the railing and prepared to jump. First he helped his wife lower herself into the water from a dangling rope. Then he clasped his two youngest daughters' hands in his and jumped. Just as they surfaced, a large man landed on them and forced them under for good. The deep heel mark later found on Maurer's head made it clear that he was knocked unconscious by the man who landed on him and most likely took his daughters down with him.

If they managed to escape the paddle wheel and the heels of those who followed them into the water, a third peril awaited them—fellow victims. People drowning are arguably in the highest state of panic possible. By thrashing desperately with their arms and legs they usually are able to keep themselves afloat for 60 to 90 seconds. All the while they look for something—anything—to grab on to. To drowning people, anything above the surface of the water looks like salvation, even if it happens to be another person's head. Filled with a primal urge to live, they lunge at the nearest person, lock them in a nearly inescapable panic clutch, and bring two lives to a quick end. This explains why modern-day lifeguards-in-training spend half their in-water time learning techniques for saving lives and the other half developing defensive skills to avoid the death lock of a drowning victim.

Panic aboard the *Slocum* had moved decent, caring people to unspeakable acts of violence and cruelty in the name of self-preservation. "In the water," remembered Susan Schultz, "it was worse." While some managed to cling to a floating plank, chair, or life belt, most of the hundreds of desperate people fighting to stay afloat in the wake of the doomed vessel attacked their fellow victims. As soon as people hit the water, one witness remembered, "there would be a skirmish of grabbing at heads and arms, and the fellows that could swim would be pulled down and had to fight their way up." Indeed, swimmers proved inviting targets for those clinging to life. "A powerful swimmer in that fearful, fighting crush of women and children," wrote a reporter, "was almost as helpless as those who could not swim."

Annie Kiesel and her husband Edward, expert swimmers both, discovered this dreadful irony as soon as they began to swim for the shore with their children. While Edward and his son made it safely, Annie was attacked by a drowning man. She fought him off as best she could, but as a reporter later described it, "the man's strength proved greater and Mrs.

Kiesel saw her little girl disappear beneath the water with the drowning man." Charles Schwartz, Jr., a seventeen-year-old who could swim, had his grandmother torn from him in a similar manner.

Bernard Miller had much the same experience. He jumped overboard with his wife and four sons and they immediately made their way toward the shore on Randalls Island. "I started after them, but had not taken more than a dozen strokes when I was surrounded by half a dozen women, who clung to me and dragged me under." A moment later all seven were saved by a rowboat, but by then Miller's family had disappeared. He would later die on June 25, grief-stricken at his total loss.

Later, during the body recovery phase, these stories of attack in the water were corroborated by grisly evidence. Time and again recoverers reached for a body only to discover two or three people locked in a final embrace. "[W]e found several women and children all tangled together," remembered one rescuer, "as if they had fallen in a panic-stricken heap in to the water . . . and gripped one another tightly in their death struggle." Some, like Emma Ottinger, who was found in the arms of a schoolmate, held fast to a terrified relative or friend; most simply died in the arms of a complete stranger.

Not everyone who clutched another person in the water went to the bottom. Indeed, some managed to buy themselves precious additional seconds above the water's surface by grabbing several fellow victims in succession before being pulled from the water. What saved them from a double-drowning was the fact that the person they grabbed managed to break free after a brief struggle. Many simply flailed about until they found another person to lock on to.

Adult survivors emerged from the waters traumatized by the things they'd seen and done, and few spoke of having grabbed others. Children, however, told a different story. Unaware of the true nature of their actions—essentially drowning another person so they might live—they freely described them to reporters on the shore. "A man and a woman were in the water where I jumped," explained twelve-year-old Sally Klein. "I caught hold of the man's hair. He went under the water, and then I caught the woman by the foot. She went down too." Young Walter Mueller recounted how he "grabbed a man's neck and he went under the water. When I came up again I seized a woman by the hair." Clara Hartman, another twelve-year-old, even expressed indignation that the man she grabbed by the neck fought her off. "He was awfully mean," she remembered, "for he tried to push me away." While children spoke of such things in innocent oblivion, adults remained silent, too ashamed to admit to their demoralized actions in the water.

Many swimmers moved by pity or valor tried to help the drowning. George Heins was swimming for North Brother Island when he saw a little girl about six years old struggling in the water. "The poor little kid's eyes were starting from her head," he remembered, "and she was calling for her mamma." He grabbed her, but "the current was so strong that I had to let go." It was a look, he said, he'd never forget. Fred Lieberman was similarly traumatized by his unsuccessful attempt to save his brother. "I caught hold of Johnny's hand and tried to save him," he explained. "He lost his hold on my hand and the last I saw of him he was looking at me with an appeal on his face that was terrible." Willie Keppler, a boy of eleven, nearly lost his life when he tried to save two women. "I had to break away to save myself."

A few succeeded in saving others and lived to tell of it. Not surprisingly, they tended to be the ones who saved young children—victims too small to overpower them. One young boy recounted that as soon as he surfaced in the water, "a little girl grabbed me by the back of my collar and held tight. I did not try to get rid of her. I swam to the shore, where one of the nurses took the child from my back." Twelve-year-old Sally Klein was the only member of her family of ten to survive, because a boy about her age "put his arm around my waist and swam around with me . . . until I was dragged up on a boat." John Muth, Jr., a boy of three, was saved by his father, who, recognizing amid the panic-churned waters his son's bright red coat, grabbed hold and swam to shore.

Adding to the struggles of those in the water was the fact that most were dressed in their Sunday best. Few had the presence of mind—or time—to remove their shoes and excess clothing. Men and boys went overboard in full suit and tie, but it was the women—and most of the passengers aboard the *Slocum* were women and girls—who had it hardest. Their ankle-length, long-sleeved dresses, undergarments, stockings, and high shoes weighed them down in the water and made it difficult even for the few swimmers among them to move.

When they failed to find something to keep them afloat—another person or a buoyant object—the people in the wake of the *Slocum* began to drown. Although it is an experience of sheer terror, drowning usually happens quickly and without extreme pain. After sixty to ninety seconds of thrashing about on the surface, a drowning person submerges for the last time. If they managed one last gasp of air before going under, they will hold their breath (apnea) for as long as possible—until they reach what experts call the "breath-hold breakpoint," the moment when their bodies can no longer tolerate the buildup of carbon dioxide in the blood (not to mention the lack of oxygen). For 85 to 90 percent of drowning victims who reach this point (somewhere between 87 and 140 seconds), their bodies' internal survival system triggers a breath. In these so-called "wet" drownings, victims inhale (or aspirate) water, causing pulmonary distress and a rapid shutdown of vital organ function leading to death.

In the remaining 10 to 15 percent of drownings, victims do not take that fateful underwater breath and aspirate. In these "dry drownings," the larynx remains closed (laryngospasm) and victims lose consciousness and die from oxygen deprivation without a drop of water in their lungs. Susan Schultz was certainly well on her way to this fate when she was somehow grabbed and revived. "[A]fter I had been in [the water] a short time," she remembered, "I felt a sort of suffocation. I could not breathe. My ears tingled and I seemed to hear sounds like music afar off." The next thing she knew, she was on the island with a doctor working to revive her.

Once a drowning victim reaches the breath-hold breakpoint and either aspirates or passes out, the fight is over. Many survivors of near-drowning experiences describe this stage as a peaceful surrender to what seems inevitable. "I gave up hope," remembered Margaret Maurer, wife of the bandleader, "thinking I was going to be drowned. I felt a ringing sensation in my head and seemed as if I were going asleep." Kate Kassenbaum related a similar experience. "I stopped struggling and didn't seem to care any longer whether I ever rose to the top or not."

It is at this point that many report the proverbial experience of having their "life pass before their eyes" (what near-death experience, or NDE, experts call a "past-life review"). If not their whole life, they recall seeing loved ones and reviewing special moments in their life. Some, of course, also speak of encountering God, deceased relatives, and a glimpse of the afterlife. Most of the *Slocum* victims who plunged into the East River never lived to tell of such experiences as may have occurred. They simply drowned in a matter of three to four minutes. Some of the victims brought to shore and pronounced dead would have been easily revived in our era, but no one knew how in 1904. The development of the technique known as cardiopulmonary resuscitation (CPR) was half a century off yet. Of the few who were brought back from drowning, only two mentioned entering into such a euphoric state. "I remember I wondered in a dreamy sort of way," recalled Kate Kassenbaum, "if any of my children were near me and if they would be saved." Clara Hartman remembered, "I had a dreamy idea that I was going to my death, and along with it was a delicious sensation of having left all mortal cares aside."

LEFT: Rev. George C. F. Haas, Pastor of St. Mark's Evangelical Lutheran Church *(author's collection)*

BELOW: The Excursion Program *(Collections of the New-York Historical Society)*

Journal for the Seventeenth Annual Excursion

— OF —

St. Marks Evan. Lutheran Church

323-327 6th Street, New York

Wednesday, June 15th, 1904

Captain William Van Schaick
(author's collection)

The *General Slocum (Robert Wilson)*

The smoldering hull of the *General Slocum* *(author's collection)*

Bodies of the dead line the beach at North Brother Island. *(author's collection)*

Stacks of hastily constructed coffins at North Brother Island *(author's collection)*

Relatives search among the dead on display at the temporary morgue. *(author's collection)*

Black Saturday: the funeral procession of the unidentified dead, Saturday, June 18, 1904
(Gustav Scholer Papers, Manuscripts and Archives, The New York Public Library)

Frank A. Barnaby, president of the Knickerbocker Steamboat Company that owned the *General Slocum*, testifies at the Coroner's Investigation a week after the fire.
(author's collection)

The hull of the *General Slocum* after its raising by a salvage crew *(Steamship Historical Society)*

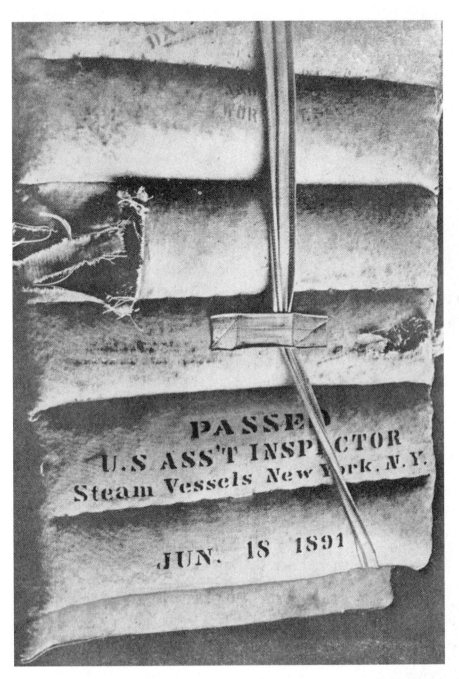

Rotten life preservers from the *General Slocum*.
The stenciled date indicates they were thirteen years old at the time of the fire.
(author's collection)

The memorial to the victims of the *General Slocum* fire, unveiled
in 1905, in the cemetery in Middle Village, Queens
(Elliott Wilshaw)

IT'S OVER WITH HER

Up in the pilothouse, pilot Ed Weaver unleashed a steady stream of whistle blasts announcing to all within earshot the steamer's distress. Van Wart gripped the wheel, his hands sweating from the rising heat, and steered the charging ship for the small island just ahead. It still looked agonizingly far off, despite making good headway. And the flames now surrounded the pilothouse.

Van Schaick shouted orders amid the smoke and flame. He faced straight ahead, eyes fixed on North Brother Island. Then he glanced toward the piers along the Bronx shore. Minutes earlier he'd rejected the idea of landing there. Now they seemed *so close*, and a nagging voice inside him said, *Do it! Hard to port and you'll be at a pier in no time!*

For a brief moment Van Schaick's fixated mind-set buckled and he gave the order to Van Wart to swing the *Slocum* hard to port. Van Wart spun the wheel and the *Slocum*'s bow turned toward the Bronx piers. In making the sudden turn, the boat heeled to starboard, a motion that sent dozens of passengers pouring pell-mell over the side.

Ten seconds later Van Schaick countermanded his own order. "Ed, it's over with her," he shouted to Van Wart. "Keep her jacked up and beach her on North Brother Island right ahead, starboard side in, so the people can jump into the shallow water." Again his pilot turned the vessel—this time to starboard—sending still dozens more into the water off the port side. "It seemed as if women and children were pouring over the sides like a water-fall," remembered one eyewitness.

The captain later claimed that he made his decision to veer away from the Bronx piers only when a tugboat captain waved him off, warning that he'd touch off an even larger inferno at the nearby lumberyard and gas works if he landed. That he ever saw—much less heard—a tugboat under the conditions then present in the pilothouse is doubtful.

In the final seconds of the race to North Brother Island, few on board the *Slocum* knew that land was at hand. Smoke and panic obscured their vision and left them disoriented. All they knew was that fire seemed to be closing in from all directions. Clothing and hair ignited in the heat and flying sparks, and more and more jumped overboard. But those who could clung to the rails, hoping to avoid death by incineration as much by drowning at the hands of a careening crowd.

Reverend Haas and his family had reason to hope that they might make it. By virtue of their position by the boat's stern railing, the point farthest from the flames, they'd been able to hang on longer than most. But as they neared—perhaps even as they hit—North Brother Island, they were carried into the water and away by a wave of terrified humanity.

When Haas resurfaced he momentarily found his wife and daughter and struggled to hold their heads above water. A moment later another torrent of desperate passengers poured down upon them, forcing them beneath the water once again. Haas lost his grip on Anna and Gertrude, and when he surfaced for the second time, "my wife and child were gone." Badly injured and in shock, Haas did not remember how he managed to avoid drowning, only that dozens around him were engaged in the same struggle. "One by one," he later remembered, "I saw them sink around me, but I was powerless to do anything." The shepherd never mentioned it, but in all likelihood his struggle to survive forced him to beat back his own flock, panic-crazed and attempting to use him as a life raft. Eventually a tug came and hauled him to safety.

In its final minute the interior of the *General Slocum* began to collapse. The hull shuddered and groaned like a wounded animal as the fire devoured wooden bulkheads and support beams that held up the decks. August Schneider, a member of the band, stood with his wife and three children on the main deck. Luck seemed to be with them, for they'd managed to sidestep a panicked group as it careened through the railing and spilled into the river. Now with the steamer's turn toward North Brother Island, the wind began to blow the flames away from them. Hearts pounding, they huddled together, hoping to hold on until the ship hit land. Suddenly and without warning the upper deck collapsed toward the center of the steamboat in a thunderous crash. The implosion sent up a huge torrent of flame and sparks. When Schneider opened his eyes he found that only he and his daughter, little Augusta, remained. His wife and two older daughters had disappeared into the fiery hole yawning before them, gone forever.

Moments later the second deck gave way toward the center. Dozens more were crushed to death by the tons of falling debris. Others not so fortunate were pinned alive beneath the wreckage, condemned to a slow but certain death by smoke or flame.

Van Wart brought the floating inferno at full throttle onto the beach at the island's western edge. He came in straight and hard and at the last minute tried to swing the vessel in such a way that would leave its starboard railing parallel with the beach. But rocks and other obstacles hampered his effort. Seconds later, to the deafening sound of the hull striking rocks, the *Slocum* shuddered to a halt like a wounded dragon, twenty feet from the shore at the bow, stern out.

EXTRA!

On shore, people watched the dreadful scene pass before their eyes. Some stood in stunned silence. Others ran to pull fire alarms or call the police. Still more jumped into boats and set out in pursuit.

One witness dialed the city desk of the *New York World*. Editor Martin Green answered the phone and in a second sat bolt upright and began scribbling in shorthand a frantically dictated account of the steamer's final minute.

"*I'm in an office overlooking the East River. There's a steamboat on fire. A sidewheeler. I can see women and children running around on her decks. . . . Smoke is rolling up. . . . Oh, God! Women and children are leaping over the railing by the dozens. . . . The ship is veering toward the shore . . . toward the Bronx around One Hundred and Thirty-fifth Street. . . . Now it's turning away . . . speeding upriver, heading for North Brother Island. . . . The whole thing is a floating furnace. . . . This is ghastly, horrible. . . . She's struck on North Brother Island and is listing. . . . She's a mass of flames . . . and all that smoke. . . . The people dying . . . dying . . . God, man! I'm sick to my stomach! I can't stand it anymore. I can't talk. . . . Good-bye . . .*"

Then the line went dead.

Green's mind raced. If it wasn't a hoax, this was a big story, perhaps even a major one. At that precise moment he was more than likely, courtesy of that phone call, ahead of the competition at the *Journal, Post, Tribune, Sun, Times,* and other dailies. But he knew from experience that it was a lead measured in seconds—a few minutes if he was lucky.

How to get there first? The caller said something about North Brother Island—what about taking a boat? A moment later and Green was speaking with Eugene F. Moran, head of the Moran Towing Company, the city's largest tugboat operator. How fast, he asked, could they get his team to North Brother Island? Not as fast, Moran replied, as simply taking the elevated railroad to the Port Morris station.

In seconds dozens of reporters and photographers were out the door, intent on being the first on the scene at the biggest disaster in the city's history.

DEAD IN THE WATER

With the *Slocum* now at rest, the armada of tugs and other boats that had fallen into line in hot pursuit of the floating inferno now went into action. Van Schaick had hoped to ground the *Slocum* broadside to the beach so that the vessel's stern—the only part not completely engulfed in flame—would lie in the shallow water. This would allow the passengers fortunate enough to have hung on during the harrowing race for the island to jump into water only seven or so feet deep. Unfortunately, the steamer hit ground earlier than expected, preventing the stern from swinging fully toward the beach. The bow rested in just seven feet of water about twenty feet from shore, but the stern jutted out more than fifty feet from shore in thirty feet of water. For people unable to swim this might as well have been three hundred feet.

Closest to the *Slocum* when it beached was the *Massasoit*, a 153-foot vessel used by the Department of Corrections to transport prisoners and guards to and from the prison on Rikers Island. But it drew too much water to pull alongside the *Slocum*'s stern, where hundreds stood pinned against the railings, moments from making the hideous choice between death by fire or drowning. Undeterred, Capt. Frederick W. Parkinson pulled within fifty feet of the raging boat and his crew leaped into action. Coxswain Carl Rappaport dove off the bow into the water below, teeming with passengers, some still struggling for life, others already gone. In an instant he was back bearing a little boy who refused to let go of his rescuer and had to be pried loose. Next came two babies—both still breathing. By the time he deposited his seventh person aboard the *Massasoit*, Rappaport was completely naked, having lost all his clothes in struggles with people in the water.

At the same time, the *Massasoit*'s deckhand, James J. Duane, put over a lifeboat. Captain Parkinson ordered another crewman to play the boat's fire hose on him while he rowed toward the inferno. Despite the overpowering heat—minimized but by no means eliminated by the waterfall from *Massasoit*'s fire hose—and the danger posed by falling debris, Duane rowed to within a few feet of the *Slocum* and pulled seven victims aboard.

The *Franklin Edson*, a tug owned by the Department of Health and used for transporting patients to and from North Brother Island, was piloted by Captain Parkinson's mentor and uncle, fifty-eight-year-old Capt. Henry Fick. He also got only to within fifty feet before its pilothouse windows cracked and paint blistered. His crew pulled twenty-five victims aboard. Overwhelmed by the sight of so many helpless forms still thrashing in the water, Captain Fick dove over the side and retrieved a woman. "I don't want any rewards or any medals," he afterward told a reporter. "I am too old for that kind of thing."

Similar scenes of selfless heroism were played out all around the blazing steamboat. From the tug *Arnot*, crewmen Olsen and Andersen jumped in and saved six women and two children. Olsen then spied three toddlers struggling for life. He swam to them and managed to drag two to the North Brother Island beach before returning for the third. The tug *Sumner* pulled up to one of the *Slocum*'s paddle boxes and off-loaded a score of cowering passengers, among them John Holthusen, the head of St. Mark's Sunday school, and his two daughters. The *Goldenrod* too made a pass at the *Slocum,* where, Captain Hillery remembered, "Men, women, and children hailed down upon my decks."

Everywhere, men tossed overboard every available life preserver, barrel, plank, chair—anything that floated—and launched dozens of lifeboats. Private boats did their part as well. The yacht *Easy Times*, piloted by off-duty fireman James C. Ward, pulled to within one hundred feet before the owner ordered him to stop—fearing the loss of his prized vessel. Ward complied but immediately put over lifeboats, allowing scores to grab hold. Captain McGovern filled his small launch *Mosquito* with five women and six children. Peter Jensen piloted his small launch *Peter* right up to a paddle box and grabbed three small children and brought them to the beach. From there he ran to the seawall and pulled forty more to safety.

Jack Wade's tug was not the first on the scene, but it immediately proved the most important. Knowing that his smallish tug drew less water than most (just four feet), Wade threw caution to the wind and ordered Fitzgerald to pull alongside the *Slocum* at the stern. In seconds they slipped past the *Franklin Edson* and *Massasoit* standing fifty feet off the burning hulk and edged closer. The heat was unlike anything they'd ever experienced—even in the Hoboken fire of 1900. It rose steadily by hundreds of degrees as Fitzgerald looked for a place to draw up. The scene before them took on a watery appearance as waves of radiated heat warped their vision.

At twenty feet off the stern, the two-thousand-degree heat caused the tug to groan, but Wade ordered his helmsman to press on. They cringed and shielded their eyes as one by one the pilothouse windows shattered, *kaposh*, allowing smoke and fumes from the *Wade*'s bubbling deck paint to waft in. Still Wade kept his eyes fixed on the hundreds of helpless passengers clinging to the *Slocum*. He could see them waving at him, beckoning him to save them from the horrible death now bearing down on them. He might share in their fiery demise, but it was a risk he was prepared to take. He wasn't going to get this close to hell only to turn away.

You'll lose your tug and livelihood, Fitzgerald shouted just before they hit.

"Damn the tug!" shouted Wade. "Let her burn."

Two of those helpless victims waving to Jack Wade were Rev. George Schultze, Reverend Haas's guest from Erie, Pennsylvania, and Mr. Muller, a Sunday school teacher at St. Mark's. To them the sudden appearance of Jack Wade through the curtains of smoke surrounding the *Slocum* seemed nothing short of a miracle. When the general panic broke out on the boat, they had managed to corral about fifty terrified children into a corner of the *Slocum*'s stern. Knowing that few of the little ones could swim, they determined to keep them on the steamer as long as possible. Despite the pitiful pleas to be allowed to jump over the railing, the men refused. They put their backs to the flames to shield the children, urging them to remain calm while silently uttering prayers of desperation. Just as they had about given up hope, Schultze spied the answer to his prayers— the bow of a small black tugboat moving steadily in their direction.

As soon as the *John Wade* nudged against the *Slocum*, Schultze and Muller off-loaded their precious cargo. "Mr. Muller and I dropped the children into it one by one," Schultze later recounted, "until there were fifty on board." Then the two men followed.

Clara Stuer described a similar moment of deliverance, though possibly by another tug other than the *Wade*. Convinced of the need to jump overboard, she'd stripped off most of her clothing to improve her chances in the water. "I started down the side of the boat," she recounted, "when I heard a voice calling me to hold on a minute. I turned and saw a man standing on the bow of a tug which was approaching." In an instant she fell to the tug's deck, followed by many more.

As the pell-mell off-loading from the *Slocum* proceeded, two of Wade's crewmen, Ruddy McCarroll and Tony Marcetti, took to the water and returned moments later with sputtering victims. Again and again they ventured out amid the frantic victims clawing at water that inexorably drew them downward. As McCarroll approached a drowning woman, he was immediately surrounded by five more. Several latched on to him, pulling him under. Luckily for McCarroll, there was enough life left in them that the quick immersion caused them to release him. Still gasping for air and vomiting water, he snared one of the women and pulled her to the *Wade,* where they were both pulled aboard. McCarroll had just passed out when the woman he'd saved suddenly came to life and began shaking him.

"Wake up! You, wake up! There is my Claus in the water!" With that she picked him up and hurled him over the side. Revived somewhat by the cold water, he made for the boy, grabbed him, and with the last ounce of strength in his big frame, pulled him to the tug's side. Back on board a second time, McCarroll passed out once again. Jack Wade then plunged into the roiling waters and saved three more.

But even Wade—as real a Jim Bludso as New York had ever seen— knew they couldn't keep at it indefinitely. He'd lost all the hair on his arms to the heat and several of his men had their shirts burned right off their backs. His tug was on fire in several places and the *Slocum* might blow at any moment, sending the rescued and rescuers alike to eternity. Reluctantly—for he could see people still trapped on the steamboat—he gave the order to back off.

Suddenly a frantic Fitzgerald was shouting something about the propeller. In all the excitement no one had noticed that they'd become immobilized, the victim of a loose line snared around the propeller. As the deckhands scrambled to fix the problem, the small fires on the tug grew larger and began to threaten the very people they'd just snatched from the *Slocum.* Now the very real possibility loomed that Wade's vessel would blow, or at the very least go up in flames. Every second counted, and they would need several minutes—likely five or more—in order to free the propeller.

At this moment it became Wade's turn to receive deliverance. Out of nowhere there suddenly came a hard stream of cold saltwater. It burst into steam upon contact with the *Wade*'s baking deck and pilothouse and stung the skin of Wade, his crewmen, and the passengers. The fireboat *Zophar*

Mills had just arrived and, seeing that its streams of water were having no effect on the *Slocum* fire, began to hose down the *Wade* and other rescue vessels that had moved in close.

Quite unintentionally, Wade's moment of peril had allowed still more victims aboard the *Slocum* to be saved. For as the *John Wade* lay immobilized yet protected by the fire hoses, dozens more jumped aboard from the burning steamer. More important, the *Wade*'s stern swung toward the shore of North Brother Island and into shallow water. "Over this bridge," a reporter scribbled later that day, "seventy-eight persons found their way to safety." Eventually, Captain Hillery threw a line to the *Wade*, and his *Goldenrod* pulled the tug to safety. All told, Wade and his six-man crew saved 155 souls.

A mong those saved that morning was nearly the entire crew of the *Slocum*. Although many would later criticize him for his decision to race for North Brother Island, none questioned Captain Van Schaick's physical courage in the face of near-certain death. Even as the flames surrounded the pilothouse on all sides and filled it with smoke, Van Schaick and his two pilots bravely manned their posts. Only when the stricken vessel ground to a halt did they attempt to save themselves by climbing through a window of the pilothouse and leaping to the rocks thirty feet below. Van Wart went first, crossing himself before jumping, followed by Weaver and last, almost reluctantly, Van Schaick. Down in the engine room Chief Engineer Ben Conklin and second engineer Everett Brandow likewise stayed at their posts until the very end. Both managed to escape with minor burns when by chance a tug drew up just as they emerged from the engine room.

Most of Van Schaick's crew, however, proved useless to the end. Incapable and in some cases unwilling to save any passengers, they somehow managed to save themselves. All but steward McGrann, the one who sank with the vessel's money, and a fireman and three members of the kitchen staff survived. But even in saving themselves, some of them proved singularly inept. First Mate Ed Flanagan, who would later try to make himself out a hero, jumped onto Jack Wade's tug. Still out of his mind with panic, he ran to the tug's line that held it to the *Slocum* and cast it off. An enraged Wade pounced and heaved Flanagan from the tug. "I went for him," he remembered almost sheepishly, "and well—oh, I just put him off the boat, that's all."

Not to be outdone, deckhand Daniel O'Neill saw a small rowboat full of people below him as he hung over the *Slocum*'s side. Despite pleas for him not to jump, he did so anyway. His impact flipped the boat, tossing rescuers and rescued alike into the water. O'Neill, who knew how to swim, paddled to shore while the victims of his recklessness struggled to stay afloat.

A few members of the *Slocum*'s crew did distinguish themselves with conspicuous acts of bravery after the beaching. One deckhand who was never identified earned the praise of Captain Parkinson of the *Massasoit*. He deserved, said the gruff captain, "all the medals which may be coming his way." The moment he escaped the *Slocum* by diving into the water from what Parkinson called "a nest of flames," he began dragging people ashore. Each time he returned to the water to pull another victim to safety. With his strength fading fast, he made one more plunge into the water and returned with three babies—two on one arm and a third in his teeth. "How he did it," said an incredulous Parkinson, ". . . I don't know." The anonymous deckhand promptly collapsed in a heap, unable to move.

Another who exhibited great courage was the *Slocum*'s African-American cook, Henry Canfield. He went overboard wearing a life preserver and was instantly attacked by several drowning passengers. Knowing how to swim, he slipped out of the life preserver—apparently one of the few good ones—and let them cling to it until rescued by a rowboat. Then he swam around and pulled several more victims to nearby boats. Just how many was never recorded, but many of the rescued noted that they were saved "by a colored man." Yet when Canfield briefly grabbed the side of a rowboat to catch his breath, the boatman lifted an oar as if to strike and shouted, "Turn loose of that." Even in the teeth of a catastrophe, racial animosity remained undiminished in the hearts of some rescuers. Canfield was eventually allowed aboard the tug *Massasoit*.

Policemen Van Tassel and Kelk displayed a similar courage and steadiness of nerve to the very end. Kelk, though badly burned, was one of the last to leave the boat. Standing on the stern of the *Slocum*, assisting people onto tugs and directing rescue efforts on the water, he appeared, according to one reporter, "as calm as though he were on parade."

His partner Van Tassel had spent the harrowing journey to North Brother Island hanging on the outside of the *Slocum*'s railing, imploring the terrified passengers to remain calm, and, when the *Walter Tracey* briefly pulled alongside, passing dozens of children onto its deck. "I stood on the outside of the rail," he said later, "passing the children into the tugs and trying to keep order." Like Kelk, he resisted the temptation to jump himself and stayed with the steamer to the bitter end. "Every time I saw a little face turning its pitiful appeal to me," he explained, "I thought of my own two children at home."

Just as the *Slocum* beached, a woman leaped from above and struck Van Tassel on the head and back of his neck with her shoes. Knocked unconscious, he fell into the water. "The water, of course, revived me," he later remembered, "and I started for the shore." Too weak to swim, however, he knew enough from his training in the marine division of the police department to float on his back. Out of nowhere a group of frantic women and children began to grab at him as though he were a small island.

Stop! he shouted, or we'll all drown. Keep calm and I'll save every one of you.

Somehow, his words penetrated the fog of panic and they calmed down. Holding on to their human raft, they floated to the beach.

BEAUTIFUL
RECKLESSNESS

E ven before the bonfire that was the *Slocum* ground to a halt just off the shore of North Brother Island, the workers there had begun to mobilize. The twenty-acre North Brother Island lay just off the Bronx shore. Like many of the city's East River islands, it held an institution city officials sought to isolate from the general population. The Riverside Hospital for contagious diseases replaced an earlier hospital established there by the Sisters of Charity in 1871. It was a comparatively pleasant place in contrast to nearby Blackwells Island, where one found not only hospitals but also a prison, insane asylum, and almshouse. By 1904 the hospital at North Brother Island cared for several hundred patients and employed 164 workers, including thirty-five nurses and six doctors. Only a few years later it would achieve notoriety as the home for Typhoid Mary.

James J. Owens, a bricklayer, was hard at work on the renovation of the hospital's exterior when he spied the burning boat as it approached 132nd Street, about a third of a mile from the island. His shouts of "Steamer afire!" as he ran for the shore were enough to draw the notice of a fellow workman who pulled the island's fire alarm. Since the staff held frequent fire drills, it was not long before a makeshift fire battalion stood ready for action atop the seawall overlooking the beach when the floating bonfire came crunching in upon the rocks.

Likewise standing at the ready or running across the lawn were doctors, nurses, and other members of the hospital staff. Some had received advance warning of the steamboat's arrival, while others simply saw it coming and dropped what they were doing. Doctors, head nurses, and other persons of authority shouted for the hospital workers to stay on the shore and wait for the people in the boats to bring victims ashore for medical attention. But the sight of so many people fighting for life in the water only twenty or thirty feet away proved too much to take, and soon staffers broke ranks and rushed into the chilly water. Most who did so were risking their lives, since few knew how to swim.

Psychologists have long pondered the question of why some people, when suddenly confronted with a situation of great peril, instinctively take heroic action while others do little or nothing, as though paralyzed by fear and chaos. Temple University psychologist Frank Farley, the nation's leading expert on the psychology of heroism, calls such people "situational heroes." It's a scenario played out not only on the field of battle, but in crises in everyday life such as car accidents and floods. Sometimes these acts of bravery involve only putting themselves in harm's way—rushing into a burning building, for example—while others include unusual exhibitions of stamina or strength that later defy explanation. People of medium build have lifted cars off of accident victims, for example, or carried injured people over great distances. Research indicates that while most people experience confusion and indecision in traumatic situations, a select few have the opposite reaction. In spite of all that swirls about them, they instantly enter what might be called a focused manic state that allows them to identify a vital problem and take immediate action with no thought to personal safety. Many who experience this reflexive heroism are later at a loss to explain how and why they did what they did, except to say in one form or another, I just had to do something.

In the case of the *Slocum* scene at North Brother Island, these feats of heroism often involved both fearlessness and near-miraculous physical acts. Lulu McGibbon was tending the hospital switchboard when a breathless messenger burst into the room and told her of the burning steamer just about to hit. In a flash, her hands rearranging the tangle of wires on the board, she made emergency calls to the police and fire departments, touching off a massive response by both services. She then called all the nearby hospitals and told them to send medical personnel.

That done, McGibbon paused to consider what to do next. Ultimately, she knew it was her responsibility to remain at her post. She was always under strict orders to never leave the switchboard unattended, especially in an emergency that might require more calls. But she could hear the commotion out in the hall as nurses, doctors, and staff scrambled to the shore, and she felt an overwhelming urge to join them. And then she was gone, down the hall and out the door, unable to restrain the impulse to do *something*. As she raced across the lawn toward the beach, nothing could have prepared her, or anyone on North Brother Island that morning, for the horrific scene up ahead. Huge clouds of black smoke billowed upward from a 264-foot-long trough of raging flame that had been the steamboat *General Slocum*. People, many of them on fire, were pouring over the sides into the river while dozens still clung to the few parts of the wreck unclaimed by the inferno. In the water, countless victims fought to stay afloat while all around them floated those who'd already lost the struggle. "They were thick as leaves in the water," remembered one witness. Boats of every description worked to pull people in while a few fortunate ones dragged themselves onto the beach and collapsed in a heap.

Lulu never stopped running, driven onward not only by courage but also by the fact that she possessed a skill quite rare in 1904: she could swim. The loose sand of the beach slowed her pace somewhat, but in seconds she was in the chilly water pulling herself toward two tiny children, one aged three years and the other six months old. The thick, layered clothing of the day made swimming difficult and threatened to drag her under. Still she pressed on, driven forward by a powerful combination of horror and adrenaline, until she reached the infants, tucked both under one arm, and swam for shore. By now dozens of workers and nurses who could not swim were wading out, forming lines by which to pass the rescued to shore. Lulu handed off the babies and returned to the deeper water choked with people fighting to stay afloat. She would save a dozen people before collapsing in exhaustion.

Joining her in the fray was eighteen-year-old Pauline Puetz, who worked as a nurse at the hospital. She too could swim, and upon reaching the shore she began pulling off her excess clothing. Her fellow workers tried to stop her, fearing she'd drown. "They tried to hold me back by my skirt," she later recounted, "but I let them pull my skirt off me and rushed into the water in my petticoat." She swam out to the *Slocum*'s stern and shouted, "In God's name, jump! Throw your babies overboard; we'll catch them." Again and again she pulled people of all ages to safety.

It was dangerous work even for the swimmers as panicked passengers lunged at them. Puetz's valor nearly cost her her life when, after making countless rescues, she returned once more when a large woman who appeared to be dead "caught me by the neck in a death grip." As they sank, she gagged on the brackish water and felt herself losing consciousness. She kept struggling, though, keenly aware that surrender meant certain death. "I had to fight for my life," she remembered, and with one last burst of strength she managed to get her hand under the woman's chin—a technique used in modern lifesaving—and pushed upward until she released her grip. Incredibly, she then swam around her attacker, grabbed her by the hair, and began pulling her to shore. Just before reaching safety the woman attacked again and pulled them both under. Fortunately, the struggle drew the attention of several rescuers, who came to her assistance. Puetz was unconscious when they laid her on the shore. She soon regained her wits and promptly began assisting nearby victims—beginning with bandaging the woman who had nearly drowned her.

The stories of these and many other heroic rescuers at North Brother Island who exhibited what one reporter called "beautiful recklessness" would be told over and over again in the newspaper accounts that followed. None drew more attention than the story of nurse Nellie O'Donnell. Unlike Puetz and McGibbon, she couldn't swim. Yet she was the first one into the water, compelled by the vision of so many people in need of help. Using an improvised stroke, she paddled out to a small boy, snared him by the collar, and pulled him to another nurse standing in four feet of water. Again and again she ventured out over her head and returned with a child until she'd rescued ten.

And then there was seventeen-year-old Mary McCann, a patient at the hospital. Born in Ireland, she'd arrived at Ellis Island only a month earlier. There, she was diagnosed with scarlet fever and sent to the Riverside Hospital for contagious diseases on North Brother Island. She had made a nearly complete recovery when the *Slocum* hit.

Like Lulu and Pauline, she could swim, but she was weak from her prolonged illness. She plunged into the water and promptly saved a young girl. The moment the child was in safe hands she was back in the water to save another girl and a boy. When heading out to make her fourth save, someone pulled her dress off. It made swimming easier, but with each rescue she moved more slowly. It was on her way back from her fifth rescue that someone grabbed her legs and pulled her under. A workman heard her cry for help and managed to pull her free of her attacker.

Those who could not swim relied on quick thinking to save dozens. Some found ropes and gave them to swimmers to take out into the water so that victims could be pulled to safety. Others jumped into some of the many rowboats about the island and proceeded to haul victims to land. At one point someone noticed that ladders were propped against the facade of the hospital and called for them to be brought to the water. "There was no one to go for them," remembered Kate White, superintendent of the hospital's nurses, "so I went." The thirty-five-foot ladders were "dreadfully heavy," but nonetheless she dragged them to the water, where rescuers waded out to their chins and then extended them to victims beyond their reach. Like so many that day, White could not account for her actions. "I never could have done it if I had been in my senses," she recalled in a manner typical of instinctual heroes. "I didn't know or feel anything."

Some of the most extraordinary exhibitions of heroism involved victims of the disaster. Many of the swimmers among them struggled to the beach and then, realizing they were at last safe from danger, turned around and went back in to pull a few people to safety. Such decisions required a phenomenal transition in their mental state from wild panic to rational action. They'd just spent twenty minutes fighting for their lives to reach shore, and now, only moments after reaching the final destination, they felt an irresistible compulsion to return to the cruel waters to save their children, their spouses, *anyone*. One thing that no doubt helped in this mental transition were the desperate shrieks of others on the shore pleading for someone to find their loved ones. Several of these would-be rescuers would not make it to shore a second time.

That was not the case of one victim-turned-rescuer named Charles Schwartz, Jr., a seventeen-year-old apprentice machinist. What made his effort so remarkable was not merely the number he saved (twenty-two), but his own story of loss and selflessness. An excellent swimmer, Schwartz had already saved two women—including Pastor Haas's sister Emma—when he saw his mother and grandmother floating facedown. He pulled both ashore and found a doctor to revive them, but it was too late. "It's no use," the doctor told him, "we can't do anything more for your people, my boy." He was devastated over his loss, haunted by the thought that he might have saved them if he'd only found them sooner. "I felt as though my heart would break," he later told a reporter.

Yet where most would be paralyzed by grief and a sense of hopelessness, Schwartz found himself inspired to do whatever he could to help those who still had a chance. Perhaps his age had something to do with it, for teenagers often possess a sense of invulnerability to personal danger. And if he was like most seventeen-year-olds, he'd also read his share of dime novels about heroes real and imagined. As he wept over the corpses of his mother and grandmother, the commotion in the water suddenly caught his attention. "I looked out upon the water and saw that there were yet men, women, and children who might be saved."

In a moment he was again in the water. He swam to a man in a rowboat and climbed in. They rowed out a ways and Schwartz dove in again and again, each time returning to the rowboat with a sputtering victim or two. Since their boat was small, they brought the rescued ashore in groups of four or five and returned for more. After Schwartz handed off his twenty-second rescue, they returned to the wreck but found no one left alive to save—they'd run out of time.

The beaching of the *Slocum* had slowed the torrid advance of the flames, but only to a degree. Crushed into an ever-shrinking portion of the boat's stern section, the desperate passengers began to jump or fall, unable to withstand the rising heat that seared their flesh and set afire their hair and clothes. Despite the nearness of the shore and the many boats now surrounding the burning wreck, most of the passengers who hit the water off North Brother Island stood little chance of being rescued.

The same desperate scenes of panic and raw terror that erupted in the wake of the *Slocum* fire out on the East River were again played out in the waters near North Brother Island. Only this time they did so with salvation in clear view, a mere twenty, forty, or sixty feet away. Some drowned in water only five feet deep—shallow enough for them to stand in if only they had the presence of mind to do so.

Some who were unable to swim found themselves alongside the *Slocum*'s paddle boxes. With the paddle wheels no longer turning, these provided a temporary refuge that kept alive their hopes of being rescued, but for no more than a few minutes. So intense was the heat that it boiled the water about them and seared their skin. "The torture was terrible," remembered Lena De Luccia. From rescue boats and the shore, victims at the paddle boxes could be seen wilting in the heat, losing consciousness, and slipping into the boiling water without a struggle.

Officer John Scheuing, the Bronx beat cop who had commandeered the soda wagon and small boat to get to North Brother Island, vowed he'd save at least a handful and rowed his boat for the paddle box. Firemen and crewmen from nearby rescue boats tried to wave him off, fearing that he'd be killed, but Scheuing remained undaunted. The heat blistered his skin and burned his handlebar mustache from his face, and still he pressed on, occasionally dousing himself with a bucket of river water. "There were five faces under that paddle box," he later explained, "that told me it was my duty to go in there. I heard voices calling out, 'Mr. Policeman, save us!' " Debris from the *Slocum* rained down on him as pulled up to one of the paddle boxes. Standing precariously balanced with one foot in the rowboat and another on a dripping paddle, Scheuing loaded five people into his boat. Then he shoved away from the groaning hulk toward the shore and watched the raging inferno recede in the distance with every pull on the oars made by his blistered hands.

By now Sam Berg was on the water. Like Scheuing, he too had been walking along a Bronx side street when he heard the fire alarm and saw people rushing down to the piers. He followed, and when he saw the *Slocum* pass all aflame, jumped in a small rowboat and with another man rowed frantically out to North Brother Island. Berg was an excellent swimmer and a highly decorated member of the United States Volunteer Life-Saving Corps, but he opted to stay in his boat and pull as many aboard as possible. By his estimate he and his partner pulled fifty victims to safety.

Stories would later emerge that some rescuers tried to extort money from drowning people before taking them aboard their boat. Others alleged that men stole jewelry off bodies as they floated in the water. While such extraordinary acts of depravity may have occurred, it is more likely that they did not. Only two people reported such incidents, both days after the fire and in one case by a woman who refused to give her name. The stories probably emerged as people on North Brother Island watched rescuers lift and then drop back into the water bodies of those already dead in their search for people they could still save.

And so it went in the precious few minutes that elapsed between the *Slocum*'s running aground and the last victim losing the battle to stay afloat and sinking into the murky waters of the East River. It was a scene of absolute chaos, with victims flailing in the water, survivors on the beach calling out for someone to save their child, husband, or sister, and rescuers working furiously to grab as many people as possible before time ran out. The latter worked in their own state of panic, keenly aware that time and simple mathematics were working against them. There were simply too many people in the water to save and not enough rescuers or time to get them out. Each trip into the water brought moments of awful choices— Whom to grab? Whom to leave behind?

Toward the end of this phase of the ordeal, as great plumes of smoke and flame poured forth from the stranded hulk of the *General Slocum* and hundreds of survivors and rescuers struggled to get ashore, someone shouted "Look!" There on the top deck a small boy about the age of six could be seen climbing the steamer's flagpole in a last-ditch attempt to escape the inferno closing in around him. For a moment there seemed to be a lull in the pandemonium around the island's shore as hundreds held their breath, watching and praying. Upward he inched as the flames grew higher. Finally he reached the top. "Hold on! Hold on!" shouted the onlookers, though none seemed to know how he might be plucked safely from his perch. They gasped as the flagpole began to tremble and sway. Still the boy hung on. Then the flagpole suddenly careened backward into the fiery cavity of the vessel, taking with it the last living soul aboard the *General Slocum.*

Part Three

SEARCHING

'Tis a sigh that is wafted across the troubled wave,
'Tis a wail that is heard upon the shore,
'Tis a dirge that is murmured around the lowly grave.
Oh! Hard times, come again no more.
—STEPHEN FOSTER

Fire is the test of gold; adversity, of strong men.
—SENECA

MAMA, WAKE UP

It was all over in a matter of minutes. Rescuers from North Brother Island, passing boats, or the nearby Bronx and Queens shores found that at a certain point in the effort to pull people from the water only the dead remained. Weeping and wailing from North Brother Island could be heard, as could the sounds of the steamboat on fire, but otherwise an eerie calm descended upon the scene. No one could be seen clinging to the wreck or heard flailing in the water. Without any official notice, rescuers became recoverers, tasked with the gruesome responsibility of collecting the bodies. William Muff, owner of the launch *Gloria* who set out from his boathouse in Queens, found he was able to save people only on his first run. "We made a second trip over the wake of the *Slocum*," he recalled. "The water was simply a mass of debris and bodies."

Even as the hopes of finding additional survivors in the water dimmed, the efforts to save lives continued on the beach. Most of the doctors and nurses of Riverside Hospital had in the course of their medical training learned the standard technique for reviving a drowning victim. But like so many other medical procedures in that era, it was a rudimentary maneuver aimed at alleviating the most obvious problem (water in the lungs) rather than addressing the larger systemic issue (oxygen deprivation). Many unconscious victims brought ashore that morning would have been easily revived by applying modern cardiopulmonary resuscitation, or CPR, which both removes the water from the lungs and provides oxygen through mouth-to-mouth breathing and circulation via chest compressions.

In 1904, however, with the development of CPR a half century off, the medical personnel did the best they could. Working in pairs, they laid a victim on her back. One worker then stretched the victim's arms above her head and quickly pulled them down to her side. A second worker pushed on the chest to expel the water. After a few rounds of this method, they then placed the victim face first over the rounded side of a barrel and pushed on her back to force more water out. On the beach at North Brother Island, there were no barrels at first, so as one nurse explained, "We rolled them over our knees." When these efforts failed—in most cases they did unless the victim had lost consciousness only moments earlier—some resorted to other traditional methods for reviving the unconscious, like vigorous rubbing of the palms, slapping the face, or pouring whiskey into their mouths. Here and there a victim vomited up seawater and opened their eyes, but most stayed on their course toward death.

Reverend Haas was one of the exceptions. He was unconscious when delivered to the beach, most likely from shock rather than drowning. Around him five medical personnel, perhaps aware of who he was, worked feverishly to revive him. Eventually his eyes fluttered and he came to. As soon as he could speak, he asked the question being heard up and down the beach that morning. "Where are they?" he asked with pleading eyes. "Where is my family? Are they saved? Are they dead or alive?" He received the same answer: no one could say.

By 10:45 A.M., approximately twenty minutes after the *Slocum* ran ashore, the medical personnel of Riverside Hospital ceased their efforts to revive any of the victims. Even with their limited knowledge of the dynamics of drowning, they knew that time had run out. Now they directed their efforts to caring for the survivors, providing everything from warm blankets and whiskey to stitches and bandages. There was no emergency medicine theory of triage in 1904, but hospital personnel made similar judgments on instinct. Serious burn victims and those in shock received first priority, those with deep lacerations and broken bones came next, followed by all the rest. As is common in similar disaster incidents, many of those treated were so traumatized by their experience, they failed to notice their injuries until they were pointed out by the doctors and nurses.

Fortunately, the first boatloads of emergency personnel had already begun to arrive. Lulu McGibbon's calls to the city's hospitals had prompted hundreds of nurses and dozens of doctors to race for the docks along the Bronx shore to board boats for the island. Dr. J. C. Ayre and two other physicians at Bellevue Hospital downtown filled an automobile with medical supplies and roared up First Avenue, followed by two ambulances carrying several more doctors. Dr. Henry Krauskopf of nearby Harlem Hospital, one of the first doctors to reach the island, was simply overwhelmed by what he saw. "There were children all about us lying dead on the grass," he remembered, and scores of injured parents, many running about screaming for their missing kin. "In the three hours that we were on the island I think we must have treated fully 150 persons."

Arriving at just about the same time were City Health Commissioner Thomas Darlington, Coroner William O'Gorman, Police Inspector Albertson, and Commissioner of the Fire Department Edward Croker. Together they worked to bring some order to the myriad activity swirling about them. Albertson posted three hundred policemen about the island and instructed them to maintain order and provide any needed help. Darlington saw to it that the medical personnel were properly supplied with blankets, bandages, and whiskey. He also personally assisted some of the injured, at one point helping a seventeen-year-old girl. She handed him a small package, asked him to give it to her mother, and promptly died in his arms. "I will never be able to forget the scene," he recalled, "the utter horror of it."

One of the largest tasks, the handling of the dead, fell to Coroner

O'Gorman. He quickly organized the retrieval of bodies from the water, hiring on the spot many of the boatmen who originally came to rescue survivors. Then he instructed teams of hospital workers and volunteers to bring the bodies from the beach to the lawn in front of the hospital. There, men from his office tagged each body with a number and placed any personal effects in a bag marked with a corresponding number. "No. 64. Woman. One gold watch" was a typical notation. In anticipation of the bloating and discoloration that sets in soon after drowning, O'Gorman also had workers examine each body and record distinguishing physical characteristics such as birthmarks or scars.

Several priests also stepped off boats and went to work. Fathers Donlin of St. Jerome's Church and Boyle and Christian of St. Luke's Church moved from victim to victim administering the Catholic sacrament of extreme unction, or last rites. Neither they nor anyone around them seemed to mind that most of the victims were Lutherans.

Also on the scene was Martin Green's force of a dozen reporters and photographers. By virtue of a chance phone call from an eyewitness and some sage advice from Eugene F. Moran, head of the Moran Towing Company, the *World*'s staff had arrived there first. The reporters and photographers realized this the moment they stepped off their boat, for they saw none of their colleagues from rival papers. None yet, anyway, for they knew that a story this big had already reached the newsrooms of the other dailies and legions of reporters were on their way. They would have to move quickly to get the first reports phoned in to fill the columns of the Extra! being prepared downtown.

The newsmen fanned out in all directions and began interviewing survivors. Most were too stunned by their experiences to take offense at the probing questions. Indeed, many seemed to welcome the opportunity to relate their story, as if the telling would make it more comprehensible, or perhaps release some of the horror flooding their minds. They poured out details faster than reporters could scribble.

Other reporters found nurses and rescue personnel and quickly transcribed the stories of heroism and quick thinking that saved so many. Photographers lugged their enormous rigs from one end of the beach to the other, pausing every so often to set up a shot of a dozen bodies lying in the water, a few survivors huddled under blankets, or the smoldering wreck of the *Slocum*. No matter how many crime scenes they had photographed in the past, none could quite believe the things they saw when they peered into the viewfinder.

Downtown at the offices of the *World*, Martin Green waited for the telephone to ring. Outside his office and far below in City Hall Park and along Newspaper Row, he could see people talking excitedly, obviously exchanging fragments of fact and rumor about the disaster far uptown. They would be among the first to plunk down a penny when his first Extra! hit the sidewalks. The men downstairs were poised to produce it; all they needed was copy dictated over the phone lines. The photographs, which had to be brought back to the office and developed, would be included in subsequent Extra! numbers.

Finally the telephone rang and Green took the first reports of the *Slocum* disaster down in furious shorthand. This was worse—far worse— than the St. Louis tornado or the Hoboken pier fire, and it was dreadful stuff to transcribe. But Green had been handed a scoop and he had a job to do: deliver the story. In thirty minutes he'd have his Extra! rolling off the presses.

As soon as he was able to stand, Reverend Haas hobbled over to the rows of the dead laid out on the grass. By now workers from the coroner's office, health department, and Riverside Hospital had pulled dozens of the dead up over the seawall and laid them out in neat rows on the grass. The sight sickened him. There under the warm midday sun lay scores of corpses, among them, he feared, his wife, daughter, and sister. As he approached the rows he saw victims in every state. Some of the dead were badly burned and disfigured, but most were not, the great majority dying by drowning. Some had contorted limbs and faces, suggesting they died struggling to the last. Others lay on the grass, hands folded on their chests, as though they'd died peacefully in their sleep. He saw several mothers with children still clasped tightly to their breasts. His missing family members, however, were nowhere to be seen.

Joining Haas in the dreadful viewing were survivors of all ages searching for loved ones. Some moved slowly, as if in a trance, while others raced about in a state of unbridled hysteria. Instinctually they turned to Haas, and he did his best to offer some measure of comfort. To those still searching, he gave words of encouragement and hope. To those bent over the bodies of loved ones, he offered prayers and consolation. It was something he'd done countless times for families in his parish when a loved one died, but this was different—not simply due to the scale of the tragedy, but also because he was directly involved. For the first time in his career, Haas received consoling words from his flock.

In a strange, subconscious way, the hideous process of searching among the dead actually boosted some of the searcher's hopes. They were engaged in a strange undertaking—a search in which they hoped not to find what they were looking for. Every corpse that turned out to be someone else's wife or child raised the prospect that theirs had been spared. As one journalist put it, "As a face was uncovered and the sheet turned back upon it, there was renewed hope that after all those sought might be saved, or at worst were only suffering in one or another hospitals." Adding to these slim hopes were the stories flying among the survivors, stories of relatives last seen climbing aboard tugboats or floating with life preservers. And everywhere, it seemed, people flung their arms around each other, indicating a miraculous reunion of people separated during the fire. The searchers clung to these images as they looked over the dead, hoping all the while not to find the irrefutable evidence that trumped all alleged eyewitness accounts of rescues—the body of a loved one.

But even those who failed to find the remains of a loved one were nonetheless traumatized by the process of seeing so many corpses. They saw countless people they knew, in some cases whole families. No one was more affected in this way than Haas, for most of these people were members of his parish family. He'd baptized, confirmed, and married most of them. In one row lay Mrs. Schwartz and her mother. In another was Amelia

Richter, flanked by several of her dead children. Not far away lay several more mothers—Louisa Hartung, Emilia Justh, Johanna Horway, and many more. There was a woman who looked like Mary Abendschein—the tireless Sunday school teacher who had handled every detail in planning the excursion. There was Henry Schnude, a deacon of St. Mark's, and George Maurer, leader of the band aboard the *Slocum*. And everywhere, babies and little children too numerous to count or name.

Nearly as haunting were the sounds of despair emanating from the rows of dead as their fellow victims recognized a wife, mother, or child. Some of the hardest scenes to witness were those involving children who found their dead mothers and fathers. Too young to comprehend what had happened, and the finality of death, they shook their mothers and pleaded, "Mama, wake up."

Despite his injuries, including severely burned hands, Haas remained among the rows of dead all afternoon, searching for his family and comforting the survivors. At one point he even ventured out in a boat to help recover additional bodies, but soon returned. Nurses and doctors tried to persuade him to get medical attention, but he refused. His flock had been devastated and he simply could not bring himself to abandon them. It was late in the afternoon when he finally collapsed from exhaustion and shock and was taken from the island, placed in an ambulance, and brought to Lincoln Hospital and later home to Little Germany.

Anna Liebenow sat on the beach with her baby Adella wrapped in a blanket. Badly burned on her left side and arm from shielding her baby from the flames before jumping onto a tugboat, she stared out into the water. She was all alone except for the baby. Her husband and two older daughters were nowhere to be seen, nor were her in-laws, the Webers, and their two children. The horrific scene in the water and the growing lines of dead on the lawn, especially the children, filled her heart with dread. Were they all gone?

Suddenly a wild-eyed woman rushed up to her, claiming that the baby she held was hers. In spite of her state of shock, Liebenow had the presence of mind to ask, "What sex is your baby?" "A boy," the woman replied. As Liebenow explained that her baby was a girl, the crazed woman ran off to continue her fruitless search.

Gradually Liebenow's husband Paul found her, followed by her in-laws Frank and Annie Weber. They cried and hugged and examined each other's cuts and burns. It was a bitter reunion, for as glad as they were to find one another, their combined stories pointed to one terrible reality: the children were gone. They still held out hope that Aunt Martha had managed to put them on a tugboat that landed elsewhere, but it seemed so unlikely. The last time they had been seen they were heading down the very stairs that moments later filled with fire and smoke. Still, it was a big boat and anything was possible. The men set out to find their children.

Catherine Gallagher was brought to the island by one of the tugboats. Suffering from minor burns and bruises, she sat on the grass in a state of hysteria. She remembered there'd been a fire and that in the ensuing confusion she'd lost sight of her mother and two siblings. She also had a vague recollection that someone had put her over the side into a passing tugboat. Now as she sat there wrapped in a blanket and looking around at the tumult among the survivors and rescue workers, she saw no sign of her family. Eventually, probably at the urging of a rescue worker, she took the first of several tours of the dead. Each time she found nothing, but the steady arrival of bodies from the beach left her no option but to wait.

At 10:55 A.M., even before the news of the disaster became general, the burning hulk that had been the *General Slocum* was raised by the incoming tide and set adrift. The floating inferno presented an enormous risk to traffic on the East River and the busy piers that lined its banks. So as it cleared the rocky shoals surrounding the island and drifted out into the channel, several tugs secured lines to the hull and towed it east to Hunts Point on the Bronx shore. Her entire upper works still ablaze, the *Slocum* began to sink as it approached the shore, weighed down by thousands of gallons of seawater pumped into it by the fireboats. Wallowing along and listing to one side, the crippled vessel began to pitch forward and then rolled on her port side about 250 feet from shore. Huge clouds of steam from the extinguished flames shot into the air, briefly obscuring the wreck. Steam and smoke continued to billow as the *Slocum* slowly sank to the mud floor below. By approximately 12:20 P.M., only the starboard paddle box, some of the upper works, and the smokestacks could be seen, shrouded in an eerie mix of smoke and steam.

At North Brother Island, rescuers-turned-recoverers found that the moving of the *Slocum* had stirred the waters and freed dozens more victims from the bottom. Men like Sam Berg, police officer John Scheuing, and young Charles Schwartz, who had saved so many victims, now worked among the dozens of men moving about in small boats and armed with grappling hooks to pull in the dead. As soon as their boats were full, they brought their dismal cargo to tugboats, which then transported the bodies to the island, landing them at a pier. As time passed, many resorted to simply towing the dead to the tugs, a move that saved time and lessened the chances of capsizing. The bodies brought in by this method cut irregular paths in the thick layer of cork dust that covered large areas of the water's surface.

Yet by 11:30 A.M., an hour after the beaching and with smoke from the *Slocum* still visible to the northeast, the retrieval of the dead slowed to a near standstill. On the island's beach and lawn lay about 150 dead. As the hours ticked by into the midafternoon with only an occasional corpse being found, it seemed to many that the worst was over. Perhaps, workers and officials thought, the death toll might not exceed 200, a ghastly tally to be sure, but far less than many had predicted given the early accounts of the disaster.

Gradually, rescue workers and medical personnel began to transfer the survivors off North Brother Island aboard the city-owned tugs *Massasoit* and *Franklin Edson*. Since Riverside Hospital was dedicated solely to the treatment of contagious diseases, officials decided to send those in need of further medical attention to several nearby hospitals. Most were taken across the river to the pier at 138th Street and transferred to ambulances for the ride to either Lincoln or Lebanon Hospital in the Bronx or Harlem Hospital in upper Manhattan, while others went directly by tug downriver to Bellevue Hospital at East 26th Street.

Also sent off the island were survivors who had few or no injuries. Many were eager to leave the island so they could notify family members and look for loved ones at hospitals, the police station, and the morgue. In a manner shocking to modern sensibilities concerning the psychological effects of trauma and tragedy, officials simply put them on trains headed downtown. Some children were escorted by policemen or transported home in a police wagon, but many were delivered to the train platform and sent home unescorted. It may have been due to the sheer number of people involved and the general atmosphere of confusion, but it also reflected the spirit of the age. Americans in 1904 thought no more of "grief counseling" than they did computer programming. Home—to the consolation of family, neighborhood, and church—was where these victims needed to be, and so off they went. Commuters on the trains could not help but notice these poor people wrapped in bandages and dressed in ill-fitting clothes provided by the hospital. Few were perplexed by the strange sight, for by now everyone in the city knew of the tragedy.

LIKE WILDFIRE

Word of the *Slocum* disaster spread with astonishing speed, even by New York City standards. Sometime around 11:30 A.M., barely one hour after the *Slocum* hit the beach all aflame, the doors leading to the loading docks behind the *New York World* building flung open. Dozens of men began hastily hurling bundles of newspapers onto the beds of trucks for delivery to uptown newsstands. At least a hundred young boys—"newsies" in the street slang of the day—jockeyed for position near a dispatch office. They pushed and shoved each other, eager to plunk down their meager cash—fifty cents for a hundred copies to sell at one penny each—and be on their way to every busy street corner in the city to hawk their Extras! telling the first details of the great disaster on the East River.

In the great race to be first, Martin Green had won.

Twenty minutes later a woman staggered off a streetcar at East Sixth Street. Weeping audibly and holding a rumpled copy of a *World* Extra!, she ran to St. Mark's Church halfway down the block. Some bystanders recognized her as a parishioner at St. Mark's and they stared as she flew by, wondering what could bring on such an undignified display of emotion. They watched as she reached the church and began pulling the door handles and knocking violently with her fists. But with more than half the parish away on the Sunday school excursion, this was one of the very rare days when the church doors were locked. She collapsed in a heap on the stairs, crying hysterically. A small crowd gathered to see what was the matter. Unable to speak coherently, she handed them the newspaper. And in the time it took to read the extra-large-font headlines, "Horror on the East River! Hundreds Feared Dead!" the neighborhood began to learn the news of the unthinkable.

At almost the same moment, George Haas, Jr., son of the pastor, heard the telephone ring. Now nineteen, he'd decided to skip this year's church excursion and was enjoying a quiet day at home. Normally on a spring weekday he could expect a relatively uneventful day, little more than answering a few phone calls and accepting a delivery or two. Nothing seemed unusual about this call, until the quaking voice on the other end began to speak.

It was a member of the parish, and in a torrent of anguished words the caller told him what had happened. There has been a terrible tragedy—a fire on board the steamboat. Hundreds have drowned or died in the flames—women, children, and grandparents. It's horrifying. And your family—your father, mother, sister, grandmother, and aunts—they are all gone.

Haas stammered out a few questions and listened to the dreadful details of the ordeal before the caller hung up. Could it possibly be true? he wondered. His father's parish wiped out in a fire aboard the *Slocum*? His entire family gone? A frantic knock at the door brought the answer. Still reeling from the news, Haas opened the door and found several parishioners standing in the doorway with tears in their eyes and looks of anguish on their faces. All at once they poured out a volley of frantic questions— Did you hear? What happened? How many have died? Where should we go? Haas just stood there in a state of shock, unable to speak.

A large crowd of distraught parishioners had by now gathered in front of St. Mark's Church. They grew more hysterical with each passing minute, their fears stoked by the bits and pieces of rumor and fact being bandied about. One woman urged everyone to stay calm—It's nothing more than typical Pulitzer-Hearst exaggeration, she said. "I've just heard from someone who was on board," she continued, "that there wasn't a single life lost." Everyone got off safely, she insisted, after the captain beached the boat.

Her words of assurance briefly calmed the crowd. But only a few minutes later, the first hard evidence that countless friends and family were gone appeared in the form of survivors returning home. Among the first to arrive was a young boy named Edwin Matzerath of 330 East Sixth Street. They gathered round the youth, noting his bruised head and singed clothing. In a halting voice he told them about the fire, the panic, and the hundreds who plunged into the water. Many, he told them, had been burned to death or drowned. At this the crowd disintegrated into panic and cries of anguish. Soon twelve-year-old Fred Baumler, also of East Sixth Street, arrived. Likewise battered and bruised, he told a nearly identical version of the tragedy. He'd come home in search of his family—had anyone seen his mother, brother, and two sisters?

With the arrival of irrefutable evidence of a massive tragedy, word spread rapidly throughout the neighborhood. Helping the process along was the arrival of an army of newsies bearing fresh Extras! containing the latest details. Friends and relatives dashed from stores to apartments to street corners telling everyone they knew the news. People poured out of their homes and businesses onto the sidewalks and into the streets. Many later recounted what it was like to learn of the *Slocum*'s fate.

Eugene Ansel sat weeping in his deli at 103 East Fourth Street. He thought his heart was about to break, for he'd just received a telegram from Germany informing him that his father had died. It was the sort of news that hit immigrants harder than others, for it stoked feelings of guilt over leaving their family and country behind for a new life in America. It had been years since he'd seen his father, and now he never would again. And on this day, he had no one in his immediate family to console him, for that morning he'd put his wife and two sons aboard the *Slocum.*

Not five minutes after the telegram boy had sped off on his bicycle, a friend burst into the store. Seeing Ansel's tears, he assumed he'd heard about the disaster and began ranting about the horror of it all and asking if Ansel had any information. Ansel, of course, had no idea what his friend was talking about, and it was several minutes before he gleaned the awful truth about the *Slocum.*

Peter Fickbaum stood behind the big wooden bar in his saloon at Avenue D and East Eighth Street. Earlier that morning he'd put his wife, four children, and a servant on board the *Slocum,* and now, as he prepared for the midday lunch crowd, he chatted amiably with a few regulars sipping their midmorning lager.

The peaceful atmosphere was suddenly shattered when his friend Nicholas Balser stumbled into the saloon. His clothes still wet and his hands and face red and blistered, he presented a bizarre sight.

"What's the matter?" asked an anxious Fickbaum. Balser and his wife Catherine had accompanied the Fickbaums on the *Slocum* excursion.

"They're lost—," he gasped, "burned—all gone." Then, before anyone had time to make sense of what he'd said, Balser gave an animated description of the fire. Hundreds had perished in the flames or in the water, including, he feared, Fickbaum's family. "My Catherine!" he repeated over and over again as men all around him slammed down their steins of beer and dashed out into the street.

Mayor McClellan was at his desk in city hall when his personal secretary John O'Brien ran into his office with news of the disaster. A steamboat had burst into flames on the East River and as many as one hundred people were dead. The startled mayor composed himself, picked up the phone, and dialed Police Commissioner William McAdoo. The two were increasingly at odds and rarely spoke directly with each other, but this was not a time for pettiness. He listened in astonishment as McAdoo confirmed the story of the fire, but upped the death toll considerably. Hundreds have perished, the commissioner predicted, perhaps more than five hundred. The mayor could hardly believe it—a blaze to rival Chicago's Iroquois Theater fire back in December. He empowered McAdoo to order up from the appropriate city departments as many medical personnel, ambulances, fire apparatus, and boats he needed. Keep me informed, McClellan said before hanging up.

THE FIX

From the moment the first survivors came ashore at North Brother Island, accusations of negligence and dereliction of duty began to fly. Rescue workers, nurses, and journalists heard the same stories over and over again. The boat, claimed the passengers, went up in flames like a paper box. The crew panicked and did nothing to fight the fire or help passengers in need. The hoses and life preservers were rotten and the lifeboats were wired in place. And the captain, they all seemed to ask, why did he not bring the boat to shore sooner?

Coronor O'Gorman heard their charges against the crew and concerning the safety provisions aboard the *Slocum* and quietly began collecting evidence even as he labored to assist in rescue and recovery work. Save anything you find that might aid in a future investigation, he instructed his men. They didn't have far to look, and by midday he had a stack of waterlogged life preservers—or at least shreds of them.

It was over an hour after the steamboat's grounding before Inspector Albertson received orders from McAdoo to consider the incident a possible crime. He was to arrest the captain and any crewmen he encountered on the charge of criminal negligence. Several police officers fanned out to make the collars, but they could not locate the wanted men. Several rescue workers pointed out a nearby tree, indicating that the captain lay there recovering after coming ashore. But neither he nor Brandow, Coakley, Conklin, Corcoran, Flanagan, O'Neill, Van Wart, or Weaver was anywhere to be seen.

The man responsible for these mysterious disappearances was none other than Frank A. Barnaby, president of the Knickerbocker Steamboat Company. A hard-nosed businessman with excellent instincts, he immediately appreciated the threat posed to his business interests by the *Slocum* disaster.

Gone were the days of the Gilded Age when a businessman could say, as Vanderbilt once famously did, "The public be damned!" Public opinion in the Progressive Era mattered a great deal. How else to explain the sensations created by muckrakers like Ida Tarbell and Lincoln Steffens? Barnaby knew that Hearst, Pulitzer, McClure, and Frank A. Munsey (publisher of *Munsey's* magazine) delighted in (and grew rich by) playing the populist crusader role against evil capitalists. Bad publicity was bad for business. If he failed to act quickly, his reputation would suffer and so would his business interests—a substantial real estate enterprise far more important to him than the piddling, two-boat Knickerbocker Steamboat Company. This he knew from firsthand experience, having been convicted of fraud in a real estate deal five years earlier.

So even before he learned of the growing howl of outrage among the survivors and officials at North Brother Island, the shrewd capitalist set in motion a scheme to contain and perhaps even stymie any effort to bring legal action against him or the company. Accordingly, he dispatched James K. Atkinson, secretary of the Knickerbocker Steamboat Company, and five other men to the scene. To the press, he would explain that they were being sent to offer any and all assistance to the suffering. But to Atkinson and his men, he described their task in more narrow and cold terms. First, find the captain and crew and get them out of there before the press and police have at them. Send them downtown to the company headquarters. They would need to get their stories straight. Second, learn as much as possible about the incident, the condition of the steamer, and what survivors were saying. The earlier he knew this information, the sooner he could rebut any accusations of negligence.

Twenty minutes later, Atkinson and his men set foot on North Brother Island and went to work taking stock of the situation and rounding up the captain and crew. They found First Mate Flanagan, Second Mate Corcoran, porter Payne, engineer Conklin, and deckhands Coakley, Collins, and O'Neill almost immediately and got them onto boats leaving the island before the police began their roundup. Subsequently they located Van Schaick, Van Wart, Weaver, and four other crewmen and likewise spirited them onto departing boats. This second group made it as far as the 138th Street pier and was about to slip away in a cab when a policeman approached and ordered them to halt. He placed them under arrest and sent them to the Alexander Avenue police station. But Barnaby's plan had not failed entirely—Atkinson's effort had impressed upon the arrested men the gravity of the situation and the need to remain unified and tight-lipped.

Downtown, Barnaby—unaware that only part of his scheme had worked—was already at work on another crucial element of damage control. He called in Miss Josephine Hall, the company's bookkeeper, and informed her that some honest mistakes had been made in some recent records regarding the purchase of safety equipment for the *General Slocum*. It was nothing major, he assured her, nothing that could not be handled with a little erasing acid (the 1904 equivalent of Wite-Out). She should see to it right away.

A few hours later, once Barnaby had time to read the newspapers and speak with Atkinson and the six crewmen of the *Slocum* who had made it to the office, he drew up a statement and issued it to the press. Faced with severe public criticism of his vessel and its crew, Barnaby opted for a full and complete denial, leavened with a few thinly veiled accusations of his own.

> *We do not feel that our employees are responsible for the disaster since their discipline was perfect, and one minute after the fire started every man was at his post. We have frequent fire and boat drills aboard, and each man acted as he had been instructed. . . .*

*The fire, I learn, started right up in the bow. Someone had placed
a bunch of bananas there and had covered it with dry meadow grass.
As soon as the blaze was discovered in it the hose was stretched and
within a minute the water was started. . . .*

*I believe that Capt. Van Schaick did all in his power to save
passengers, and will back him in whatever course he pursued.*

The Slocum *was fully supplied with all life-saving devices and I
cannot understand why the passengers did not avail themselves of
them. At the vessel's recent inspection we were told that she could safely
remove all of the passengers she was licensed to carry.*

In just a few lines of text, Barnaby set forth the company's strategy for the
coming legal battle. It rejected any suggestion that the crew failed in its duties and that the captain used poor judgment in heading for North Brother
Island. Further, it denied that the boat's safety equipment and emergency
training were inadequate. More important, Barnaby tried to shift blame
from the company to the passengers. *Someone*—i.e., a passenger—had
started the fire by placing bananas and grass in the bow. Then, when the
fire raged out of control, the passengers *did not avail themselves*—i.e., they
panicked—of the ample life preservers and boats aboard. In this latter
point, Barnaby sought to play the gender card, suggesting the whole
fiasco had been caused by hysterical passengers, most of whom were
women. The next day in a subsequent statement of denial, he made this
point more explicit. "A hundred failed in doing what a single man could
have done."

Not far from Barnaby's office, about half a mile down Broadway at 17
Battery Place, officials of the United States Steamboat Inspection Service
had commenced their own scramble for cover. The man in charge of the
USSIS's Second District (which covered the East Coast of the United
States from Virginia to the Canadian border) was Robert S. Rodie. The
forty-three-year-old was a classic self-made man—of the bureaucrat sort.
After a brief stint in the private sector as a clerk in the Pennsylvania Railroad's marine division, Rodie secured a position as assistant supervising
inspector of steam-powered vessels in New York. By 1901 he'd risen to his

current position as supervising inspector of the Second District. Given the nature of the USSIS, he was perfectly suited for the job. He was fiercely loyal to the service and resistant to any attempt at reform. And one additional thing made him ideal as head of the Second District office: he had absolutely no training in the design and workings of steamboats. Like Lundberg, he'd become an "inspector" merely by watching other "inspectors."

Assisting Rodie in overseeing the district were two deputies, Gen. James A. Dumont and Thomas H. Barrett. Like their boss, they were classic placeholders, only with decades of bureaucratic service behind them. Dumont, inspector of hulls, was eighty-five years old and had spent nearly three decades with the service. Barrett, the inspector of boilers, was seventy years old and had been with the USSIS for the past fifteen years. Despite their titles, neither man did any actual inspections. They rarely left the office and mainly occupied themselves with signing certificates of approval based on work carried out by assistant inspectors like Lundberg and Fleming. Both men had signed the certificate attesting to the seaworthiness and safety of the *Slocum* back in May.

Dumont had actually held the top position in the USSIS of supervising inspector general in Washington, D.C., until March 1903, when he resigned under pressure from the secretary of Commerce and Labor. No one in the service seemed to think it odd when Dumont took the inspector of hulls job in New York—just the thing for a man with "experience" and a desire for light work.

All three men shared a desire to protect the USSIS from the scourge of the era—the good-government reformer. Unfortunately, Dumont's replacement, George Uhler, was one such man. From the start he proved distressingly keen on revamping the service and had already made waves the previous year when he noted in his annual report the permissive culture within the USSIS that allowed most fines for violations to be reduced or waived altogether.

Of course, Uhler's scrupulous attention to the most minute details also meant that he provided the seasoned men in the field with endless laughs. On one occasion he demanded that Rodie repay the service five cents for overstating the reimbursable mileage for a trip. The distance from Albany, New York, to Portland, Maine, he testily informed Rodie, was not 281 miles, but 280. On another, he upbraided an official for discussing two separate matters in one letter. "Hereafter," he insisted, "you will confine each letter to one subject."

Still, a man of Uhler's position was not to be taken lightly. It was already well known that Congress was contemplating tougher inspection laws, and Uhler intended to demand more rigorous enforcement of them by his inspectors. The *Slocum* disaster threatened to put the spotlight on the service and expose its many flaws—unless Rodie, Dumont, and Barrett acted to contain the controversy.

As a massive, fossilized bureaucracy, their containment effort would be less nimble than Barnaby's, but then again their task was somewhat smaller: find Lundberg and Fleming, the USSIS men who had inspected and certified as safe the *Slocum* five weeks earlier. Lundberg in particular would have to prepare for the onslaught of questions from the media and eventually investigators from the coroner's or district attorney's offices. If he exposed the service for what it was—a corrupt patronage mill that had long before lost focus on assuring the safety of steamboats—he might go to jail. Or worse, Rodie, Barrett, Dumont, and countless others in the service might lose their sinecures in a general housecleaning.

Lundberg was soon found and spirited into the offices of the USSIS past a group of reporters, who received no answers to their rapid-fire questions. Two hours later, after having had the chance to "collect" his thoughts, Lundberg emerged and took a few questions from the press.

How did you examine the life preservers? they asked. "I first counted them until I found that there were 3,000 in all," he began. "Then I made the pile into lots of forty each and each fortieth preserver I examined." Nearly every one, he asserted, was in good shape and "able to support the weight of any person in the water for a long while." How did he explain, the reporters asked, the innumerable reports of rotten life preservers? "If any two people try to get a life preserver and struggle for its possession," said the beleaguered inspector in a blame-the-victims explanation strikingly similar to Barnaby's, "they could easily break it apart and make it useless."

Had he been shown the *Slocum*'s fire drill procedure? Yes, he replied, "it was in my mind perfect in every way." The steamboat was, he concluded, "in first-class A-1 condition and had complied with every requirement of the law. Every life-raft was in good condition. Every life-boat swung freely on its davits." Lundberg's statements were greeted with a skepticism that would only grow in the coming weeks.

That Barnaby's and Rodie's instincts were sound became clear by the later afternoon when the Extras! being cranked out by the city's newspapers began to include accusations of corporate negligence, cowardice, and poor judgment. "Captain Arrested with His Pilots" proclaimed the headline in Martin Green's *Evening World*. The front page of Hearst's *Evening Journal* carried the headline "Life Preservers Old and Useless."

Then came the statement from Coroner Joseph Berry at North Brother Island. Filled with seething indignation at the rising death toll amid mounting evidence of negligence and dereliction of duty, he approached a group of reporters and began speaking. "You may be sure," he began, "that this most terrible calamity will be investigated by all departments of the City Government." The district attorney, coroner, and police department, he continued, were cooperating in the effort to fix responsibility for the dreadful calamity. But he made it clear that he had a firm idea where the blame lay. The effort to extinguish the fire, he charged, had been botched. "Had the fire been handled properly, it could have been extinguished without trouble." Short of that, the crew should have done everything in their power to quell the panic and distribute life preservers. "But this they seem to have overlooked entirely," the disgusted coroner concluded, "in their mad desire to escape themselves." The coroner's point was lost on no one: the fire aboard the *General Slocum* was indeed a disaster—but it was no accident.

I MAY YET FIND
MY DARLINGS

A s soon as word of the *Slocum*'s fate reached Little Germany, relatives and friends of those on board raced uptown to the Bronx on elevated trains. Before long, thousands crowded around the piers near 138th Street. In the distance they could see the armada of boats large and small off the edge of a beach filled with rescue personnel. Smoke from the *Slocum*, now long-departed from the scene, rose off Hunts Point to the northeast. Prevented from reaching the island by policemen, desperate relatives waited for the boatloads of survivors to arrive.

A second huge crowd massed outside the nearby Alexander Avenue police station, where the first bodies were brought. By 3:00 P.M., one hundred policemen were at work near the station, trying to keep order among a crowd of several thousand people frantic to view the thirty-seven bodies transported there from the island. "Men were cursing and shouting," wrote an eyewitness of the pitiful scene. "Women were crying, embracing one another, calling out through the crowd to know if any one had heard of this or that one, begging the police to let them in to set their fears at rest."

In charge of this makeshift morgue was Bronx coroner Joseph Berry. Surveying the surging crowd outside, he quickly recognized the need for a larger facility—a much larger one—and notified O'Gorman and other officials at North Brother Island to devise an alternative plan. In the meantime he would let as many anxious relatives in to view the dead as possible, but only in clusters of six at a time to prevent overcrowding.

Most seemed to be men, the fathers, sons, and brothers who went to work that day while their wives, daughters, and sisters enjoyed a day at the shore. Many of these same men, who normally prided themselves on their German stoicism, broke down completely. Eugene Ansel, the deli owner who had learned of his father's death just minutes before hearing about the *Slocum*, arrived at the police station on the verge of insanity. He approached a corpse of a woman in her twenties, lifted the sheet covering her face, and fell to his knees. It was his beloved wife, Louisa, he exclaimed. A moment later he repeated the same lamentations over the body of a different woman. Three more times he declared a different body to be that of his wife before two policemen pulled him aside. They had already seen several men do the same thing. Another man could not remember his wife's name, while another found that the stammering he had conquered as a youth had returned to render him incapable of speech. Ansel was nearly as difficult to understand, but the policemen managed to learn that his wife wore a wedding ring with her initials engraved on the inside. Twenty minutes later the body of a sixth woman—previously misidentified—was identified as Louisa Ansel by her wedding ring. The bodies of Ansel's two boys, Alfred and Eugene, Jr., were not there, and Ansel left to look for them in the hospitals.

Not long after, Paul Liebenow and his brother-in-law Frank Weber rushed in. Like many survivors that afternoon, they entered covered in bandages and exhibiting cuts, bruises, and burns. They looked wildly around the station for their missing children but found nothing. Seeing their distress, Coroner Berry approached and asked several questions about the children in an effort to help, but the men were so distraught they were unable to speak coherently. After examining the remaining bodies, the two dashed out the door headed for one of the hospitals.

Not all the news was bad at the police station. Every now and again a relative found a survivor in the rooms set aside for the injured and those young children without parents. One of the latter was a little three-year-old named Lizzie Kregler, clad in a bright red dress. She'd been one of the lucky ones plucked from the paddle wheel box after the steamer beached. For four hours she sat in stunned silence in the station house until she suddenly perked up at the sight of a man searching among the dead.

"Papa!" she called out.

The voice at first startled the man, one Charles Kregler, but he quickly scanned the room and saw his youngest. He rushed to her and took her up in his arms, exclaiming, "My dear Lizzie, my dear Lizzie, how glad I am to find you." With tears running down his face, he left with his daughter to search for her mother and three older siblings (he would find only a second daughter).

By far the most remarkable piece of positive news at the police station involved fifteen-year-old Clara Hartman. She'd been found facedown in the water at North Brother Island and presumed dead. The small launch that found her was already filled with bodies, so the men simply towed her to shore. There a worker tagged her as body no. 24, wrapped her in a tarpaulin, and placed her with the dead. She was taken to the police station where, four hours later, a woman bent over her and unfolded the tarpaulin. She wanted to record a few identifying features of the young girl to assist in later identification. As she examined the girl, something made her pause. This body, she thought, somehow seems different from the others, but she couldn't say why. The startling answer came a moment later when she undid the girl's corset and detected breathing.

"Be quick!" she shouted to several startled workers. "Hurry! This girl is alive!" Doctors rushed into the room and took measures to revive her. Gradually Clara's breathing deepened. Presently she opened her eyes and within five minutes was fully conscious and able to speak a few faint words. It was one small miracle in an afternoon of unrelenting misery, and it left many workers at the station momentarily frozen in their tracks. A few sharp commands from one of the doctors and they jumped back to work, wrapping the young girl in blankets and calling for an ambulance to take her to Lincoln Hospital. Just before she was carried out, one of the doctors took out his scissors and snipped off her body tag with the number 24 written on it.

While thousands waited for admission to the police station, others headed for one or more of the several hospitals to which the injured were sent. "I have five children," a distressed Frances Iden said to the policemen guarding the entrance to Lincoln Hospital, "the oldest nineteen, and the youngest five. They were all on the excursion. Let me pass." They stepped aside and she bolted up the stairs and down the main corridor, pleading for someone to show her where the *Slocum* survivors were being held. She moved from ward to ward, carefully examining the occupants of each bed until finally she came upon a young girl almost completely covered in bandages. It was her twelve-year-old Anna. They recognized each other instantly and embraced in a tearful reunion. "I had five children this morning," Mrs. Iden explained to the nurses gathered round them. "Now I only have this one." As it turned out, Iden would later learn that one of her sons had survived without injury.

Anna Iden was hardly the only young survivor waiting alone at Lincoln Hospital to discover the fate of their family. Eleven-year-old Dora Kregler had boarded the *Slocum* with her mother, brother, and two sisters (one sibling survived uninjured). Twelve-year-old Rose De Luccia, a member of an Italian immigrant family that attended the excursion, listened to the people around her sobbing in German and wondered what had become of her mother and three siblings (only her mother lived). Ten-year-old Frances Richter lay in her bed worrying about the fate of her mother and six siblings. All had been killed, and she was eventually found by her older brother, who did not go on the trip.

Carl Kircher arrived to discover that his wife and two sons were alive and likely to recover. But his only daughter, Elsie, the only member of the family given a life preserver, was gone. Paul Port, the laundry owner, found his wife at Lincoln, but his two sons were missing. Frederick Zipse, accompanied by his son William, located his wife Sophia, but none of their five children who went on the trip (all had died). Conrad Muth found his brother John and nephew John, Jr., the only survivors of a group of fourteen.

Amid these scenes of anxious waiting and searching, a few counted their blessings. As each distraught parent passed by her bed, Emma Firneisen realized just how lucky she was. She was burned, battered, and suffering from shock, but she and her three children had survived. Marie, age seven, and Henry, age ten, were in the hospital with her, while William was uninjured. In a nearby bed Mary Kunster reflected on her good fortune. Her sons Charles, seventeen, and William, twelve, were with her at Lincoln Hospital, injured but alive. They perhaps more than most would feel the sharp prods of so-called "survivor's guilt" in the months and years to come.

Similar scenes unfolded at nearby Lebanon Hospital, where Anna Liebenow lay in a bed moaning under the pain of burns on the left side of her body. With her was Adella, her six-month-old baby who miraculously survived the ordeal. In a nearby bed was Annie Weber, her sister-in-law. Her burns were much more serious and included severe damage to her lungs. Drifting in and out of consciousness, the two women wondered if their husbands had found their missing children.

Twelve-year-old Henry Oellrich waited until his father found him. He had no answer when his father asked of the fate of his mother and four siblings (none survived). Not seriously hurt, Catherine Gallagher waited for hours for word of her mother and two siblings. Toward 8:00 P.M., two women convinced her to go home and they accompanied her on the elevated train as far as East Fourteenth Street. From there the eleven-year-old ran home alone.

Anna Frese, the fifteen-year-old aspiring concert pianist, was too badly burned to leave so quickly. When doctors looked at her scorched hands, they announced that amputation was necessary. Fortunately, Anna had her parents with her. Her father adamantly refused to let them amputate, and they left the hospital as soon they could. Anna's piano-playing days were finished, but her hands eventually healed. Fourteen-year-old Martha Kutsch, all alone in the hospital, accepted the same diagnosis of the doctor who examined her crushed hand. It was amputated later that evening.

And in a ward separate from the passengers lay the *Slocum*'s captain, William Van Schaick. A policeman stood nearby, a constant reminder that he was under arrest. Van Schaick writhed in pain from the burns he had suffered and the broken foot sustained when he jumped from the burning boat. But the mental anguish was nearly as bad. Over and over he replayed the frightful scenes in his mind. Incessantly the sounds of the ordeal—what he said were "the cries of people suffering from burning to death"—echoed in his head. And then there were the nagging doubts about his decisions— Full ahead into the wind? Make for North Brother Island instead of something closer? Never conduct a fire drill?

For most, Harlem Hospital was the last stop before the journey downtown to the morgue. Located in Upper Manhattan, it was the farthest from the scene of the accident. Still, those who entered were not yet ready to give up. "In their faces," wrote a journalist, "could be read the forlorn hope that still lingered, in spite of a tireless search of hospitals in the Bronx, that those whom they sought might possibly be in the Harlem institution."

All afternoon and into the evening they came, alone and in groups. Inside they joined the procession of searching relatives moving through the wards past countless bandaged survivors, many of them friends and neighbors. Most left disappointed but still hopeful. One large man fought to hold back his tears as he spoke with a doctor about his fruitless search for his wife and five children. "For four hours I have looked for a trace of them, but to no purpose. God is good, though, and I may yet find my darlings."

And off he went to the morgue, the place everyone dreaded most.

HARVEST OF THE DEAD

At around 3:00 P.M. the outgoing tide began to sweep away any hope of a death toll under two hundred and lay bare the stunning scope of the disaster. Scores of bodies began to appear as the waters receded. In just one hour, between 4:30 and 5:30 P.M., workers found fifty bodies. Over the next few hours the rate of what one reporter starkly termed the "harvest of the dead" soared to one body per minute. Even men accustomed to the grisly aftermath of murders and accidents, like Coroner O'Gorman, were shaken by the experience. "No one who stood on the beach Wednesday night," remembered O'Gorman, ". . . will ever forget the scene. It is the kind of thing that a man will wake up nights and see again before him in the darkness."

The same terrible reality was dawning east of North Brother Island at the sunken wreck of the *Slocum*. As more and more of the vessel was exposed by the lowering tide, workmen from the Merritt Chapman salvage company began to recover dozens more victims. They also began to pull apart the paddle box and sections of the cabins. Soon the naval reserve launch *Oneida* pulled alongside the wreck bearing a team of four divers. They immediately donned their 175-pound armored suits and descended into the hull. There they saw scenes that made them shudder, and a few of them cry. Charles P. Everett, a veteran diver who six years earlier had explored the wreck of the U.S.S. *Maine* at the bottom of Havana harbor, gave a heartfelt account of what he saw on his first dive into the hull of the *Slocum*. The vessel was so completely destroyed, he said, had he not known what caused it to sink he would have guessed a huge explosion. "The appetite of the fire," he reported, "must have been insatiable." Once inside "the tomb," as he called it, he saw scores of bodies trapped in the wreckage. "All [were] caught in that implacable, fatal grip supplied by the crunching together of beams and stanchions and wooden supports" when the decks collapsed. Most were women and children, many still clinging to each other in a final embrace. "They tell me I was down in the tomb about an hour and a half. That must be a mistake. I was down there a year." A reporter from the *Times* noted that Everett "blanched as he described to us the horror." The story was, the journalist agreed, "a tale to make strong men weep."

Within an hour Everett and his fellow divers managed to bring more than two hundred bodies to boats waiting at the surface. No one doubted anymore the early predictions of more than five hundred dead.

E ven before the official death toll began to surge, Coroner O'Gorman set in motion plans to establish a giant temporary morgue downtown on an enclosed pier owned by the Department of Charities and Corrections. The choice was a wise one as the pier, located at the end of East 26th Street, stood adjacent to the city's official morgue. Better still, it was close to Little Germany.

The morgue was a large brick building with an exuberant, Moorish look that belied its dismal purpose. On normal days it might contain the remains of as many as half a dozen persons, mostly criminals who died in prison, the impoverished too poor to afford a funeral, homeless people with no identification, or murder victims. Most were destined for burial in one of the city's potter's fields.

Ever since the first telephone calls that morning had shattered the normally sleepy routine of the facility, the morgue staff had been working fever-ishly to prepare the Charities Pier for the arrival of hundreds of dead. They had an enormous and unprecedented task before them. The Charities Pier was ideal in terms of sheer space, for the massive covered pier was designed to operate like a temporary warehouse, protecting cargo from the elements as it came and went from boats. Assisted by dozens of city employees from agencies like the coroner's office, the morgue staff established a viewing area where relatives could identify their loved ones, and a station where death certificates and body removal permits could be written up. They also ordered supplies—chiefly several tons of ice with which to preserve the bodies, and hundreds of coffins. The latter would prove difficult to obtain in such numbers, and eventually men were set to work knocking together pine-board coffins.

At 3:50 P.M. the tugboat *Fidelity*, one that had saved so many lives in the minutes after the *Slocum* hit North Brother Island, drew up to the Charities Pier with the first cargo of dead. Deckhands jumped from the boat and secured its lines. A team of morgue workers waited by a massive stack of rough pine coffins of every possible size. One by one the bodies were lifted from the tug, wrapped in blankets or tarpaulins. On the pier, workers hastily removed these makeshift shrouds and placed the bodies in coffins. Then two men carried each coffin into the temporary morgue and set them down in two long rows. Wooden blocks were placed under the heads of the coffins to raise them for easier identification. Ice was immedi-ately poured over the bodies, filling in the empty spaces and leaving little more than the faces exposed. A photographer from the coroner's office then snapped a picture to aid in future identification. The ritual was re-peated thirty times until the tug was empty. At 4:55 the tug *Massasoit* ar-rived with eighty more.

By now the crowd outside the Charities Pier exceeded ten thousand. With the *Slocum* ordeal now nearly seven hours old, people were increasingly agitated and hundreds of policemen were on hand. Many of those waiting pushed and elbowed each other in a struggle to get near the doors, and it took hours for the police to transform the mob into something resembling a line. Many were survivors, determined in spite of their injuries to wait as long as it took to enter the morgue. Others were relatives who had spent the day waiting and searching for missing family members. After a confusing day spent searching in several locations in Manhattan and the Bronx, all now knew that the morgue was the final stop, the place where their agonizing questions would be answered.

While they waited, they cried and offered each other words of consolation and hope. Some kept calling out to anyone who would listen, asking if they had seen their missing relative. Those who possessed them brought photographs and held them out to anyone who would look. Many families had split up during the day in order to check several locations at once. Now all were convening at the morgue. People walked about scanning the line in search of kin, hoping the others had good news. Journalists and photographers—by now every paper in the city had gotten into the act—also swarmed the area, interviewing searchers and taking pictures. Many let their hunger for gripping copy get the best of them. "The so-called journalists ran around with pencils poised," one irate mourner remembered, "human bloodhounds sniffing a trail. . . . As a group they showed neither tact, pity, nor concern for the bereaved, plying weeping mourners with all sorts of questions about the deceased."

Suddenly above it all arose the jaunty beat of a band playing popular tunes. In all the confusion no one had thought to cancel the nightly concert on the nearby East 24th Street recreation pier. It was some time before the band was stopped, right in the middle of a rousing rendition of "The Monkey Wrapped His Tail Around the Flagpole."

A steady procession of horse-drawn vehicles convened upon the scene. Some were teamsters bringing ice and coffins to the morgue. Others were ambulances coming to bear away those who fainted or went mad. But the largest group by far were undertakers. Every few minutes another horse-drawn hearse *clip-clopped* up to the morgue, where it joined a long line of like vehicles. Among them were the four principal undertakers who served the St. Mark's community, Jacob Herrlich, Hermann Kipp, F. Obendahl, and Philip Wagner, men to whom Mary Abendschein sold advertisement space in the excursion program. They were there as businessmen, to be sure, but it was not the sort of opportunity any of them would have wished for. All undertakers inevitably handle the affairs of people they know well. But on this night they'd already lost track of how many friends, neighbors, and fellow parishioners had called upon them to handle their affairs. They were overwhelmed emotionally, but also practically, and the latter would soon force them to turn away countless people they wanted to help.

Other undertakers, however, especially those not from the Little Germany neighborhood, viewed the *Slocum* disaster as a phenomenal business opportunity. These were not evil men for the most part. They were entrepreneurs competing in the everyday marketplace of death, and demand for their services had suddenly peaked. They were lined up to serve people in need. It was understood in 1904, just as it is in our day, that this would necessarily include a certain amount of bill padding and overcharging. But it was also understood that this would be done with a certain dignity and propriety.

Some of them, of course, lacked such restraint—so much so that critics would later charge they lacked even a soul. Like hardware store owners who triple the price of shovels during a snowstorm, these men viewed the *Slocum* disaster as a blizzard of death, a brief window of opportunity in which to reap tremendous profits at the expense of the weak, desperate, and uninformed. They arrived at the morgue with runners—men and boys armed with reams of contracts and business cards—and set them to canvassing the crowd in what one journalist described as "a shameless rivalry for business." Their goal was simple enough: make a killing on the killing.

They spread rumors to induce panic buying—that is, to get people to sign contracts for an undertaker to remove a body and handle all the subsequent duties related to the wake, funeral, and burial. Undertakers are overwhelmed, they told the crowd. Sign now, went the pitch, and you need not worry that your loved one's remains will be properly taken care of. Be advised, they warned, state law stipulates that only a licensed undertaker may remove the dead from the morgue. Do you want your wife or child languishing in that warehouse while you wait for an overbooked undertaker? We guarantee prompt service.

Dazed by grief and compelled by the fear expertly stoked by the agents, many in the crowd signed such contracts. Most did so thinking they were merely procuring transportation of the body to their homes, but the contracts contained language calling for complete undertaking services, from removal of the body from the morgue to transportation to the cemetery. They also failed to stipulate prices for these services, allowing for price gouging on a massive scale. Not surprisingly, given the bonanza of opportunity outside the morgue that night, several fights over customers broke out between these unscrupulous undertakers, or between irate mourners and undertakers, resulting in arrests and indignant headlines the next morning.

Finally at 7:00 P.M. the word came down that everything was in order and that people could begin entering the building to claim their loved ones. Stretched in two neat rows down the center of the long rectangular building were hundreds of pine coffins. Shafts of fading, late-evening sunlight shone down through large dusty windows located near the ceiling, reflecting off the inch-deep water left by the tons of melting ice. Over in one corner stood a table at which sat officials prepared to fill out death certificates and issue the permits required before an undertaker could remove a body. Every few feet along the rows of the dead stood morgue personnel and policemen, ready to intervene should anyone become hysterical at the sight of a dead family member. They would not have long to wait.

At one point in the preparations, Frederico DeStephano, a *Herald* photographer, asked Coroner Gustav Scholer of Manhattan to pose for a picture. Scholer, a pillar of the German community, stood in serious pose, dressed in a white suit and wearing a white broad-brimmed hat that gave him the appearance of Theodore Roosevelt. Before him were five open coffins containing the remains of children, each the picture of angelic calm and repose. Later that evening some of the women at the scene would add to this effect by placing flowers in the coffins holding children.

Policemen outside announced that relatives were to enter the building two abreast in groups of fifty and walk down the aisle between the coffins to view the row on the right, then peel off to the left and head back toward the entranceway allowing them to view the other row. Strict order would be enforced, the officer announced, and at the first sign of crowding or pushing the doors would be closed. Then the heavy steel doors swung open. Those toward the head of the line had been waiting nearly six hours and they suddenly felt overwhelmed by conflicting emotions—they were desperate to get inside but dreaded what they would likely find. They walked in slowly, with halting steps that showed them to be filled with apprehension.

As at North Brother Island, it was a harrowing, trying sight. More than two hundred coffins filled with victims in every imaginable condition and position (although those burned beyond immediate recognition were held in the morgue proper). Searchers clutched each other as they shuffled down the watery aisle, scanning warily the field of misery at their feet. They passed countless people they knew, but kept moving. Occasionally they lingered over a coffin, drawn by some personal feature or article of clothing that suggested the person inside might be their parent, child, or sibling.

Peter J. Fickbohm, the man whose tranquil saloon received early word of the disaster, was one of the first to enter the morgue. Like so many others in the crowd, he had already been uptown to canvass the police station and hospitals. He now knew that one of his children, ten-year-old Fred, was alive and lying in a bed at Lebanon Hospital. He braced himself as he entered the morgue, knowing that his wife and two children were most likely somewhere in the line of death ahead. It took only a minute to find his wife Marie. He fought to keep his emotions in check, but as he knelt by the coffin he began to sob uncontrollably. A few moments later he stood up and walked with a morgue official to the table, where he filled out a death certificate. Then he rejoined the procession of searchers filing past the dead, now more certain than ever that his two missing children were among them.

Other identifications followed. Eugene Ansel, the deli owner who'd learned of his father's death earlier in the day, searched for his two sons. Hours before he had found his wife at the Alexander Avenue police station. When he found his son Alfred, he simply knelt down and stroked the boy's cold forehead. "Poor little boy," he said in a barely audible voice, "poor little child. Why, oh, why did you go?" Not far away from him Mary King found the body of her sister. She too reacted with calm, quietly kneeling by the body and placing a rose on her sister's chest.

Not everyone was able to contain their emotions. Frederika Weaver was already trembling and sobbing before she viewed her first coffin. "She had just started down the line of the dead," wrote a *Journal* reporter, "when she gave a shriek terrible in the depth of emotion sounded."

"I have found my Helen!" she wailed. "I have found my Helen!" Workers would have removed her to the hospital, but she insisted she be allowed to search for her two remaining daughters. She paced back and forth in a futile effort to compose herself, crying loudly all the while. Eventually she pressed on and at the end of the row found two coffins bearing Esther, age five, and Mamie, age seven.

"I have found them!" she called out. "I will go insane! I know I shall! . . . I shall die with grief, I know I shall."

Many searchers lost their minds as soon as they saw their dead loved ones and tried to commit suicide by jumping in the river. One of the first was Catherine Diamond, who upon finding the body of her mother let out a shriek and bolted for the edge of the pier. She nearly made it over the side, but was caught by an alert doctor. It eventually took four men to restrain her. Jacob Denesch attempted to jump in the river after identifying the badly burned remains of his wife. Bernard Miller, the man who lost sight of his wife and four sons in the water when he was attacked by drowning women, tried to jump and was caught. He begged the policemen, "Let me go. Let me die. I am without all that was dearest to me in life. I must die with them." Lena Von Rekowski tried to jump *with* the coffin holding her ten-year-old daughter. Surrounded by morgue workers, she pulled out a bottle of carbolic acid—a popular method of suicide in 1904—and managed to drink some of it before being subdued. The dose was not fatal.

Over and over, these "scenes terrible, heart-breaking, indescribable," as a *Times* reporter put it, broke out in the morgue. After a few hours they "made even the emotion-hardened morgue attendants wipe their eyes and turn away their heads."

Morgue officials also faced another problem: some of the workers and volunteers were stealing from the dead. From the moment the first bodies were brought ashore at North Brother Island, Coroners O'Gorman and Berry had taken steps to prevent this all-too-common occurrence. Huge quantities of jewelry, watches, cash, and in some cases bankbooks and banknotes were removed from the dead and placed in sealed envelopes bearing a number that matched the body's. This measure, they hoped, would prevent theft and assist in identification. Nonetheless, they received many reports of theft by workers throughout the day and into the night and requested the police to post additional detectives on the island and at the morgue.

As the night wore on and darkness enveloped the city, workers broke out dozens of portable lamps. Their glow heightened the macabre atmosphere of the morgue as searchers held them near the faces of those in the coffins to assist in identification. Despite the late hour, the crowd showed no sign of abating and indeed seemed to actually grow toward midnight.

Among those admitted at this time was Henry Kassenbaum of Greenpoint, Brooklyn. His wife Kate had presided over a large family reunion of eighteen Kassenbaums, Torniports, and Schnudes aboard the *Slocum*, a group that included his daughters, their husbands, and his grandchildren. Now only two remained: his wife and his daughter Henrietta, age thirty, in Harlem Hospital. Over the next twenty minutes he would find the bodies of five of his family members.

Many searchers like Kassenbaum were distressed to leave the morgue without finding all their family members, but others, at least on this first night when the disaster was still only hours old, did not despair. Until they found a body, they clung to the hope that their loved ones were safe—perhaps waiting in a different police station, or lying unconscious and unidentified in a hospital not yet visited. This was especially true of those who heard from survivors that their spouses or children had made it ashore, or onto a boat. Robert Wallace was one such man. His only child, eleven-year-old Rose, had gone on the excursion alone and not been found. Still, he believed she was alive, for one of the neighborhood boys said he saw her on North Brother Island. But Wallace had looked everywhere—the island, the Alexander Avenue police station, local hospitals, and now the morgue—but to no avail. "I fear she is among the dead," he confided to a reporter outside the morgue, "but I cannot keep from hoping that maybe after all Otto really did see her, and that eventually she will be returned to me." The next day he returned to the morgue and found Rose's body.

Others clung to even thinner reeds of hope. Walter Peters, for example, found his wife's body at the morgue, but not that of their seventeen-month-old baby, Lillian. But Peters had reason to believe she might be alive. "I know Lillian didn't die with my wife," he explained to officials at the morgue. "My wife was drowned, but she looks peaceful and there's a smile on her face. She'd never have looked that way if she hadn't known that the baby was safe." A few hours later Peters's hopes were dashed when he found his daughter among the dead.

Feeding these hopes were the occasional reunions of searchers and the sought in front of the morgue. Early in the evening, for example, three women stood in the line near the entrance, huddled together consoling each other. Suddenly people near them stirred and, looking up, they saw one of many they sought. There stood their eleven-year-old Minnie Weiss in a blue dress now streaked with water stains and mud. She'd just stepped off one of the tugboats delivering more bodies to the morgue. Minnie noticed her relatives at the same moment they saw her and broke into a run. The women burst through the line of policemen and threw their arms around the dazed girl in a scene witnessed by hundreds. Soon they were back in line, for thirteen members of the extended Weiss family had gone on the trip and all but Minnie were missing.

O utside the morgue, along what observers now began to call "Misery Lane," the crowd continued to swell. It also became more agitated as those searchers who toured the rows of dead returned to the street and the anxious questions of those still waiting—Did you see my wife? My children? My brother? Countless members of the crowd learned, even before entering the morgue, that inside lay the body of the one or ones they sought. Their cries of anguish and despair stirred the crowd and deepened its collective fear. "It was a mad, excited crowd," wrote a *Times* reporter, "frenzied with grief to a point that meant self-destruction if unrestrained." In other words, many tried to jump in the river and were stopped by a cordon of police.

By now it was clear to the policemen detailed to crowd control that many, perhaps a quarter or more, of the people outside the morgue had not lost a friend or relative on the *Slocum*. They were curiosity seekers, people motivated by a ghoulish desire to see the carnage up close. This startling development represented the darker side of the phenomenon of mass entertainment being pioneered at places like Coney Island and the Polo Grounds. The morgue offered a similar experience to that found at Luna Park's smash hit exhibit Fire and Flames, just ratcheted up several notches and free of charge. The curiosity seeker could immerse himself in a scene of horror and literally stare death in the face. Unlike Coney Island, this spectacle involved real people rather than actors and had no happy ending. But the spectators among the mourners nonetheless walked away with the same sensation of excitement and relief felt upon exiting the Johnstown Flood exhibit or Fire and Flames.

As the night wore on, more tugboats arrived bearing additional bodies. No one in the crowd in front of the morgue could see the boats docking, but word of their arrival nonetheless spread quickly, causing renewed chaos. But it was the arrival of the *Franklin Edson* at 9:00 P.M. that nearly touched off a riot. Many of those who had already toured the rows of the dead once refused to go to the back of the line, which now stretched for blocks. Those who had not yet gained entry protested with equal vehemence that no one should get in ahead of them. Pushing and shoving broke out, and moments later the line disintegrated and the crowd charged the doors. Only with the greatest effort and restraint—they implored the crowd not to make them use of their batons—did the police manage to push them back. The doors slammed shut once again. No one would get in, the police announced, until calm returned. Half an hour later the line was restored and the doors reopened.

At 11:15 P.M. the tug *Minnahannock* arrived at the pier with eighty-three additional bodies and word that still more were on the way.

ARE THERE NO MORE?

All afternoon and late into the evening the streets of Little Germany pulsed with frantic movement. As word of the disaster spread and became widely known, people poured out of tenements, shops, and factories onto sidewalks seeking more information. Initially there were only rumors, Extras!, and fragmentary evidence provided by the first survivors. But by 1:00 P.M. a few members of St. Mark's opened an information bureau at the church where relatives could check a list of the injured and killed. More than twenty policemen were on hand to help maintain order along the line and keep an eye out for pickpockets. Reporters were also there, taking detailed notes that would be used to publish lists of the dead, injured, and missing in the papers. It was a grim detail, but far easier than one at the morgue.

Alone and in clusters the searchers shuffled their way up the stairs and into the church. As one journalist described it:

> Men and women bent with age, tottering weakly on the weary feet
> that had borne them all night long in constant search at hospital and
> Morgue, their wrinkled faces blank with misery, their eyes run dry of

tears; mothers whose faces were tortured with anguish and little
children with wondering fear and terror written on their tear-stained
faces, gently jostled one another as they pushed their way to the church
door and made their heart-rending inquiries.

Those who learned the cruel fate of their loved ones from these hastily scrawled ledgers of death made for the morgue. The rest—a majority on the day of the disaster—kept moving in a continuous cycle that took them from St. Mark's to the morgue, to home, and back again.

Another stopping point was the elevated train station at East Eighth Street. Nearly all the survivors who returned that day and evening came by this line, and consequently an enormous crowd of several thousand gathered there to keep vigil. As soon as they spied a survivor, distinguished by their bandages and damaged clothing, they crowded around and peppered them with anxious questions about others still missing. Occasionally those who detrained at the station were met by relatives, but most simply answered a few questions and staggered home alone.

Out of sympathy for those affected by the *Slocum* disaster, the elevated train company ran a special train for survivors, express to Eighth Street, that arrived toward 8:00 P.M. "My heart went out to the pitiful band limping toward us," said one policeman on duty. "Some were bandaged; some could barely totter; all seemed at the point of collapse." Policemen and relatives stepped forward to assist them and in a few minutes the platform was all but empty. All that remained was a crowd of several hundred searchers. "Are there no more?" one of them wailed plaintively. "In God's name, is that all?"

All afternoon and long into the night, the neighborhood's streets vibrated with the incessant rattle of horse-drawn vehicles. Carriages and cabs brought relatives home from work in search of news about their families. Ambulances brought home the injured from the hospital. And everywhere black hearses transported the dead to funeral homes for preparation and then on to the homes of their families.

One of those who came home in an ambulance was Reverend Haas. Treated for his injuries at Lincoln Hospital, he was released and sent home around 6:00 P.M. His sister Emma, suffering only minor injuries, had arrived hours earlier. The trauma of his experiences in combination with his painful injuries left him agitated and incoherent. Sent straight to bed for rest, he had recovered sufficiently by about 9:00 P.M. His doctor allowed his brother and son to break the news to him: his wife was dead and his daughter still missing. So too were his mother-in-law and sister-in-law and her son. "It is as I feared," he replied, "and only as I was prepared to hear."

To calm the fears of his parishioners over his condition (rumors abounded that he had gone insane and was on the verge of death), his doctor issued a statement. Reverend Haas, it began, has suffered a terrible blow, but is making a rapid recovery. "He is now in full possession of his faculties," he continued, "and has plans to rejoin the recovery efforts in a few days. The news of his wife's death and the uncertainty as to his daughter's fate was broken to him this evening and he bore up as a brave pastor should."

His parishioners tried to do the same. Throughout the vicinity of St. Mark's, they could be seen moving hurriedly between the church morgue, home, and train station. Others huddled on the sidewalks and at corners to exchange news and console one another. Cries of anguish pierced the air as dreaded news reached family after family.

Some were so overwhelmed by the news, they tried to end their lives. John Woll, whose wife and children were missing and presumed dead, staggered about the streets begging for someone to kill him. Another man tried to kill himself with a butcher knife, but was restrained in time by friends. These and other despondent searchers were brought home by friends and placed under all-night watch. Nonetheless, in the coming months and years at least half a dozen of these men and women would succeed at killing themselves.

Reporters combed through the neighborhood looking for stories and information for the morning editions. One who had earlier in the evening seen Mrs. Diamond attempt to drown herself in the river, called upon her at home. In the several hours since her suicide attempt, she'd regained her sanity but was still struggling to comprehend the magnitude of the disaster.

"All of us are gone. Look across the street. There's a grocery store closed on account of death. Do you see the sign? Look down the block. At the corner of Rivington Street, from one house, six people are dead. Mr. and Mrs. George Gerdes, and their daughter; Mrs. Margaret Fackman and her two little girls—all dead. Next door, at No. 341, Mrs. Meta Hardkopf and her son Henry are gone and Mrs. Kester and her two babies. Up at Mangin and Houston Streets, Mr. Frese, the saloon-keeper, lost his family. Not a block from here, Mrs. Halpmann's four children are gone. We all knew each other; and now—all dead!"

Not everyone had given up hope so completely. An old gray-haired man named George Hansen refused to surrender hope that his daughter and granddaughter lived. While others raced about in search of information at the church and morgue, he maintained an all-night vigil at the elevated train station. All day and night he stood on the street below scanning the survivors as they descended the platform in all manner of conditions. None had heard or seen anything of his daughter and granddaughter. Still he kept his eyes fixed "in pitiful expectation" on the stairwell leading down from the platform, hopeful that his persistence would be rewarded. Exhausted, he fell asleep standing against an iron beam for support. Finally at about 3:00 A.M. he awoke to the familiar sound of his granddaughter's voice—"Look, Mama! Grandpa is waiting for us!" He opened his eyes and promptly fainted.

B y that late hour, recovery efforts at the scene of the disaster had been halted until sunrise. Earlier in the evening, as darkness began to set in, Police Commissioner McAdoo phoned the Metropolitan Street Railway Company to see if they would lend some of their portable flare lamps normally used to assist in emergency repairs made during the night. Within an hour a boat bearing eight lights docked at North Brother Island. These were quickly set up and soon the main section of the beach was suddenly flooded in an eerie blue light, giving the proceedings there a surreal and haunting quality. "It was a ghostly and unreal scene," one witness reported, ". . . the sputtering arc lights cast a weird glow and I shall never forget the dripping swimmers stumbling out of the water bearing limp burdens in their arms." Nearly seven years later these very same lights would be used to illuminate the scene of the tragic Triangle Shirtwaist Factory fire of March 25, 1911.

Diving at the *Slocum* wreck was suspended at 11:00 P.M., but the men in boats patrolling the waters near North Brother Island continued through the night. Searchlights from patrol boats swept back and forth across the waters. Every now and again the sighting of a body or two encouraged them to press on.

At about 2:00 A.M., with the remaining workers on North Brother Island nearly faint with exhaustion from sixteen hours of ceaseless toil, work was suspended until daybreak. Most simply stayed on the island and slept on cots set up in the hospital. The body count stood at nearly five hundred, and everyone knew that sunrise would bring still more. They nodded off to sleep to the steady sounds of men hammering nails into pine boards—an all-night crew of carpenters hired to construct hundreds of coffins in anticipation of the next day's work.

THE MORNING AFTER

T he steel wheels of the elevated train screeched to a halt at the Eighth Street station. Out onto the platform stepped eleven-year-old Willie Keppler. A light, cool drizzle fell on him from a cloudy early-morning sky. The station was all but deserted—strange, for a weekday. Descending to the street below, he noticed the same thing—Little Germany was nearly silent, not unlike a Sunday morning. Stores remained shuttered and a smaller than usual number of commuters could be seen heading for work.

Keppler found the eerie calm unnerving but hardly puzzling, for he knew perfectly well what had caused it. He had been on the *Slocum* the day before and survived because he could swim. But because he'd disobeyed his father and gone on the excursion against his orders, Willie stayed in Harlem all day, afraid of the whipping he would receive. He eventually spent the night in a park and might have stayed away longer had he not picked up a copy of the *World* and seen his name listed among the missing. That convinced him to head home, preferring "to get the licking instead of breaking me mudder's heart."

As the boy trudged home to meet his parents, evidence of the *Slocum* disaster was everywhere. "Walk where one would," wrote one reporter, "from Third avenue to the river on the east and from First Street in the south to Tenth Street to the north, the scenes of death, of mourners seeking their dead or wailing over their lost ones' bodies, of remnants of families all but obliterated, with those left behind scarcely able as yet to realize the *Slocum* tragedy, were yet constantly before one." Black hearses and wagons rattled through the streets bearing coffins. Here and there he passed people dressed in black hurrying, he soon discovered, in the direction of the morgue. Occasionally he heard crying and moans of despair coming from open tenement windows.

Finally, Willie reached his home. Slowly he ascended the stairs until he reached his family's apartment. He hesitated as he gripped the doorknob—fearing his father's wrath. Yet when he entered he was greeted—to his shock and delight—by his stunned parents with a shower of hugs and kisses. "And me fadder," he explained with a smile, "give me a half dollar for being a good swimmer."

Throughout the neighborhood, however, evidence abounded that the Kepplers' experience was the exception to the rule. Despite the catastrophe of the previous day, the district's many public schools were open that morning. Like the rest of the neighborhood, they were uncharacteristically quiet. Their flags were at half-mast and several policemen stood out front.

It was inside the school buildings, however, where the impact of the *Slocum* disaster was most evident. That morning teachers and administrators took attendance with particular care and found scores were absent. This was the first indication of just how many children perished in the fire—51 from P.S. 25 on East Fifth Street; 21 from P.S. 122 on East Ninth; 19 from P.S. 129 on East 19th; 14 from P.S. 104 on East 16th, and many more. It was but part of a much larger toll that totaled 356 children under the age of fourteen.

On hand were no grief counselors or extra staff. Instead, Superintendent Maxwell sent out a memo to all the city's schools noting how the

Slocum disaster provided teachers and principals with "the opportunity to admonish their pupils to remain cool and collected in the presence of sudden danger, which is always imminent in a great city; not to risk their lives unnecessarily; to learn to swim; and always to be ready to lend a helping hand to those weaker than themselves." The lesson-minded Maxwell did, however, call for flags to be flown at half-mast and for graduation ceremonies to be postponed until the following week.

The parents and relatives of many of these missing and dead children could be found at St. Mark's, where volunteers continued to collect and make known the lists of the dead, missing, injured, and unscathed. Outside the church a long line stretched down the block in near-total silence. In the morning drizzle women stood with shawls over their heads, men with their collars turned up and hats pulled low. They shuffled forward as if in a trance, many having not slept in more than twenty-four hours. "At times a woman would scream and the rest would look up inquiringly for a moment," observed one reporter, "then drop their eyes again to the sidewalk."

At the top of the stairs they read a note from Pastor Haas posted on the front of the church. "In a common loss, we have a common hope. I wish I could be with you, but I am stricken just as you are." Inside, searchers posed their questions to the volunteers. A few received word of a loved one's body being found, but most received only "the shake of a head and a few kindly words of the clergymen." Then it was back home or to the morgue, or simply to the back of the line to ponder what one reporter called their "fathomless misery."

All night long, while the people of Little Germany had searched and waited for answers, the city newspaper editors prepared the morning editions. For most of Wednesday their presses churned out updated Extras! every hour. It was news coverage by piecemeal. The morning editions, however, would offer the first chance to tell the whole story—at least as much as was known by the early-morning hours. This meant not merely publishing the first accurate numbers regarding the probable death toll, but also a fuller range of stories based on extensive interviews with survivors and rescuers. Equally important, it provided the first opportunity to weigh in editorially on the tragedy, its cause and meaning.

The papers were unanimous in their expressions of horror over the disaster. It was not merely the volume of death—estimates of the toll ranged from 600 to more than 1,000—but also the setting and victims. "That a Sunday School picnic should all at once become a hideous massacre," wrote the *Times*, "is revolting to the imagination." It was particularly distressing, the papers agreed, that in the words of the *World*, "those of the weaker sex and of tender age" were the fire's chief victims. So too was the fact that the disaster happened, observed the *Eagle*, "a few yards from shore."

But the papers differed in the assessment of blame. It was still early yet and the full scope of the *Slocum*'s unsafe conditions and cowardly performance of its crew was not widely known. As a result several papers urged caution. "It is now too soon," offered the *Tribune*, "to censure anybody." The *Sun* concurred—"Judgment should be suspended until all the facts are brought out." There was no question, however, the *Sun* editors stressed, that one or more people were responsible for the disaster. It was not "an act of God."

Most of the city's dailies, however, felt enough evidence was at hand to allow for some preliminary accusations. Nearly all agreed that a significant factor in the disaster was the weak and ineffective body of law governing steamboat construction. How else to explain the fact that a steamboat certified as safe on May 5 could go up in flames like "a mere tinder heap of painted wood" on June 15, as the *World* put it. Many agreed that steamboat regulations should be raised to the level of transatlantic liners, but the press went further, demanding the indictment of the inspectors.

Surprisingly, given the fury yet to come, only one paper criticized Captain Van Schaick. "His decision to head for North Brother Island," wrote the *Brooklyn Standard Union*, "caused the loss of many precious lives." In contrast, most of the papers praised the captain and his pilots for staying at their posts until the very end. "That they behaved with physical courage," asserted the *Sun*, "is not in dispute." Some papers even praised the crew for their performance in fighting the flames.

The papers that morning also restrained themselves when it came to assessing the culpability of the Knickerbocker Steamboat Company. Nearly all mentioned the allegations of defective life preservers, but deferred judgment until more evidence was at hand. None used, as they soon would, words like "murder" to describe the disaster. That would change in only a few hours, as overwhelming evidence of negligence and dereliction of duty accumulated.

THAT MAKES
NUMBER 522

M ayor McClellan spent the night at his regular home in Washington Square. Traveling out to his new summer cottage at Long Branch was out of the question, given the enormity of the tragedy and the fact that recovery operations were ongoing to find some five hundred missing passengers. After a shorter than usual sleep, he rose, dressed, and walked to city hall in a drizzle, his mind fixed on the troubling matters that awaited his attention. Even if he had wanted to think of something else, it would have been impossible, for on every corner, newsies called out the morning headlines.

"499 Known To Be Dead!" (*Herald*)

"Horror in East River!" (*Tribune*)

"Many Gallant Rescues of the Drowning!" (*World*)

McClellan arrived to find city hall busier than usual, with all activity focused on matters related to the disaster. Key department officials filled the hallway leading to his office, as did three times the usual number of reporters. He politely brushed off their questions, promising to give a statement and entertain questions shortly.

His assistant John O'Brien greeted him with a stack of telegrams and expressions of condolence from President Roosevelt, the mayor of Philadelphia, and countless others. "Chicago sends to New York her heartfelt and honest sympathy on account of the terrible calamity which has just happened," read a typical message. "Our own recent catastrophe [Iroquois Theater fire] makes us mournfully appreciative of the sorrow in which your city has just been plunged." That same morning in Washington, D.C., President Roosevelt was receiving the first of many telegrams from foreign heads of state. "Profoundly moved by the awful catastrophe of the General Slocum," wrote the president of France, Émile Loubet. "I have it at heart to address to your Excellency my sincere condolences and to send to the families of the victims the expression of my sorrowful sympathy."

McClellan hastily dictated responses to the most important ones and then called in the heads of the departments responding to the *Slocum* crisis. He directed Commissioner Darlington to make arrangements for the burial of all unidentified bodies at the Lutheran cemetery in Middle Village, Queens. To Police Commissioner McAdoo, the mayor emphasized the need to relieve the suffering of those affected by the disaster. Any investigation into the causes of the fire and subsequent death toll could wait a day or two.

Next he dictated a letter to Reverend Haas.

> *On behalf of the people of our city and myself I express to you and to your stricken flock the sentiments of sorrow which pervade the community at the awful calamity which has come upon you.*
>
> *In the hope that we may lessen, in some degree, the anguish which you and your people suffer, I have appealed to the generosity of our fellow citizens to render financial aid to those who may need it to care for their sick and to decently bury their dead.*
>
> *We all hope that courage may be given to you to bear up under your great affliction.*

Finally, after consulting with his advisers, the mayor drafted a proclamation announcing the creation of a relief fund and plans to create a committee to oversee it. It also called for the flags at city hall to be put at half-mast. Then, after answering several questions from reporters, McClellan excused himself and prepared to make a trip he did not want to make, but knew he must—a tour of both North Brother Island and the morgue.

It was going on noon when the mayor and several high-ranking officials stepped into a cab on Park Row for a short ride to the pier at the end of Fulton Street. Waiting was the tugboat *Manhattan* to take them to North Brother Island. Looking up as he stepped aboard, the mayor noticed the boat's flag and asked that it be lowered to half-mast.

By now the overcast skies and drizzle had given way to bright sunshine and warm steamy temps. McClellan stood in the pilothouse and pressed the tug's captain about the last journey of the *Slocum*, where the fire had started, and where, based on the wind and tides at the time of the fire, he would have run the steamer aground. The captain didn't hesitate in his answer: "Sunken Meadows, not North Brother Island."

Thirty minutes later the *Manhattan* docked at North Brother Island. McClellan was given a brief tour of the island by Health Commissioner Darlington, who also provided a detailed recount of the rescue response. At one point they passed the enormous stretch of coffins constructed during the night. The gloomy sight shocked the mayor and caused him to pause in silence for nearly a minute. A more upbeat moment awaited at the hospital, where he greeted and congratulated the staff for their heroic efforts the day before.

From there McClellan asked to be taken to the beach where the *Slocum* had run aground. He found dozens of men working in boats with grappling hooks, looking for bodies. They had been at it since daybreak, but with limited success. But now as the tide began to run, the rate of recovery increased. Just minutes after McClellan arrived at the beach, a worker shouted that he had found a body. The mayor and his entourage watched as they lifted the frail form of a nine-year-old girl from the water and rowed it to shore.

"That makes number 522," a coroner's office clerk informed the mayor.

The sight made his stomach turn, and he struggled to retain his resolute bearing. "It is awful," he muttered.

A lunch had been prepared for the mayor and those with him, but he balked. The things he had seen on the island, he said, had "robbed him of his appetite." Instead, he took the opportunity to thank the men engaged in the recovery effort. "I can only regret the necessity that prompted it."

With that, they headed for the tugboat *Manhattan*. McClellan felt a sense of relief as they departed North Brother Island, but he was hardly at ease. He had one more appointment to keep, and it was one he sorely wished he could avoid: the morgue.

LIFE KILLERS

The searching for bodies had begun again at daybreak despite the drizzle and choppy water. Toward midday, sounds of commotion on the floating diving platforms near the *Slocum* wreck caused salvage and recovery workers to look up. They could not believe their eyes at first, but after a few seconds it was clear they were not imagining it. Thundering upriver toward them was the *Grand Republic*, sister ship to the *General Slocum*, carrying over a thousand joyous passengers from two Harlem churches. Apparently the previous day's disaster had failed to move Barnaby to cancel any bookings. Such a decision would not only cost the company money, but might also be taken as a sign of weakness, or worse, guilt.

The workers' amazement at Barnaby's decision quickly turned to outrage. Unlike the many steamers that had passed since dawn, the *Grand Republic* did not slow down. Nor did its captain order the band on board to cease playing. Indeed, as the boat approached the wreck, its passengers began cheering and waving hankies. They may have meant it as a sign of support and encouragement, but the men for whom it was intended took it as a gesture of derision. So too did the crowd of anxious relatives gathered on the Hunts Point shore hoping for news of lost loved ones.

Furious, Inspector Albertson began waving his arms and shouting to the pilot to veer off and slow down. Ignoring the warnings, he maintained top speed and stayed on course, clearly intent upon giving his passengers the best possible show by drawing as close as possible to the wreck. The steamer passed within a hundred yards of the wreck, sending a huge wake over the diving floats and disrupting the recovery effort for several minutes. "I thought I knew human nature," commented Albertson, "but people are more callused than I ever thought them."

The passing of the *Grand Republic* was merely the worst of many similar incidents on the East River that morning. Several more steamers would pass with bands playing and flags flying, their starboard rails jammed with gawkers, before the day was through. None came as close to the wreck as the *Grand Republic*, and several slowed down and silenced their bands as a sign of respect. Far worse were the scores of small boats filled with curiosity seekers and souvenir hunters. Some of the latter even pulled up to the wreck and tried to rip off pieces of the paddle wheel box. Albertson eventually had police boats establish a line beyond which none but official vessels could go. Word was also sent to the city's excursion lines that captains of steamboats failing to slow down and steer clear of the wreck would be arrested.

The incident with the *Grand Republic* only served to spur on the efforts of Coroner William O'Gorman. Deeply affected by all he had witnessed in the twenty-four hours since the disaster, he was now more determined than ever to nail the Knickerbocker Steamboat Company and its callous president, Frank A. Barnaby. He'd heard enough from the survivors and seen enough useless life preservers to determine the chief cause of the disaster. To prove his case he needed evidence, and he instructed the divers to be on the lookout for anything that might shed light on the *Slocum*'s safety equipment and the efforts of the crew to fight the fire.

Not long after his first dive, John Rice surfaced with a long section of pipe. It was the standpipe that ran along the boat's starboard side to supply water to two fire stations. Just as O'Gorman had suspected, the valve was shut tight, indicating that no effort had been made to fight the fire from that station, even though it was on the side initially free of flames. His face flushed with anger, he turned to several reporters. "I don't put a bit of stock into the pretty tales of heroic fire fighting reported by the crew when it was all over."

Nearby stood a pile of equally damning evidence. "I found today more life preservers, or life killers rather, with rotten canvas coverings split, and rotten granulated cork half dribbled out of the place where good, honest, solid cork ought to have been." Other life preservers were intact but water-logged, taken from bodies pulled to the bottom of the river. What further evidence was needed, he fumed to the reporters, to show the *Slocum*'s owners and crew to be guilty of "criminal neglect, criminal carelessness and criminal cowardice"? His office, he warned, was committed to bringing the truth to light. "I have smoked a cigarette and tried to keep a smile going all the time, but when these things come to light, I get mad all over." His anger would only intensify over the next few hours as subsequent dives brought up reels of fire hoses never unfurled and lifeboats wired tightly to davits.

Mad as he was, O'Gorman would not be the one to lead the first investigation into the disaster. That duty fell to fellow coroner Joseph Berry. He too was outraged by the mounting evidence that the *Slocum* carnage had resulted from negligence and cowardice.

Everyone agreed on the need for a formal investigation of the *Slocum* disaster, but there was considerable confusion over which level of government had jurisdiction in matters pertaining to steamboat accidents. Earlier in the day, McClellan had promised an investigation, but he wondered aloud whether the city had the legal standing to prosecute any wrongdoers, since steamboat laws were written by Congress and administered by the federal USSIS. George B. Cortelyou, Secretary of Commerce and Labor, the department that oversaw the USSIS, vowed to personally conduct a federal investigation leading to indictments of any guilty parties. William Travers Jerome, the flamboyant crusading district attorney for New York County, likewise promised to investigate. "I shall not rest until the guilty are punished," he declared. "On my honor, I shall see them stew in prison!"

But until the questions of authority and jurisdiction were settled, only

Coroner Berry possessed the authority to impanel a jury, issue subpoenas, and conduct hearings into the incident. By law, coroners were empowered to investigate any and all deaths involving questions of negligence or criminal activity.

B erry began his work immediately, and on Thursday, June 16, barely twenty-four hours after the *Slocum* ran aground, he began conducting preliminary interviews with key people associated with the disaster at his office in the Bronx. The first man called was Henry Lundberg, the USSIS inspector who certified the *Slocum* and its safety equipment as safe and up to standard.

"When did you last inspect the *Slocum?*" Berry asked. Lundberg, a large, broad-shouldered man, shifted uncomfortably in his chair, glanced at his lawyer, and spoke.

"I decline to answer that question," he answered Berry, "by advice of counsel." Berry immediately served him with a subpoena to appear before a coroner's jury on Monday, June 20. He'd have no choice but to testify then. Nor would the members of the crew, officials from the Knickerbocker Steamboat Company, survivors, rescuers, and others—some two hundred in all—served with subpoenas over the next few days. But already, in addition to Lundberg's refusal to speak, Berry had noticed a disturbing fact. The *Slocum*'s crewmen arrived at their interviews accompanied by high-priced lawyers paid for by the Knickerbocker Steamboat Company.

Clearly Barnaby was going to take no chances.

JUST ONE MORE

Mayor McClellan arrived at the Charities Pier at about 2:00 P.M. to inspect the morgue. North Brother Island had been disturbing, but he knew to expect far worse here. No sooner had the anxious mayor stepped onto the pier and removed his hat than his fears were realized. A woman who had just identified the body of her young daughter threw up her hands and fainted at his feet. Less than a minute later he was knocked off balance when two workers carrying a coffin bumped him on the shoulder.

A far more jarring experience awaited him inside the enclosed pier. In silence the mayor toured the facility, his shoes *plip-plopping* in the ice water that covered the floor, runoff from the coffins. The faces staring up at him from the open coffins—especially the children—affected him deeply. He and Mrs. McClellan had no children, but the image of so many dead innocents was seared upon his memory. "I shall never forget the horror of the scene . . . (at) the emergency morgue," he wrote three decades later in his memoirs. "One little girl had gone down with her pet kitten in her arms, another was clutching what was evidently her best hat."

He put on a good face, thanked the workers for their magnificent efforts, and left as soon as possible, haunted by the scenes he'd witnessed and the dawning realization, as he later put it, "that there was so pitifully little that could be done."

Not long after he departed, the orderly routine he witnessed was shaken by a near-riot outside the facility. Nearly one hundred policemen had worked to control the crowd, which grew larger as the day wore on. To keep out as many curiosity seekers as possible, the police cordoned off the area for two blocks around the morgue and allowed only those seeking their relatives to pass. The problem, of course, was that there was no reliable way to determine which seekers were legitimate and which were not. As a consequence, about six hundred or so legitimate searchers were prevented from getting to the morgue, and by 4:00 P.M. their desperation reached the breaking point. All it took to unleash their pent-up frustration was news that another tugboat bearing thirty-nine more bodies had arrived. The crowd surged forward, broke the police line, and raced for the doors leading to the pier. "With desperation born of distraction," reported a journalist, "they fought to get entrance." Normally the hardened blue-coats would have pulled their batons and pummeled the crowd into retreat, but they were under strict orders to use restraint given the horrific event that brought out the distressed masses. But when two elderly women at the head of the line were trampled, the batons were pulled out and orders given for the crowd to retreat. Slowly the anxious mourners fell back and re-formed a line.

A short time later the crowd was again put in a frenzy when a gleaming carriage pulled by four black horses drove headlong into the line of mourners. Inside was the well-known banker William Hoffman, his wife, and several guests. Clad in formal attire and heading for an evening of fun at the Sheepshead Bay racetrack in Brooklyn, they looked as startled as anyone. Apparently Hoffman's driver thought the ferry they wanted left from the East 26th Street pier. Fortunately no one was injured, and after profuse apologies Hoffman and his party retreated, their ears ringing from the denunciations of the crowd.

Apart from these incidents, the identification process at the morgue went surprisingly well throughout the day and into the evening. Despite continued suicide attempts and nervous breakdowns, searchers identified hundreds of bodies and made arrangements for their removal. A few of the identifications drew special attention. For example, Christian Schoett, an organist at St. Mark's, was found in a coffin right next to one holding his fiancée. Margaret Gerdes was found, her relatives charged, without the $300 of jewelry she had worn on the trip. William Pullman, treasurer of St. Mark's Sunday school, was found with a soggy $350 check in his pocket made out to the Knickerbocker Steamboat Company.

By midnight Thursday the body count stood at 561, including 130 as yet unidentified at the morgue. That still left as many as 500 persons missing and presumed dead. Their relatives maintained their vigils at the morgue, growing more desperate by the minute. The trauma of losing loved ones in the disaster was now compounded by the fear that they might never recover a body. There is in most people a deep-seated need in such circumstances to find the remains of a loved one. Until they do, the tragedy seems unresolved or, in modern parlance, it lacks "closure."

Adolph Molitor searched for forty-eight hours for his wife and three children, but with no result. "I searched high and low for them," he told a reporter, "but can get no trace. I believe they are drowned and are floating somewhere in the Sound. It is very mysterious and I am almost heartbroken over their loss." The great fear of searchers like Molitor was that their loved ones had been washed out to sea or that they were among the dozens burned beyond any hope of recognition.

Paul Liebenow and Frank Weber experienced the same feeling of hopelessness. Both men, brothers-in-law in search of two children each, had suffered severe burns in the fire but stayed for hours on end at the morgue, pinning their hopes on each new body delivered by the tugboats. They no longer had any illusions of seeing their children alive again. Indeed, that morning, before heading for the morgue, Liebenow had stopped at the local haberdashery to buy black armbands and other trappings of mourning. He was waited on by the same clerk who two days before had sold him a new suit and hat for the church excursion. Liebenow eventually located the body of one daughter, three-year-old Anna, but his six-year-old Helen and Weber's two children remained unaccounted for.

The growing desperation of the searchers began to show not merely in their faces but also in their judgment. By Thursday evening morgue officials were wrestling with several agonizing cases of missing bodies. Adolph Hill, for example, identified two of his nieces, Christine and Lydia Richter, but when he returned with an undertaker their bodies were gone. The same thing happened to the Koeppler family, prompting them to take out ads in several newspapers.

> *Lilly Koeppler, 17 years of age, not found yet, but identified with burned left cheek and hair. All parents will kindly make another examination of their dead to give sorrowful and heartbroken mother information to find her child. Henry and Elsie Koeppler, 192 First Avenue.*

Between sheer exhaustion and rising desperation to find a body, some searchers clearly made false identifications that the overwhelmed morgue staff failed to catch.

One body of a missing child, in one of the more bizarre events associated with the disaster, actually found her family. Late Thursday afternoon, friends of Henry Heins located him at the morgue where he'd been searching for two daughters (having already found his wife and another daughter). Margaret, his seven-year-old, they explained, had been found floating in the East River near the foot of Clinton Street. Incredibly, it was eight miles from where the *Slocum* ran aground, but one block from her family's home at 300 Front Street.

The scenes of greatest chaos and turmoil, however, were not found at the morgue, but rather in the many undertaking establishments surrounding St. Mark's. Customarily, in keeping with the elaborate wake and funeral rituals that developed in late-nineteenth-century American life, bodies were moved only one at a time. Undertakers, or "morticians" as many now liked to be called, usually prepared a body for waking and burial, a process that by 1904 included embalming, dressing the deceased in a dignified outfit, and positioning them in a peaceful pose. But by the evening of June 16, the neighborhood's undertakers were overwhelmed with families requesting their services. Normally accustomed to handling less than a half dozen cases in a typical week, these small family-run establishments now received scores of requests for their services. By the evening the signs of strain had begun to slow.

Jacob Herrlich's modest undertaking establishment held fifty-two bodies; his brother's, twenty-six. Philip Wagner had twenty-three. In some cases coffins lay stacked on sidewalks in front of funeral homes while hearses and even common delivery wagons pressed into emergency service could be seen bearing as many as seven coffins at a time, stopping from house to house as if delivering milk or ice. By late Thursday evening, the grieving were informed, embalming and other rituals of preparation were no longer available. Remains were brought straight to the family's home. Countless parishioners had to be turned away despite their heartrending pleas to take "just one more." Regretfully, they were forced to deal with undertakers from beyond the boundaries of St. Mark's whose service and prices were untested. Complicating matters even further for the undertakers was the fact that so many families had not found all their dead. They refused to go ahead with funerals until everyone was found. It made planning funerals nearly impossible.

SACRIFICED TO GREED

A t 5:00 P.M. the evening editions of the papers hit the streets. It was just twelve hours since the morning editions had come out, yet the difference in tone and emotion of the disaster commentary had changed dramatically. Gone were the editorials urging the public to avoid a rush to judgment as to who might bear responsibility for the hundreds of lives lost. The steady accumulation of evidence attesting to the dismal condition of the *Slocum*'s safety equipment and eyewitness statements regarding the utter uselessness of the crew during the emergency had outraged the public. So too had the shocking news that Inspector Lundberg refused to answer Coroner Berry's questions. The editorialists stood by their assertions in the morning that the laws governing steamboat construction and inspection were inadequate and in need of change, but now shifted their focus to the inspectors and, more important, the owners of the *Slocum*.

None surpassed the vehemence of William Randolph Hearst. His *Evening Journal* seethed with indignation, charging Barnaby and the other directors of the Knickerbocker Steamboat Company with wholesale murder:

It is the old, the usual story of such events in this country, where money laughs at the laws made to protect life—where the dull, sordid, unimaginative love of money deadens the conscience and despises costly safety.

It is almost unnecessary to go into details. Every American can guess them. . . .

The lifeboats were inadequate—there might as well have been none.

The life preservers were old, rotten, useless.

LIFEBOATS COST MONEY.

LIFE PRESERVERS COST MONEY.

Human life is cheap.

They will regret the deaths—they will, perhaps, send flowers to some of the hundreds of funerals—unless their lawyers advise them that that might be an admission of guilt. They will soon forget the incident that interrupted a business career.

Next to his editorial was a graphic cartoon depicting a dead child laid out on a mortician's slab. At her feet was a man, clearly Frank A. Barnaby, counting his profits. At her head stood the grim reaper. Above her frail form floated an image of the burning boat. Accompanying the cartoon a caption read: "The life of this child and many hundreds of others were sacrificed to Greed in the General Slocum disaster. Death and Greed count the profits. When will a day of reckoning come for the criminals that are responsible for the deaths?"

This tidal wave of collective outrage was precisely what Barnaby had hoped to avoid. Still, he knew how quickly the public tended to forget scandals. And then there was the coming legal battle. He'd already hired a top-notch lawyer and brought the *Slocum*'s crew into line regarding their testimony.

"Will the guilty go unpunished as usual?" asked Hearst. "Probably—the money that breaks the law knows how to evade it."

Barnaby certainly hoped so.

At 6:00 P.M. the mayor's office announced that more than $5,000 had been collected for the relief fund. It was an astonishing sum for a fund roughly six hours old, and it reflected the widespread horror felt by most New Yorkers over the disaster. Donations came in every size. British sportsman Sir Thomas Lipton, who happened to be in New York, gave $1,000. President Roosevelt pledged $500. But most were modest contributions made by countless ordinary citizens who journeyed to city hall or St. Mark's in an outpouring of mass sympathy that impressed even the most cynical New Yorker. "I never suspected the generous heart beneath the hard-boiled exterior of our city," wrote one *World* reporter. "New Yorkers of high and low station trooped to St. Mark's by carriage, street car, el train, automobile and on foot. . . . Here a beshawled Jewish immigrant woman dropped a crumpled dollar bill into the collection barrel . . . there a dignified Wall Street broker gave fifty dollars . . . the line of donors stretched around the block and grew longer every moment . . . workers, rich men, poor men, beggars, and perhaps thieves gave to the fund . . . it was an emotional outpouring. . . . Never again will I believe our city has no heart." By 10:00 P.M. the fund topped $9,000.

Shortly before midnight, the tugboat *Fidelity* arrived at the Charities Pier with five more bodies. As workers placed the coffins in the now small rows of unidentified dead, Health Commissioner Darlington ordered the morgue closed and relatives sent home until the morning. Just as soon as the last searcher was escorted from the building, a team of embalmers set to work embalming all the bodies as yet unidentified or uncollected by an undertaker. Their work soon took on the atmosphere of a gothic horror story as a violent thunderstorm enveloped the city. Brilliant blue-white flashes of lightning preceded violent claps of thunder that shook the steel-frame structure.

Far across New York harbor, at the Knickerbocker Steamboat Company pier on Staten Island, the *General Slocum*'s sister ship *Grand Republic* rocked in the wind and waves kicked up by the storm. Suddenly a bolt of lightning sliced through the sky and hit the pier with a tremendous explosion. A small fire broke out, but was quickly extinguished by an alert watchman.

FRIDAY, JUNE 17

F riday morning found the streets of Little Germany once again hushed by what one reporter called "the great calm of grief." Stores remained shuttered and shades drawn while only the occasional wagon or hearse kicked up the dust from the streets.

Inside their small apartments throughout the neighborhood, members of St. Mark's parish were waking—if they slept at all—to the realization that any family member now unaccounted for was certainly dead. While the horrific total was still uncertain because of the great number of missing— estimates ranged from 800 to 1,200 killed—individual tallies were more certain. Henry Cohrs, Fred Baumler, Edwin Fitch, and John Finkenangel, for example, each lost a wife and three children. For William Oellrich, Magnus Hartung, and Edward Muller it was a wife and four children each. Joseph Justin lost his wife and five children. Many of these losses ran even higher when extended families were taken into account. Twenty-nine members of the extended Kohler family, for example, were lost.

Despite the notable absence of people, especially children, from the neighborhood's streets and sidewalks, evidence of the tragedy abounded in the doorways of every block. Attached to many doors were small white cards with a somber black border that read We Mourn the Loss of Our Friends. They had been printed and distributed for free by a local printer. On the doors of buildings of families who lost loved ones in the disaster were hung clusters of ribbons, white for children and black for adults. But even these were often poor indicators of the suffering going on inside. One tenement five doors down East Seventh Street from Pastor Haas's home had five white ribbons attached to its front door, even though fourteen had died. Some families, too poor or too distraught, hung no ribbon at all.

Activity in the neighborhood would pick up soon enough, as those in search of the nearly five hundred victims still missing headed yet again to the morgue. Others, now considered "fortunate" because they had found the remains of their loved ones, made preparations for the first funerals, scheduled to begin at midday.

Despite the fact that five hundred people remained unaccounted for, the situation at the Charities Pier was relatively calm. The crowds still remained huge, but the passions of those who'd spent the last two days frantically searching for loved ones had been cooled by the stark reality that too much time had elapsed for any to be found alive. Word had also spread throughout the crowd that nearly all the bodies collected had been identified. By noon Friday only twenty-five remained unidentified on the pier, and by 6:00 P.M. only nine. Thirty bodies burned beyond any hope of recognition were being held in the morgue proper adjacent to the pier.

Many who visited the Charities Pier that day had already found most of their missing relatives and had funerals scheduled for the next day. They checked in at the morgue hoping to find the last ones so the family might be buried as one. This was the goal of Conrad Muth. His brother and nephew, John and John, Jr., survived the fire, but John's wife and three children were lost. So too were his mother-in-law, three nieces, and a sister-in-law. John had broken his leg in the fire, so it fell to Conrad to locate the missing. "All of the family who have been found," he told a reporter, "will be buried tomorrow afternoon at the same time in the Lutheran Cemetery. I am waiting here to see if I can't find some of the others."

Even quieter was the scene at St. Mark's Church. The information bureau established in the first hour of the disaster was all but deserted, for it had no information to offer. Anyone unaccounted for by Friday morning was certainly dead. Still, a little more than one hundred people stopped in to make inquiries, and one young boy released from Lebanon Hospital felt compelled to drop by to add his name to the list of survivors.

A little before ten o'clock the quiet at the church was disturbed by the arrival of more than one hundred clerics of all faiths from churches and synagogues across the city. They came to express their sorrow for the tragic loss of life suffered by St. Mark's and to pledge their help, especially in conducting the hundreds of funerals expected over the next week. It was agreed that given the circumstances, no public funerals would be held in places of worship. Rather, simple funeral rites would be performed in homes or at undertakers' establishments. Later, a full-blown public memorial service would be held to honor all the dead. The gathering also agreed that the unidentified dead at the morgue would be buried in a mass grave the next day, Saturday, June 18, with records of valuables and effects kept at the coroner's office in the event that a later identification was possible.

These decisions were made by this gathering of clergy for a very simple reason: the leadership of St. Mark's had nearly been wiped out. Reverend Haas had survived, but was still incapacitated by injuries and grief. The church's secretary and treasurer had died in the fire, as had the chairman of the poor committee, the sextant, and the choir leader. Seven members of the board of trustees and three members of the board of elders had also perished. As for the church's Sunday school, apart from the hundreds of children killed, both superintendents (of the German and English sections), its secretary, and several teachers were gone. In all, St. Mark's lost sixteen of twenty-one parish officers. Until St. Mark's recovered—if it ever recovered—the ministers in attendance pledged their assistance and leadership. "The calamity," said Rev. William R. Huntington of Grace Episcopal Church, "has made Lutherans of us all."

Shortly after the meeting adjourned, Reverend Kraeling, one of several associate pastors at St. Mark's, left the church and walked east one block to 242 East Sixth Street. Tucked under his arm was a book containing all the rites of the Lutheran ministry—most of them joyful: baptism, confirmation, marriage. Today, however, his marker was placed at the Rite of the Dead. The hour had arrived for the first funeral.

Upstairs in a typical cramped East Side tenement, he greeted the Harris family and took his place next to the body of Agnes Bell. The Harrises were Orthodox Jews with whom Bell had boarded. She had gone on the trip with their ten-year-old daughter Sylvia. Both were killed, but Sylvia's body had yet to be recovered. Kraeling offered no eulogy and finished the simple ceremony in fifteen minutes. Two men from the undertakers closed her coffin and carried it to a waiting hearse at the curb. Minutes later, as a small crowd looked on in silence, the vehicle pulled away, headed for the Lutheran cemetery in Queens.

Ten more funerals would take place that afternoon, a mere glimmer of what lay ahead the next day.

Farther downtown, while Kraeling recited prayers over Agnes Bell, Mayor McClellan met for the first time with the men he'd named to the relief committee the previous day. Although donations had already begun to pour in, theirs would be the official relief fund. The eighteen men chosen were some of the city's foremost business, civic, and philanthropic leaders, including Jacob Schiff, Robert A. Van Cortlandt, Morris K. Jessup, George Ehret, and Isaac N. Seligman. Their goal was simple enough: raise a fund sufficient to provide short-term relief, including funeral expenses, to families victimized by the disaster and long-term support to the many orphaned children. Immediately they drew up an appeal for donations that asked the citizens of New York for "a generous response to the necessities caused by this calamity."

While to the modern mind this appeal for financial help in the wake of a disaster seems only natural, in 1904 it was done with some reluctance. People were not accustomed to giving money to causes not immediately at hand, with the possible exception of missionary work in Africa. New Yorkers discovered this back in the 1870s when the Statue of Liberty languished in crates because Americans failed to raise enough money to pay for the pedestal. Only when Joseph Pulitzer took the lead in raising money (and newspaper sales) by announcing that he would publish the name of every contributor, even if they only gave a penny, did money pour in. Americans, especially the middle class and wealthy, were by nature suspicious of such funds, regardless of the cause. In part this was due to their belief that charity was something every able-bodied person should avoid at all costs. There was always the danger, even in a calamity like the Galveston hurricane of 1900 or the Johnstown flood of 1889, that charity distributed to victims might undermine their work ethic, warp their values, and ultimately hamper their return to normal life. Hermann Ridder, chairman of the relief committee, recognized these concerns and endeavored to allay them. "The work of the relief will be systematic," he told the press, "and while we will be exceedingly liberal with all who come to us for aid, all cases will be thoroughly investigated and dealt with according to thorough business methods." Translation: fear not—no waste and no freeloading will be permitted. McClellan's selection of the city's leading men to serve on the committee was likewise intended to boost confidence in its handling of the money.

The aversion to charity was plainly evident among the victims themselves. Later in the day when the relief committee opened an office in the basement of St. Mark's, almost no one showed up. Even in their grief and destitution, the people of Little Germany were too proud to ask for help. Only when dozens of volunteers conducted a door-to-door campaign to convince people to take advantage of the fund did people begin to do so. Even then there were instances of men who sold all their possessions to pay for funeral expenses. Many months later, when all the money had been allocated, the people of St. Mark's agreed to burn the lists of relief recipients so that none, especially the children, would bear the stigma of having taken a handout.

But for now the focus was on raising money, and the people of New York responded with an outpouring of generosity. Taking a page from Pulitzer's Statue of Liberty campaign, the dailies published the names of contributors in the hope that it would stimulate wider giving. Contributions came in from retail magnate F. W. Woolworth ($100) and Wall Street tycoon Bernard Baruch ($250), but also from thousands of average citizens moved by the stories of suffering and despair in Little Germany. Their one-

and two-dollar contributions helped swell the fund to $15,000 by day's end. Even children did their part, as evidenced by a note that accompanied a donation of 85 cents.

> *Dear Mayor McClellan: I send herewith the 60 cents I was saving for the Fourth of July. Please give it to the poor children who are suffering on account of the appalling fire on the General Slocum.*
>
> *Sincerely yours,*
> *W. B. Joyce, Jr.*
>
> *P.S. My little brother sends 25 cents that he had.*

NO STONE LEFT
UNTURNED

G eorge B. Cortelyou, Secretary of Commerce and Labor, arrived at midday Friday from Washington, D.C. The dapper forty-two-year-old had come a long way from his modest origins. Originally a teacher, he taught himself stenography and at the age of twenty-seven started a new career as a private secretary to a series of increasingly influential men. By 1895 he was President Cleveland's stenographer, a position that subsequently landed him a job as President McKinley's personal secretary. When Roosevelt assumed the presidency after McKinley's assassination, he retained the likable and efficient Cortelyou. Two years later Roosevelt tabbed him to serve as the first Secretary of Commerce and Labor, a newly established cabinet position. He brought to his job the spirit of Rooseveltian Progressivism and began at once to revamp several of the departments and agencies under his authority, including the USSIS. One of his first initiatives was to remove the ancient and ineffective James Dumont and replace him with the reform-minded George Uhler.

Cortelyou was a native New Yorker who welcomed every opportunity to return to the great city. But this particular trip was to be all business—and politics, of course. His mission was damage control in the service of a

Roosevelt administration desperate to avoid scandal. The *Slocum* disaster both moved and outraged the president, but it also made him nervous. This was an election year, a chance to be elected president in his own right. The last thing he needed was a scandal in one of his departments—an incident of corruption or incompetence that would undermine his image as a reformer committed to making government work for the people. With the spotlight now focused on the USSIS, he issued a statement calling for a thorough investigation and dispatched the Secretary of Commerce and Labor himself to the scene as an indication of his administration's seriousness.

Cortelyou's immediate task was to erase the impression of bureaucratic stonewalling so ineptly conveyed the day before by Supervising Inspector of the Second District Robert S. Rodie. When asked by a reporter whether, in light of the allegations made in the *Slocum* disaster, he planned to order a reinspection of the city's steamboats, he haughtily dismissed the idea, saying:

> *They will not. When we inspected them we found that the requirements of the law had been complied with and granted certificates. There is no necessity for an additional examination, and none will be made. They will all be inspected at the end of the year when their certificates expire, and if everything is found satisfactory another certificate will be granted.*

No sooner had these words reached the newsrooms of the city's daily papers than Inspector General Uhler, speaking to reporters in Washington, let fly with an unusually frank statement about the problem of political influence being brought to bear on the USSIS to reduce fines levied by the service on boats in violation of safety codes. "What's the use of having the laws?" asked the exasperated reformer. "They no longer act as a deterrent." Once a fine is levied, the "violator of the law appeals to a Senator or Congressman . . . [and] the fine is reduced." Uhler spoke the truth, but his statement caused great embarrassment to the administration. Taken with

Rodie's obstinate remarks, they produced a firestorm of criticism and charges of a cover-up. That morning's edition of the *Times* demanded a thorough and independent investigation "to determine whether the Steamboat Inspection Service is as rotten as it is generally believed to be." Cortelyou arrived in New York for the sole purpose of allaying any concerns of a cover-up.

Over the next few hours Cortelyou met with Rodie at the USSIS office on Whitehall Street near the Battery. Joining them was Inspector General Uhler, who likewise made the trip from Washington. After making clear to them the displeasure their remarks to the press had caused him and the president, Cortelyou informed them that a formal investigation would begin immediately and that they must issue a statement to that effect. "You may be assured," following the release of the statement, "that no stone will be left unturned in order to ascertain the whole truth in regard to this awful calamity." It would not be left to subordinates like Dumont and Rodie. "I should hold this inquiry myself," pledged Cortelyou, "and I shall have the assistance of the most efficient men in the department."

While Cortelyou, Rodie, and Uhler promised an investigation into the *Slocum* disaster, Coroner Berry pressed on with his. Accompanied by Terence J. McManus, counsel for the Knickerbocker Steamboat Company, several members of the *Slocum*'s crew filed into Berry's office in the Bronx to make preliminary statements in anticipation of Monday's formal inquest before a jury.

The first man questioned was deckhand John J. Coakley. Berry began by asking what he knew of the fire's origin. When asked this same question by journalists on the day of the fire, Coakley had spun a tale about seeing porter Walter Payne run from the lamp room just before the fire was detected. Since Payne was black, Coakley doubtless thought his lie might find a receptive audience.

Now under the scrutiny of formal legal proceedings and no doubt fearing for his future, Coakley told the truth. He explained how he discovered the fire in the hay on the floor of the lamp room after a small boy had told him of the smoke. After several futile attempts to put out the flames, he said, he went and found Flanagan.

Up until this point his testimony, while informative as to the details of the fire's origin, was not especially noteworthy. It was when he detailed the effort to fight the flames that he made statements very damaging to his employer, the Knickerbocker Steamboat Company. The battle against the fire lasted only a few minutes, he explained, and ended when the hose burst. "When the hose burst, I guess I lost my head." Coakley followed with a spirited defense of Van Schaick's decision to head for North Brother Island, but the damage was done. The company line as asserted by Barnaby the day of the fire that the crew's "discipline was perfect" had been shredded by one of the key participants. Subsequent statements made by Second Mate Corcoran and First Mate Edward Flanagan only added to the emerging image of a steamboat staffed by incompetent cowards and outfitted with defective safety equipment. Corcoran topped everyone when he asserted that he had seen a woman give birth in the midst of the fire and jump overboard with her baby. Hearst's *Evening Journal* summed up the proceedings in its banner headline "Slocum Employees Make Startling CONFESSIONS." Public outrage was on the rise and had begun to focus on two primary figures: Inspector Lundberg and Frank A. Barnaby. Both could only hope that Monday's formal inquest before a jury would bring no further troubling revelations.

BLACK SATURDAY

As the first light of dawn shone over the low hills to the east of the Lutheran cemetery in Middle Village, Queens, small groups of men could be seen walking through its grand entranceway. Slung over their shoulders were the tools of their trade—pickaxes and shovels. They were grave diggers, arriving to continue their thankless task in preparation for what people were already calling Black Saturday—the day when the largest number of *Slocum* victims would be laid to rest.

In the distance, toward the southern end of the sprawling cemetery, they could see the flickering flames of torches and hear the sounds of digging. An all-night crew of some one hundred men was nearing completion of a huge trench intended for the burial of the thirty unidentified victims. These newly arrived diggers, many of them temporary workers eager to earn a few extra dollars, were slated to continue this work as well as the excavation of dozens of individual graves needed over the next few days.

Several miles away in Lower Manhattan, a team of reporters gathered in the offices of the *New York Times*. Each held a list with scores of names

and addresses on it—one segment of the city's master list of dead and missing compiled at the St. Mark's information bureau. They listened as an editor explained their assignment. The *Times*, the editor told them, was
convinced that the list was seriously flawed, with some people appearing
on it two and three times with different spellings and others long since
found alive and well listed as missing. These errors, noted the editor, had
led to a grossly inflated death toll of nine hundred or more. To correct this
error and arrive at an accurate count, they were being sent out into Little
Germany to verify the accuracy of the list and make appropriate changes. If
they were diligent in their duty, he said, the city would have an accurate list
and the *Times* Sunday edition would outsell its rivals.

A few minutes later the reporters stepped out into the early-morning
sun now filling Park Row and took a short walk to the elevated station to
catch nearly as short a ride to Little Germany. Once there they spread out
and began their canvass of what their paper now routinely referred to as
"the stricken district."

The scene in Little Germany was markedly more animated compared
to the previous two days. Most shops remained closed, but the streets and
sidewalks were full with what a *Times* reporter called "the mournful pomp
of death." The first funerals, all simple affairs in homes, began at 8:00 A.M.
and ran all day long at a peak rate of one every four minutes. By 6:00 P.M.
the remains of some two hundred victims had been sent to the Lutheran
cemetery.

Police Commissioner McAdoo assigned six hundred policemen to the
area to maintain order and prevent traffic tie-ups. To minimize the latter,
many of Little Germany's streets were closed to all vehicles except hearses
and carriages bearing relatives to the cemetery. The bluecoats wore white
gloves and full dress uniforms out of respect for the occasion. On special
orders from headquarters they also carried no clubs, lest they be tempted
to use them if a disturbance broke out. "No rough business today," ordered
Inspector Max Schmittberger. "I want you to remember that this little
community is heartsick with grief. Your business today is to lend a helping
hand and to say a kind word to these people." The plan was to have at least
ten policemen at every funeral to prevent the crowds of onlookers from get-

ting out of hand. Someone at St. Mark's furnished the police department with a tentative schedule of funerals so as to allow detachments of policemen to be moved from funeral to funeral.

Throughout the district, hearses lined the curbs, sometimes as many as three abreast. They were a unique and relatively recent addition to the growing number of rituals and trappings of funerals at the turn of the century. They bore elaborate ornamentation, including brass lanterns, carved designs in the exterior woodwork, and plush interiors. Nearly all had glass windows on both sides to allow bystanders to view the coffin (increasingly known by the more refined term *casket*). Hearses came in two colors, black for adults and white for children. Even the horses were "dressed" for the occasion, draped from head to tail in a fancy netting of either white or black.

Inside the tenements flanked by hearses, several dozen ministers performed brief funeral rites. In some buildings, funerals occurred simultaneously on several floors. For those who could afford it, German bands set up outside to "play the soul away," as the German custom termed it. Policemen held back crowds of sympathetic mourners and kept a watchful eye out for that ubiquitous nuisance found at all public events, the pickpocket. One such miscreant apprehended in front of a tenement on Avenue A had to be spirited away from an enraged crowd that threatened to lynch him. But for the most part, the day was free of disturbing incidents.

Yet there were problems, especially for those families intending to bury their dead. In several homes, families gathered for a scheduled funeral only to be kept waiting hours for a hearse to show up. Despite bringing in countless hearses from all over New York and even New Jersey, undertakers struggled to meet the demand brought about by more than one hundred funerals in a single day. Compounding this problem, many undertakers misjudged how long it would take for hearses to make the round-trip to the cemetery in Queens and failed to account for traffic and delays at the cemetery. More than one family was told, after hours of waiting, that their loved one's funeral would have to be postponed until Sunday.

Part of the hearse shortage could also be attributed to the tradition of using only one hearse for each body. Indeed, more than tradition, it was a firmly established rule adhered to by the city's undertakers to prevent discount funerals. Faced with such extraordinary circumstances, however, many undertakers ignored the rule and put as many as four coffins in a single hearse. "What can we do?" asked one exasperated undertaker. "The union says there must be a hearse for each body, but rules cut no figure on this awful day!"

Rules might not have, but greed surely did. "To all the harrowing features with which the catastrophe is replete," wrote one reporter, there was added "the rapacity of some undertakers in the death district." Funerals that only a week before had cost $50 now ran for $100. The cost of renting carriages to convey mourners to the cemetery jumped from $5 to $15 or even $25. One factor that contributed to this price gouging, in addition to the fact that nearly all the undertakers charging extortionate prices came from outside the St. Mark's neighborhood, was the widespread but erroneous belief that all funerals were being paid for by the mayor's relief fund. Hermann Ridder, chairman of the Relief Committee, vowed to expose the price gougers and subject them to a boycott. "We are quite willing to pay and pay liberally for their services," he explained, "but we will not stand for extortion." He appealed to the daily papers to print the names of the offending undertakers and threatened the latter with boycotts. "For the present we are at the mercy of the undertakers. . . . but when this emergency has passed, we will go over every bill carefully . . . and give notice that the name of every undertaker who has made an exorbitant charge will be punished. No earthly law can reach him, but I am sure no man who presumes to charge extra now could continue to live and work in this district."

One couple, either out of poverty or disgust, decided to do without the services of an undertaker. They were seen at midday walking toward First Avenue dressed in mourning, with the husband carrying a tiny white coffin under his arm. Bystanders stared at the extraordinary scene and watched with curiosity when a teamster stopped at the corner and spoke to them. "I'm going to the cemetery," said the grizzled man, "and I'll take that for you." The husband and wife exchanged glances and looked for a moment like they were about to decline the offer when the husband nodded in assent. The driver quickly cleared a space for the coffin amid his cargo of potted flowers and motioned for the couple to join him on the seat. A moment later they drove off, leaving behind a crowd of onlookers moved to tears by the incident.

Most families, however, brought their loved ones to their final rest in a hired hearse. They could be seen on almost every street, some parked in front of homes, others heading in the direction of the new Williamsburg Bridge followed by one or more carriages filled with mourners. Thousands, including a great many New Yorkers not directly affected by the disaster, joined the crowds lining the sidewalks leading to the bridge. They turned out as a gesture of sympathy and support to those devastated by their losses, standing for hours in the hot sun and dabbing their eyes each time a funeral cortege passed. Even though they'd all read the accounts of hundreds of children killed, most still found it shocking to see the seemingly endless processions of white hearses pass, their tiny contents visible through the side panel windows. The sight frequently caused bystanders to faint.

Black Saturday and the days of countless funerals to come were especially hard to endure for those who still waited for the bodies of their spouses, siblings, parents, and children to be found. Mrs. Stockerman, for example, lay in her apartment, prostrated with grief over the loss of her four children, none of whom had been found. All day she lay in her bed waiting for her husband to return with news, tortured to the verge of insanity by the sounds of passing funeral corteges and bands.

Amid such a vast display of sorrow and despair, two funerals drew special attention: that of Pastor Haas's wife and the unidentified dead. The former was held in the parlor of Haas's home. A single black hearse waited outside 74 East Seventh Street as the police held back an enormous crowd that pressed in from all directions.

More than two dozen fellow ministers attended the ceremony, including Haas's brother, the Reverend John Haas. Although his doctor pleaded with him to remain in bed, Reverend Haas insisted on attending the funeral. Grimacing with pain, he hobbled down the stairs and took his place beside his sister Emma, who was carried downstairs on a stretcher, her head still covered in bandages.

The service began at 1:00 P.M. with Rev. J. W. Loch of Brooklyn reading the funeral prayer, followed by a reading of the Ninth Psalm by Rev. Hugo Hoffman. Reverend Alexander Richter of Hoboken then offered a brief sermon that urged the living to accept the will of God, no matter how trying the experience.

> We should all be good Christians, recognizing in this tragedy, no matter how appalling, the inscrutable hand of Providence. Everything that has happened to us has happened with God's will. We as Christians should bear with composure whatever the good Lord sees fit to inflict upon us. In times like this we should show the world that our faith stands conquering and supreme on the ruins of our shattered homes. All we need to know is that God did not prohibit this accident. Whether it was due to the negligence of the owners or anybody on board cannot be said at the present time, but God has His hand in it and we must recognize that.

Just before the service ended, a messenger arrived with a dramatic announcement: the body of Mrs. Haas's sister, Mrs. Sophia Tetamore, had been identified at the morgue. Remembering a birthmark he'd seen on Mrs. Tetamore during an operation he performed the year before, the Haases' family doctor went to the morgue and examined the thirty bodies believed to be burned beyond recognition. He found her and immediately sent word to the Haas household. Arrangements were hastily made, and in less than an hour the body arrived at the Haas residence. After a second service, the coffins were removed to the hearses, followed by family members who stepped into the black carriages at the curb. Again Haas's physician and several ministers pleaded with him to return to bed, but he remained adamant in his determination to see his wife brought to her final resting place. "She was a devoted wife," he explained, "and though it kills me, I shall pay her this last tribute." Even in his frail condition, he felt compelled to be true to his calling as husband and shepherd.

The unusually large crowd gathered on East Seventh Street near the pastor's house gasped when they saw him shuffle out onto the stoop, his son and brother on each side. They were moved, as they had been on board the *Slocum* during the panic and at North Brother Island in the aftermath, by his unbending sense of duty and courage. They'd been told he was near death and now here he was, burnt hands swathed in bandages and scorched face covered in medicinal powder, preparing to make a long, jolting ride to the cemetery to bury his wife and sister-in-law. Even in this moment of extreme personal grief and suffering, Haas found strength in the crowd's remarkable display of support and sympathy. Though it only added to his sorrow to gaze out across the ocean of grief-stricken faces as he descended the brownstone stairs to the curb, he nodded silently to them, acknowledging their condolences and offering his own. Haas then gingerly stepped up into the black carriage and took his seat. One of the attendants from the undertakers closed the door and signaled the driver of the lead hearse. Slowly the cortege pulled away, the weeping crowd gradually filling in the street behind it.

One hour later, at 3:00 P.M., mourners and sympathizers gathered by the thousands to witness the most moving spectacle of the sorrowful day. Starting from the morgue at East 26th Street, thirteen hearses moved in somber formation south along Second Avenue. All traffic, even other funeral processions, were stopped to let pass the ten black and three white vehicles bearing the remains of twenty-nine unidentified victims. Only one carriage followed, carrying two men from the health department under orders to make an accurate map of the burials should any of the coffins need to be disinterred.

Aware that with hundreds of victims still unaccounted for, and that many grieving relatives of the dead would identify with these unknowns, officials arranged for the procession to wind its way through the streets of Little Germany, making certain to traverse East Sixth Street past St. Mark's Church. From the sidewalks mourners threw flowers in front of the hearses and called out the names of their missing kin. Many knelt on the hard sidewalk as it passed. Reporters noted that even the policemen wept as the vehicles slowly rolled by on their way to the Williamsburg Bridge and the burial ground.

By the time the cortege of the unknown *Slocum* dead arrived at the Lutheran cemetery in Middle Village, Queens, at about 4:30 P.M., thousands of mourners and dozens of hearses and carriages jammed its narrow lanes. Many, like the Haases, were on hand to bury their dead, but a great many had made the trek to attend the burial of the unknowns. Among them were those whose loved ones remained unaccounted for and who just might be among the twenty-nine burned beyond recognition. They looked upon each casket with expectant eyes that asked, in the words of one reporter, "Does it hide one of mine from me?"

A full hour passed before the coffins containing the remains of eleven children, seventeen women, and one man were placed in the long trench dug the night before. Shortly after the last worker climbed out, Rev. D. W. Peterson of nearby Trinity Lutheran Church raised his hand. Silence fell over the scene as thousands fixed their eyes upon the minister. "We are gathered here under the shadow of common grief," he told the crowd in a voice that broke with emotion, "and we will join in the singing of 'Nearer, My God, To Thee.' " With a trembling voice he began the song that all knew by heart. Gradually the crowd joined in, sending the mournful strains of the song out across the rolling hills of the cemetery. By the end of the first verse, the crowds assembled throughout the cemetery at eight other funerals had joined in, as had the grave diggers, journalists, and policemen. For several minutes all set aside their individual sorrows to join in a common expression of faith and forbearance. When at last the final lines were uttered, Reverend Peterson again raised his hand to speak some final words of encouragement. "Remember that the Lord does all things well. His ways are mysterious but they work out His own glorious ends." Then, in spite of himself, he dissolved into uncontrolled sobbing. Like the song of a moment before, the minister's tears set the crowd to crying and wailing. Then in groups and as individuals they came forward to murmur a final prayer and toss handfuls of dirt into the trench before turning to walk away.

QUESTIONS AND ANSWERS

While the people of Little Germany struggled in what one paper termed "one complete web of woe," the work of city officials, fund-raisers, investigators, divers, and journalists continued unabated. In the case of the latter, no group was busier than the investigative team sent out by the *Times* to establish an accurate list of the dead and missing. In apartment after apartment they found grieving relatives. Most proved willing to provide the reporters with the information they sought. Many of these interviews took place next to one or more coffins awaiting burial. Others, like that with Fred Diehl of 200 East Fifth Street, occurred in an atmosphere of despair. Diehl jumped to his feet when the reporter knocked, but immediately collapsed in a chair when he realized he'd misinterpreted the intention of the caller. "Oh, I thought it was someone bringing them to me," he said, referring to his missing wife and three children.

I have almost walked my feet off looking for them and I can't find
a trace of a single one. If this keeps up much longer I shall go crazy. I
walk through the house and at every step a pain goes to my heart.
There are their schoolbooks, just where they left them. I open a closet

door and see their clothes, and I have to turn away. I cannot believe
that they will never return. Oh, they must come back! This is just a
bad dream I'm having, and soon I'll wake up.

The reporter recorded his information and left the despondent man to continue his vigil in his dark and empty apartment.

Other knocks went unanswered, as many families were out visiting the morgue, making funeral arrangements, or attending funerals. Neighbors answered questions and corrected errors on the list. As expected, the reporters were able to strike several hundred names from the list, mostly because multiple spellings or erroneous addresses had resulted in several families being listed twice. The *Times* also noted that many addresses were clearly fraudulent, doubtless supplied by curiosity seekers in order to gain entry to the morgue.

But to their great surprise, the reporters found themselves adding nearly as many names to the list as they took off. One child listed as Agnes Alga, for example, turned out to be two girls, Agnes and Olga Grolke. In addition, the reporter also learned that a third girl previously unaccounted for, Mamie Ryan, had gone with the Grolke sisters and not returned. More startling, however, were the discoveries of families not on the list because every member had perished in the fire. A widow named Johanna Vassmer, for example, went on the excursion with her daughter and never returned. Only a chance mention by a neighbor to a *Times* reporter led to the discovery and the addition of two more names to the list.

At the end of the day, the reporters returned to the *Times* offices and began comparing notes. Over the course of the next few hours, they fashioned a new and far more accurate list. Whereas in Saturday's morning edition the paper listed 560 bodies recovered and 448 missing with an estimate of 900 killed, the adjusted totals in Sunday's paper would read: 581 bodies recovered, 270 missing, and 812 estimated dead. The *Times* canvass had clarified the picture considerably, but its goal of dramatically reducing the death toll estimate was not realized. The "extreme estimate," the paper feared, would prove correct in the end.

Far downtown at the USSIS offices, Robert S. Rodie faced a different set of reporters. Perturbed by their probing questions, he once again inflamed public opinion with his arrogant and officious responses. Would he, they asked, consent to public demand for the *Grand Republic*, sister ship of the *Slocum*, to be reinspected? No, he answered curtly, the USSIS will only reinspect a vessel if requested in writing by its owner. "The board," he informed the reporters in an irritated tone, "does not devote its time to attending to the wants of the public." Two hours later, doubtless aware of the anger generated by his dismissive remarks, Rodie notified reporters that henceforth he and other officials would communicate with the media only through written statements.

It was this attitude of indifference to the suffering of hundreds that spurred Coroners O'Gorman and Berry on all day in their relentless search for evidence of negligence and wrongdoing on the part of Barnaby and the officers and crew of the *Slocum*. O'Gorman made arrangements for a local captain to take him and other officials on an excursion retracing the *Slocum*'s ill-fated journey. He also collected more physical evidence from the wreck, most notably a section of cheap and worn fire hose. Berry issued more subpoenas and interviewed several witnesses in preparation for the formal inquest on Monday.

At city hall the most pressing matter was an emerging dispute over how best to recover the several hundred bodies believed to be still trapped inside the sunken *Slocum*. There were two options—dynamite the wreck, as the divers recommended, or hire a salvage company to raise it. Frank Barnaby, McClellan was told, was blocking either move, claiming that the *Slocum* was no longer owned by the Knickerbocker Steamboat Company, but rather by a marine insurance company. If he gave permission to dynamite the wreck, he explained, his company would forfeit the $70,000 claim that, he assured everyone, he intended to donate to the relief fund. Barnaby likewise tried to block the effort to raise the *Slocum*, claiming that his company was bankrupt and unable to afford the expected

$10,000 fee (this move was part of Barnaby's overall plan to dissolve his company and thereby leave no assets that might later be seized in a lawsuit). The boat's insurers were willing to offer only $5,000.

McClellan bristled at the news of Barnaby's obstinance. "There is no time to be lost," he explained. "Red tape can not enter in to this matter." Grieving family members must not be made to wait to receive the remains of their loved ones. Raise the wreck immediately. The city will put up whatever funds are necessary. "These bodies must be taken out at once. . . ." Turning to Police Commissioner McAdoo, he authorized him to contract with the Merritt Chapman salvage company to raise the boat as soon as possible.

The mayor's Relief Committee reported that as of Saturday evening, more than $22,000 had been collected. Already over one hundred families had been given assistance. "The visitors have found the people affected," a representative of the committee assured the public, "to be self-respecting and not the kind who would ordinarily accept aid from any committee."

O ut on the East River, divers and boatmen extracted twenty more bodies from the water. Now more than ever, as the effects of seventy-two hours' submersion began to render the bodies less and less recognizable, morgue officials took note of any small clue that might lead to a positive identification. One woman in her late twenties wore a wedding ring marked "F.H. to A.T. Jan. 28, 1892." A young boy carried a piece of stamped metal that read "Frank De Luccia goes to P.S." Another woman bore no identification, but drew the attention of nearly everyone because she was found tangled in an American flag. A little boy was found with a small flag in his pocket on which was stitched the motto "Be thou faithful unto death."

All were taken by tug to the Charities Pier and immediately embalmed. Identifications began almost as soon as the doors were flung open to admit the searchers. Only seven remained unclaimed when the morgue closed at 10:00 P.M. Nearly five hundred had yet to be found.

Several hours later the police received a call from a citizen reporting a disoriented man wandering the streets talking incoherently to himself. The officers who responded to the call found Walter Watson in a state of sheer madness. The twenty-nine-year-old morgue attendant had been on duty at the Charities Pier since Wednesday. "I can't identify that body," he said to some imagined figure. "Take it away. Bring me another one. No, I can't identify that, either. Take it away." The officers took him into custody without a struggle. He was later committed to the psychiatric ward at Bellevue Hospital.

THE ACT OF MAN

H e could hear their cheerful voices echoing down the tiled hallway of Lebanon Hospital. The sound pulled him out of the delirious fog that had enveloped his mind since his arrival Wednesday night. Captain Van Schaick had slept only intermittently since then, in between intense bursts of pain from his broken heel and burned skin and the haunting, harrowing memories of the fire that destroyed his boat and more than three-quarters of its passengers.

The cheerful chattering grew louder and then stopped just outside the door to his ward. Then in filed fifteen or so young girls dressed in Sunday best. They were members of a group called the Christadora Club from Little Germany. They had come to bring flowers and treats to the victims of the *Slocum* disaster still recuperating in the hospital. By chance their first stop was at the bedside of Captain Van Schaick.

Their innocent faces, full of life and devoid of judgment, were a welcome sight to the weary mariner. He'd had regular visits from his son and other well-wishers, but also less welcome calls from the press and the coroner's and district attorney's offices.

With tears in his eyes, the old captain thanked the girls for their kindness, but gently declined to accept their offerings of flowers and fruit. Give them to the victims whose injuries and sufferings were greater than his, he told them. Somewhat hesitantly they retrieved their gifts and went on their way.

The captain had had few pleasant moments since the fire. Confined to a bed in a dreary ward, he'd had little to do but relive over and over in his tormented mind the dreadful final minutes aboard the *Slocum*. Each time as the events replayed in his mind he could hear the screams of women and children and see the flames chasing them overboard. No matter how many times he assured himself that he'd done all that he could, voices of doubt whispered in his head. He went over the options and every time came to the same conclusion: beach her on North Brother Island. Convincing himself that he'd made the right decision, however, did little to stop the traumatic images unfolding over and over again in his mind. And then there was the matter of the *Slocum*'s safety equipment and the readiness of his crew. How would he answer the inevitable questions that would surely arise during the coming coroner's inquest?

The one bright spot in all this gloom was the chance reunion of the captain and a former love. Van Schaick had been married briefly in his younger days, but had lived the life of a bachelor for more than thirty years. Handsome and affable, he'd dated a succession of women, but each relationship dissolved for one reason or another. So it had been with Grace M. Spratt, a nurse twenty-five years his junior. They'd courted for seven years when the relationship finally dissolved. Several years had elapsed since their parting when their paths crossed a second time at Lebanon Hospital. It seemed a small miracle to Van Schaick that such horrific circumstances could produce so welcome a result. Perhaps it was his helpless condition, or maybe just the fact that he was a bit older now, but he realized how much he cared for her—needed her. He looked forward to her regular visits and warm words of encouragement. He sensed that she still harbored feelings for him. And, he learned to his great relief, she was not married.

Sunday morning, scarcely a pulpit in the city failed to take up the subject of the *Slocum* disaster. Some ministers, like Rev. John B. Remensnyder, president of the Lutheran Synod, urged his listeners to accept "this fearful visitation" of God's hand. "God's ways," he reminded them, "are higher than our ways, and His thoughts higher than our thoughts, . . . let us not question them."

A far more common theme, however, focused not on God's ways but on the actions of His deeply flawed people. "If a cowardly crew," thundered Rev. John L. Belford of Saint Peter and Paul in Brooklyn, "seeks its own safety instead of fighting the fire or saving the helpless, the disgrace is not due to Providence, but to selfish and base humanity."

To drive a boat at full speed with a burning furnace in her bow seems madness. To expect God to change the laws of nature would be presumption. The disaster was not the act of God. It is the act of man. It comes from greed, neglect of duty, from defiance of law and conscience.

Still others hit harder, bringing forth a theme then gaining wider currency in the reform-minded Progressive Era: the evil of the impersonal and unreachable corporation. "With the growth of corporations," noted Reverend Huntington of Grace Church, "there is a tendency to eliminate the individual, so that no one person will be held responsible when something goes wrong." Reverend James Oliver Wilson of the Nostrand Avenue Church in Brooklyn agreed, but was more blunt in his assessment of guilt. "Sin did it," he declared, "sin in the individual, and sin in the corporation. But for sin in the Knickerbocker Company, the sin of greed and carelessness, the boat would not have burned." "We wonder at times," lamented Rev. C. D. Case of the Hanson Place Baptist Church, "whether many a corporation does not do the least possible and not the most for the good of the people. If a corporation can prove that it simply obeyed the law, it feels morally free." At a minimum, most clerics agreed, the guilty should be brought to justice, tougher codes for steamboat construction should be enacted, and an honest system of inspectors put in place. In most churches, special collections were taken up for the relief of those affected by the tragedy.

The most extraordinary service on Sunday was attended by neither sermon nor collection. At 10:00 A.M. a modest crowd, half the normal size for a typical Sunday, filed into the pews at St. Mark's Church. While outside the edifice "the fluttering emblems of death" were everywhere in the form of flower arrangements and black bunting and crepe, inside, the church gave no indication of the extraordinary fate that had befallen its members. "The pews were gaunt and crypt-like in their empty desolation," recorded one journalist, "the walls were undraped and the altar . . . was naked and bare. On the lectern only were a few black bows."

Ghostlike, the afflicted members of the flock stood silently in the church, praying and waiting for the service to begin. In the distance they heard the joyful peals of church bells calling together some congregation, sounds that only accentuated the sorrowful setting.

A few minutes after the hour, uncharacteristic for St. Mark's or any German church for that matter, the simple service began. Reverend Holstein, a retired minister from Brooklyn, entered and faced the tearful assemblage. With half the parish choir dead, along with the organist, there would be no music, even if desired. Instead, he recited the lines from J. S. Bach's Cantata 27, "Who Knows How Near Is My End."

Just as the last words were read, the small, silent crowd stirred. In the doorway leading to the vestry was Pastor Haas, covered in bandages and held up by his son and brother. Without prompting everyone rose in a wordless expression of sorrow and gratitude. For a few seconds all was still, then as one witness remembered it, "the long pent-up storm of emotion broke," and everyone began to cry. "From all directions, came the sound of weeping, of sobs low and heartbreaking, sobs childish and tearful, sobs dry and hard and terrible." Haas took his place in a pew, bowed his head in prayer, and listened as Holstein proceeded to read several selections from the Bible, including the 39th Psalm:

And now, Lord, what wait I for?
My hope is in Thee . . .
Remove Thy stroke away from me.
I am consumed by the blow of Your hand.

When it was over, all remained standing until Reverend Haas hobbled through the doorway leading to the vestry. Then with heads bowed and shoulders slumped, the parishioners shuffled out into the sunlight of a gorgeous Sunday morning.

All day the scenes of Black Saturday were repeated as hearses filled the streets and mourners lined the sidewalks of the neighborhood. One hundred fifty-nine people were buried, including Mary Abendschein, the woman who organized the excursion. By evening, officials at the Lutheran cemetery estimated that some fifty thousand mourners had thronged there to witness burials or lay flowers on the graves of those already interred. In the most moving service, two hundred children from the nearby Trinity Lutheran Church each carried a potted plant into the cemetery, placed it on the grave of the unidentified dead, and sang "Nearer, My God, To Thee."

In spite of it being a Sunday, Coroners O'Gorman and Berry continued their investigation in preparation for the next day's formal inquest. They devoted the main portion of their day to a trip retracing the *Slocum*'s last journey. They brought with them on the police boat the *Slocum*'s assistant pilot, Edwin H. Weaver. Pleased to be out of jail, Weaver took the helm of the police boat and went over the course, answering questions put to him by the coroners as well as Inspector Albertson and an ex–fire marshal. When the key question of the day was put to him—what would he have done if he had been captain—Weaver answered without hesitation, "I would have run her in at the foot of East One Hundred and Twenty-ninth Street," he asserted, "which could have been done in a few minutes' time." His statement both sickened and thrilled O'Gorman and Berry, for it meant that Van Schaick, on top of operating a firetrap staffed by incompetents, had committed a fatal error in judgment in deciding to run at top speed into the wind for North Brother Island. They'd believed this since the day of the fire, only now they had confirmation of it from one of the principal men in the pilothouse. Weaver's challenge to Van Schaick's version of the story would be a crucial piece of evidence when repeated under oath at the coming inquest. "I am perfectly satisfied with the results of the trip," O'Gorman told reporters when the police boat docked.

Federal authorities were also on hand for their own fact-finding cruise on the East River. Secretary of Commerce and Labor Cortelyou was joined by USSIS inspector general George Uhler and supervising inspector for the Second District Robert S. Rodie on a tug that left from the pier at East Third Street. Retracing the *Slocum*'s voyage, they proceeded to North Brother Island, where they paused to watch workers remove twenty bodies from the water. Next they visited the *Slocum* at Hunts Point and watched as three bodies were removed from the wreck. Satisfied with the recovery and investigation efforts under way, Cortelyou left for Washington later in the day, leaving Uhler and Rodie under strict orders not to speak with the press. The two did issue a brief written statement assuring the skeptical public that the coming federal investigation would be "complete and thorough in every respect."

The effort to recover the bodies of some four hundred missing victims continued in earnest, but the results were frustrating. Forty-seven remains were recovered from various locations in the river and in the wreckage and transported to the morgue, where a crowd of ten thousand waited. Now, four days since the fire, many searchers feared that the missing bodies had been swept out to sea by the tides. Still there was reason to hope that the raising of the wreck later in the week would lead to more recoveries. By midnight Sunday, 22 bodies remained unidentified out of 628 recovered. Little Germany's undertakers faced several more days of nonstop work.

Late Sunday evening, as a steamer passed Seabright on its way home from an all-day excursion at the shore, a man fell overboard. Alert passengers and crewmen threw life preservers to him as he flailed in the water. But each one sank as soon as it hit the water, and the man drowned.

A TANGLE OF
CONTRADICTIONS

O ver the course of the next week, news of the *Slocum* disaster continued to fill the pages of the city's dailies. Martin Green and his
fellow editors sent out legions of scribes and photographers to
gather the stories and images a horrified but fascinated public demanded.
Although competition for scoops and unique stories was keen, there was
little to distinguish the coverage of one paper from another.

Each day readers scanned a table printed on page 1 as though check-
ing a box score or stock index. It listed the ever-rising number of bodies recovered, bodies identified, persons listed as missing, and the probable
total. On Monday, June 20, the *World* announced that the "latest figures"
from the police showed 669 bodies recovered and 353 missing. On
Wednesday the updated figures read 855 recovered and 200 missing, but a
new canvass launched that morning of the Little Germany neighborhood
by one hundred German-speaking policemen promised the most accurate
tally to date. When the results were made public on Saturday, June 25, the
estimated death toll stood at 1,031 (the official death toll was eventually set
at 1,021). The *Slocum* incident now held the unenviable distinction of being the deadliest peacetime maritime disaster in U.S. history.

A key factor in driving this grim number upward was the sudden and quite unexpected appearance of several hundred bodies beginning on Monday. This merciful turn of events was likely due to the buildup of gases within the decomposing corpses, but workers attributed it to a violent thunderstorm on Monday. Their conclusion was based on a long-standing belief that loud thunder or explosions could raise a submerged body, allegedly by causing the spleen to burst, which in turn caused bloating leading to buoyancy. Eager to try anything that might hasten the recovery effort, O'Gorman ordered the river "sounded." All day Tuesday the East River echoed with the report of two artillery pieces mounted on a float and towed by a tug. On Wednesday, spectators along the shore and in boats were treated to a series of spectacular dynamite explosions that sent plumes of water more than one hundred feet into the air. Scores of bodies surfaced during the day, as did countless dead and stunned fish.

As before, all recovered bodies went directly to the Charities Pier at East 26th Street. But their condition was such that identification was possible only by clothing, personal effects, and photographs. Remarkably, nearly two hundred were identified in this manner before Wednesday afternoon, when fifty-two unknown victims were buried at the Lutheran cemetery. Any remains later identified from clothing and effects were exhumed and buried in family plots. Pastor Haas's daughter was identified in this manner on Saturday June 25, as was Frank Weber's son Frank, Jr.

On Thursday afternoon, with the rate of recovery once again slowed, Commissioner James Tully ordered the temporary morgue at the Charities Pier closed and disinfected. Any future recoveries, he announced, would be handled in the official morgue adjacent to the pier. The next day seventy-five photographs of bodies, clothing, and personal effects went on display at the police station on East Fifth Street.

One of the biggest stories of the week concerned the monumental effort to raise the *Slocum*. It took longer than expected for the salvage experts at the Merritt Chapman Company to free the hulk from its resting place in five feet of mud, but by Wednesday evening they had five chains under the hull. The next morning, through a combination of hoisting and pumping, they brought the charred wreck to the surface. Officials, workers, and curiosity seekers stared at the sight, both awed and horrified by the completeness of the fire's destructive work. Almost nothing remained of the boat's upper works. Three decks, cabins, pilothouse—all were gone. As a *Times* reporter described it:

> *Much of the water has been pumped out of the Slocum and her bulk is high out of the water. Her big walking beam looms out of the wreck like an enormous gallows. Part of her starboard wheel is still intact, and her port wheel driving rod still has a few blades of the wheel adhering to it. The big boilers, covered with rust, stand like two towers in the middle of the hulk.*

On Friday the *Slocum* was towed to a shipyard at Erie Basin in Brooklyn where investigators began poring over it to find the source of the fire and additional evidence of negligence on the part of the vessel's owners and crew.

That evening some fifteen hundred people turned out at the Grand Opera House for a charity performance by vaudeville stars like Lillian Russell and an up-and-comer named George M. Cohan. After deducting expenses the event raised $3,000 for the relief fund, which by the end of the following day surpassed $107,000. Contributions ranging from pocket change to hundreds of dollars poured in all week, from Mrs. Francis Smith and J. Rabinowich, who each contributed a dollar, to Tammany Hall and the Coney Island Jockey Club, who turned over checks for $2,000 and $1,000 respectively.

Hermann Ridder, chairman of the relief fund committee, announced that a grand total of $150,000 would be needed to pay for hundreds of funerals and provide relief for families left destitute. A special effort would be made to establish a long-term relief fund for the dozens of children orphaned by the disaster. In addition to money, many organizations such as the Association for the Improvement of the Condition of the Poor, the Children's Aid Society, and many women's clubs organized food deliveries and child care for homes left motherless.

Investigations on the federal level moved forward with the creation on Thursday, June 23, of a special United States Commission of Investigation Upon the Disaster to the Steamer General Slocum. Acting under the auspices of Secretary Cortelyou, the five-man commission included one high-ranking officer each from the navy and army and three top officials from the Department of Commerce and Labor, including USSIS inspector general Uhler. They were charged by President Roosevelt and Cortelyou with making "a careful and thorough investigation of the disaster" to determine its cause and make recommendations for reforming the USSIS and crafting new legislation regarding steamboat safety. Many were pleased by the news, aware that regulations of steamboat safety rested almost exclusively with the federal government. They took their trust-busting president at his word when he vowed that justice would be served. But others, particularly those loyal to the Democratic Party, dismissed the commission as mere election-year window dressing. "What a farce!" snarled the *Journal of Commerce*. "Mark you, every man on Cortelyou's commission is an administration toady."

The following day, Friday, June 25, United States District Attorney Henry L. Burnett held a joint news conference with State District Attorney William Travers Jerome to detail the forthcoming criminal proceedings related to the *Slocum* disaster. As the city and state of New York lacked any authority or standing in the case, a federal grand jury would convene the following week to review evidence, listen to testimony, and, if warranted, hand down indictments. Jerome and Coroner Berry promised their full cooperation.

The real story of the week, however, the one that dominated headlines and stoked public indignation, was the coroner's inquest that began on Monday morning, June 20. Coroner Joseph Berry arrived early at the Second Battery Armory at Bathgate Avenue and 177th Street. Normally he conducted inquiries in the hearing room at his office, but experience from the past five days convinced him that a larger venue would be necessary.

The drill room at the Second Battery Armory was ideal, though it required a few temporary modifications before the inquest could begin. Carpenters were still hammering together the platform for the witness stand and the jury box when he strode into the imposing edifice.

One of his first tasks was to ensure that his evidence was at hand. To his relief he found several visibly defective life preservers, coils of rotten and worn fire hose, lengths of standpipe with unopened valves, and a section of railing that four dead people were found clinging to. He could only wonder how the Knickerbocker Steamboat Company would attempt to dismiss such damning evidence of criminal negligence.

Although the hearings would be held before a jury charged with listening to the testimony and rendering a verdict of guilty or not guilty, the coroner's inquest did not have the standing of a court of law. Its chief purpose was to gather as much evidence and testimony as possible, render a verdict, and then turn the matter over to the slower-moving federal investigation and prosecution. For this reason, all the participants took the proceedings very seriously, knowing full well that all testimony and evidence gathered would very likely be used by federal prosecutors. Indeed, many federal officials, including U.S. Assistant District Attorney Henry Wise, were on hand to personally hear the testimony.

By 9:00 A.M. the key participants began to arrive. Among the first was State District Attorney Francis P. Garvan, who entered with an entourage of staffers and lawyers. The week promised to be a big one in his career, as he, through a prior arrangement with Berry, would handle most of the questioning of witnesses. But the twenty-nine-year-old Garvan was motivated by more than mere ambition; he carried with him the anger of a reformer confronted with the dreadful consequences of corruption and greed run amok. "I don't care whose toes I step on!" he told the press over the weekend. "I'm going to find out who was responsible for this ghastly occurrence. The truth will be exposed."

Frank A. Barnaby followed Garvan, accompanied by his counsel, ex-judge Abram Dittenhoeffer. Attorney Terence McManus, counsel representing the Knickerbocker Steamboat Company, arrived, as did Inspector

Henry Lundberg and his lawyer, Mr. S. J. Gilbert. More witnesses and lawyers followed, until all were seated. At 9:45, Berry gave the signal to admit the spectators. Given the huge crowd gathered outside the building, only the relatives of people killed in the *Slocum* disaster or survivors were admitted. The curious, the sympathetic, and the outraged would have to read about the inquest in the evening papers.

Everyone stared as the forlorn mass shuffled into the spectators' gallery. Many were wrapped in bandages and used crutches and canes to walk. Others showed no indication of physical injury, but their haggard faces and red, sleepless eyes told of their suffering and loss. They were there seeking answers.

Shortly after 10:00 A.M., Frank A. Barnaby was called as the first witness. Nattily dressed in a gray summer suit, the forty-eight-year-old businessman did his best to appear at ease as Garvan began his questioning. The latter opened with some perfunctory questions about Barnaby and the Knickerbocker Steamboat Company, but soon homed in on the crucial question of whether the life preservers aboard the *Slocum* were useless, as so many had charged. What evidence did Barnaby have, asked Garvan, to justify his contention that the *Slocum* carried hundreds of new life preservers? Barnaby reached into his coat and coolly drew out some bills and handed them to the young assistant DA. Garvan scanned them as he asked that they be noted as evidence.

"You know of your own knowledge that these bills are for *Slocum* apparatus," asked Garvan with his eyebrows slightly raised to suggest some doubt.

"I do," answered Barnaby curtly.

"I find here five bills," continued Garvan, "they are for life preservers— about 350 of them—and they are dated May 14, 1902; April 30, 1903; May 1903; April 1904; and May 1904. You are sure all these were for the *General Slocum*?"

"Yes."

Garvan paused and then pounced.

"If that is the case," he asked suddenly, "how is it that I find in some of these bills the name *'Grand Republic'* scratched out or taken out with acid and the name 'Slocum' inserted? One of the bills still stands in the name of the *Grand Republic.*"

"I don't know about that," snapped Barnaby. "I suppose that some bookkeeper must have done that."

"What is the name of that bookkeeper?" demanded Garvan in a tone that indicated he knew he'd just cracked the aura of invulnerability most corporate executives enjoyed.

"I don't know," stammered a flustered Barnaby. "Separate accounts are kept for each boat. The books will show to which one the life preservers went."

"Any erasures in them?" asked Garvan, looking knowingly in the direction of the jury. Barnaby gave no answer, so Garvan continued to press the witness, who was by now sweating profusely.

"How do those bills show on your books?"

"As for life preservers bought for the *Slocum.*"

"Did all these preservers go to the *Slocum?*"

"No, but our books will show how many went there and how many went to the *Grand Republic.*"

"These bills show all the purchases of life preservers since 1902. Is that correct?"

"Yes."

"Can you give us the accounts showing the purchases of life preservers for the *Slocum* since 1891?"

"I don't know. The books, except for the past three years, are in storage in Brooklyn. We will try to get them if they are needed. I believe they are there, but usually we do not keep books except for a season's business."

Garvan paused to let Barnaby's words register fully with the jury before hitting him with a stinging shot. "Is it customary for a large concern to destroy its books?"

"I don't know" was Barnaby's mumbled reply.

Garvan posed a few more questions, but satisfied that he had seriously damaged Barnaby's credibility, let the witness step down.

James Atkinson, secretary and general manager of the Knickerbocker

Steamboat Company, next took the stand. When asked about the matter of life preservers aboard the *Slocum,* Atkinson denied knowledge of equipment purchases, company records, or erasures made on bills. "I can't tell anything about it," he explained. "I got the bills from the bookkeeper and handed them to Mr. Barnaby."

When Atkinson divulged that the company had but one bookkeeper, a Miss S. C. Hall, Garvan turned to the crowd and asked if she was present. Atkinson explained that she was downtown minding the company office.

"Well, Mr. Atkinson," said Garvan testily to a man twice his age, "you go downtown and keep the office, and let Miss Hall come up here and tell us something about those bills. And tell her to bring all the company books."

As Atkinson slunk off the stand, Berry announced a one-hour recess for lunch.

It was not yet 12 noon on the first morning of the inquest, and already he and Garvan sensed victory. They plainly had Barnaby and company on the run. Grilling the crew, they anticipated, would only add to their case.

The afternoon session began with a start as Captain Van Schaick was called to the witness stand. As the jury and spectators looked for the man whose picture they'd seen day after day in the papers, word was sent to Berry that the captain remained in the hospital, too weak as yet to testify. He might be available later in the week.

Berry then returned to the witness list and called up the first of four of *Slocum*'s crewmen. John Coakley, the deckhand who first learned of the fire, took his seat on the witness stand. Clearly nervous and unused to wearing a suit and tie, he removed his coat and folded it across his knee. Garvan wasted no time in establishing several key points.

"Were you ever present at a fire drill on board the *Slocum* at any time?" asked Garvan.

"I never was."

"Were you ever instructed as to what to do in case of a fire?"

"Never."

"How long have you been on the *Slocum*?"

"Eighteen days at the time of the accident."

When asked what his duties were aboard the boat, Coakley replied that he was "to keep the children from climbing where they should not be." Asked what he was doing when informed of the fire, Coakley replied that he was drinking a beer.

He then went on, at Garvan's prodding, to explain how he tried unsuccessfully to put out the fire himself and then notified First Mate Flanagan. After the hose burst, he continued, he ran to warn passengers and distribute life preservers. Then, he asserted, "I lowered one of the lifeboats."

"What's that?" interjected Garvan, with an incredulous look on his face. By the time of the inquest it was widely known that none of the *Slocum*'s lifeboats had been launched. "Do you mean to say that you lowered a lifeboat?"

"Yes," answered Coakley.

Garvan fired several more follow-ups regarding Coakley's patently false claim about the lifeboat, but the deckhand stood by his statement.

Berry then took over and moved on to ask about the lamp room where the fire began. When asked about its contents, Coakley ticked off a list of highly flammable items, including lamp oil, lubricants, wood, charcoal, oily rags, and on June 15 barrels full of hay—each one prohibited by federal law pertaining to steamboats.

"Did you ever light matches when you went down where the oil was in the forward cabin?"

"Why sure, if I wanted to see," answered Coakley.

"Did the rest of the crew do the same?"

"Sure they did."

Satisfied that the deckhand had provided ample evidence in favor of the prosecution, Berry dismissed Coakley, who was immediately returned to the house of detention.

More damning testimony followed. Deckhand Tom Collins explained that he too never saw a fire drill aboard the *Slocum*. He flatly contradicted Coakley's assertion that any lifeboats had been launched. Second Mate

James Corcoran corroborated Collins's statements, but admitted further that part of the problem with getting the fire hose to work properly may have resulted from his failure to remove a solid rubber stopper, or flange, from the standpipe before attaching the hose.

"The fire hose would be useless with that rubber flange in there?" asked Garvan.

"Yes, sir," answered Corcoran.

"Was this rubber flange taken out when this fire started?" the district attorney pressed.

"I don't know," came the somewhat sheepish reply.

"You didn't take it out?" Garvan demanded incredulously.

"No, to tell the truth, the rubber stopper was not taken out at all."

Garvan and Berry were having a field day with the witnesses, but they'd saved the best for last. Late in the afternoon the *Slocum*'s first mate, Edward Flanagan, took his place in the witness chair. Peppered from the outset with questions about the contents of the lamp room, the rubber stopper in the standpipe, and the effort to extinguish the blaze, Flanagan answered repeatedly that he did not remember. Frustrated, Garvan asked him caustically what had happened to his memory.

"Well, if you went through what I did," he replied in a distressed voice, "your memory might be bad, too. I can't sleep nights. I imagine I see the whole thing before me—"

But Garvan would have none of it and he cut him off and resumed his questioning. Because of Flanagan's senior position on the boat, the district attorney was particularly keen on exploring the issue of the life preservers and Lundberg's inspection on May 5.

"Were there any new life preservers on board the boat this year?"

"I don't remember."

"What kind were in the racks?"

"They were all good, I guess. Some of them might have been bad."

"Were you present when the inspection was made?"

"I didn't go round the boat with the inspectors."

"Did you see them inspect the life preservers?"

"Well, the inspector went around and he had a stick in his hand. He poked some of the life preservers in the racks. He ordered me to take down about twenty or maybe ten."

"Then all he did was to poke the life preservers with a stick?"

"That's all I remember."

"You had charge of putting up the preservers?"

"Yes."

"Were there any new ones?"

"I can't remember."

"Did they inspect the fire hose?"

"I don't remember."

"Now, isn't it a fact that you saw no life preservers on that boat except those which were stamped 'passed Sept. 28, 1891'?"

"Yes, that's right."

Coroner Berry then jumped in: "Isn't it a fact, that when the inspectors were on board you took twenty new preservers and put them on a bench and led the inspector to them and told him they were all like that and he passed them?"

"I can't remember that."

Flanagan, visibly wilting under the pressure being applied by Garvan and Berry, had only a moment to catch his breath when Assistant U.S. District Attorney Henry Wise stood and was recognized by the coroner. Did Flanagan, he asked, possess a license, as required by law, to serve as first mate aboard the *Slocum*. No, he replied reluctantly, he'd never bothered to get one.

When the first day of the inquest came to a close a few minutes later, Garvan and Berry were elated. It had seemed almost too easy, as witness after witness made damaging statements about the Knickerbocker Steamboat Company and their own performance during the disaster. Perhaps the most striking was the number of times they made statements that contradicted each other and their own earlier versions of events. To Garvan, Berry, and the press, these inconsistencies highlighted the degree to which many of the witnesses, doubtless at Barnaby's instigation, were lying. "As is usual in the case of men instructed to tell untruths," observed the *Times*, "they are becoming involved in a tangle of contradictions."

Little that transpired the next day did much to undermine this perception. Several more crewmen were interviewed, but the most notable testimony came from Miss S. C. Hall, the bookkeeper for the Knickerbocker Steamboat Company. The thin, frail-looking woman arrived with the company's books dating back to 1902, the rest having been destroyed, she explained. Under relentless questioning from the district attorney she admitted to using acid to change the name *Grand Republic* on the bills for life preservers to *General Slocum,* but insisted she had done so prior to the fire. "It was my custom to use acid," she explained, but when pressed she could offer no clear explanation as to why she'd changed the life preserver bills.

"Is it not a fact," he asked sharply, "that not one life preserver has been bought for the *Slocum* or put on board her since 1895? Don't your books show that?"

"The books only show what occurred since 1902."

"I want an answer from you, Miss Hall," Garvan roared. "Do your books show the purchase of any life preservers for the *Slocum* since 1902?"

"I can't find any entries," Hall answered, as she made a halfhearted shuffle through her books.

Garvan asked that the books be put in evidence. This brought Terence McManus, lawyer for the company, to his feet in protest. Garvan glared at him and asked mockingly why he objected to so routine a request. "Are there any hideous secrets concealed in them?" McManus backed down and Garvan resumed his questioning of the bookkeeper.

"Now, you say that you know there were no life preservers bought for the *Slocum* since 1902. Explain to me then why you changed these bills to make them appear as if the purchases of these preservers were for the *Slocum,*" Garvan demanded.

Cornered, Hall grew incoherent, unable to complete a sentence.

"Who told you to get out the bills for the life preservers?" asked Coroner Berry.

"I can't remember."

"Now, there are only two persons who could give you that order—the president or Mr. Atkinson. Do you mean to say you can't remember who ordered them?"

"I cannot," Hall responded.

"Why did you choose the life preserver bills and not those for other supplies?" the coroner wondered.

"I don't know. I thought they might be wanted."

Berry told Hall to step down and immediately head for the company office to retrieve all relevant books and documents. To ensure her speedy return, he sent a policeman to accompany her. As she left the makeshift courtroom, two representatives of the Kahnweiler & Sons life preserver company took the stand and stated unequivocally that no new life preservers had been delivered to the *Slocum* since 1895, and possibly as far back as 1891, the year the vessel was launched. But when one of the witnesses, Otto Kahnweiler, insisted that one of his "Never-Sink" preservers lasted twenty years if properly cared for, Garvan seized upon the occasion to make a dramatic point to the jury. When the district attorney placed a decrepit life preserver in his lap, Kahnweiler responded, "I'll trust myself to that belt now with hands and feet tied." Garvan gave a tug on the straps, tearing them off effortlessly. As cork dust poured onto Kahnweiler's feet, Garvan turned to Berry and said, "That will do."

Pilot Ed Weaver led off the afternoon session and produced a great deal of consternation when he defended Captain Van Schaick's decision to beach the boat on North Brother Island. "Did you not tell me on Sunday," asked Berry, referring to the trip aboard the police boat over the course taken by the *Slocum*, "that if it had been left to you the *Slocum* would have been beached at 129th Street?"

"I did not," retorted Weaver, in spite of the fact that all the major dailies had published accounts of his statement criticizing Van Schaick's decision.

The biggest sensation of the day came in the middle of the afternoon when Inspector Harry Lundberg was called to testify. The burly thirty-eight-year-old invoked his Fifth Amendment right against self-incrimination and refused to answer any questions.

Turning to the jury and gallery, Garvan made clear his outrage. "This is one of the most remarkable spectacles that I have ever witnessed. An officer of the United States Government taking any such stand is unparalleled."

On Wednesday, the third day of the inquest, Garvan and Berry continued to build their case against Barnaby and the company. Reverend George Schultze, the minister from Erie, Pennsylvania, who had attended the *Slocum* excursion as the guest of Reverend Haas, testified that the crew made no effort to help the passengers and that all the life preservers he found were rotten. Ben Conklin, the *Slocum*'s chief engineer since she was launched in 1891, said he'd never seen a fire drill aboard the boat. Captain John A. Pease, captain of the *Grand Republic* and commodore of the Knickerbocker fleet in charge of keeping the boats in full working order, said the *Slocum*'s life preservers "looked all right" to him but he'd never actually examined them. Nor had he, contrary to testimony by others earlier, bought any fire hose for the *Slocum*.

But the key moment for the prosecution came when Miss Hall was recalled to the stand. Garvan had declared earlier for the benefit of the jury that he could prove that no new life preservers had been purchased for the *Slocum* since 1895. The answers elicited from Miss Hall in the next few minutes would indicate whether or not he could deliver on that promise.

Garvan's confidence, already high, rose still higher even before Miss Hall opened her mouth. For he could plainly see that despite her announced intention the previous day to locate company books and documents that would corroborate her version of events related to the altered bills, she took the stand empty-handed. No, she answered, sheepishly, she had no evidence. Nor did she, upon further questioning, have any bookkeeping system at all.

With Miss Hall on the ropes regarding the altered bills for new life preservers and the possibility looming that she might divulge the fact that

Barnaby had ordered her to doctor the books, Terence McManus, counsel to the Knickerbocker Company, rose from his seat. All eyes turned in his direction at the sound of his chair scraping the floor. "In order not to prolong this investigation," the veteran lawyer said, "my clients will concede that no new life preservers have been put on board the *General Slocum* since 1895." Before these words had time to fully register with his astonished audience, McManus proceeded to outline the company's new legal strategy. Having failed at outright fraud and deceit, it would now hide behind the USSIS's sham inspection system. "We did not believe that any [life preservers] were needed, and relied entirely on the inspection made by federal authorities that everything on the boat was in first-class condition."

Garvan smiled and said he was pleased by the admission, "as we would have proved the fact, if we have not already done so." In fact, officers from his office had gone aboard the *Grand Republic* the day before, he explained, and found all of the 350 life preservers referred to in the altered bills as having been sent to the *Slocum*.

"Yes, and stole the logbook," sputtered an indignant Dittenhoeffer, leaping to his feet. "You stole the log, and have not returned it. That's an indictable offense, I'll have you know."

To Dittenhoeffer's petulant rant, Garvan responded only with a taunting grin that said—case closed.

The next day, Thursday, June 23, came off as "hero day" at the inquest, as one daily put it. North Brother Island heroines Lulu McGibbon and Mary McCann told their stories to a rapt audience, as did tugboat captain Jack Wade. The latter had particularly harsh words for Flanagan and the *Slocum*'s crew, but firmly upheld the decision of Van Schaick to beach the boat on North Brother Island. "He couldn't have done any better," said Wade in his endearingly blunt manner. This assertion was later challenged by another veteran pilot, Capt. John Van Gilder, who insisted that Van Schaick should have landed the *Slocum* at 131st Street. Van Schaick himself made a dramatic entrance into the armory on a stretcher, but after consulting with medical personnel and the captain's lawyer, Berry declined to have him questioned and sent him back to Lebanon Hospital.

Several survivors also took the stand, including Paul Liebenow, who showed the jury his badly cut hands—injuries resulting, he explained, from his effort to free life preservers from the wire mesh that held them in place.

At 5:00 P.M., Berry announced the day's proceedings closed and that no further hearings would take place until Monday, June 27, four days hence. Neither Garvan nor Berry offered an explanation for suspending the hearings, but the truth was that it came at the behest of the jury. They had seen and heard enough, the foreman explained, to render a verdict. Having examined only a fraction of the more than two hundred witnesses subpoenaed, Berry and Garvan decided to temporarily suspend rather than formally end the inquest. This would allow for the gathering of additional evidence and perhaps even testimony by Van Schaick.

Nonetheless, a sense of finality permeated the air as the evening papers hit the newsstands. The people of New York read not only of the inquest's suspension but also that the *Slocum* had been refloated, the Charities Pier closed, and Cortelyou's federal commission formed. On Friday the U.S. assistant district attorney announced the formation of a grand jury, and on Saturday the police department released its updated list predicting a death toll of 1,031. On Sunday, Pastor Haas summoned all his strength and preached for the first time since the fire. On Monday the coroner's jury, instead of hearing testimony at the armory, took a tour of the *Slocum* wreck to see the evidence firsthand. On Tuesday morning all the papers predicted that the jury would render its verdict by day's end.

GUILTY

Everyone who attended Tuesday's session of the coroner's inquest understood that the case would go to the jury that day. As a result, an atmosphere of impatience suffused the steamy drill room as still more witnesses were brought forth to nail down final points in Garvan and Berry's case. The calling of two final witnesses in the afternoon temporarily sparked renewed interest among the jury and spectators.

Julius Mayer, counsel for Inspector Lundberg, sent a jolt through the audience when quite unexpectedly he called his client to the stand. Despite invoking his Fifth Amendment right against self-incrimination and refusing to answer questions on two previous occasions, Lundberg was now eager to tell his story. To no one's surprise, he painted a picture of a diligent inspection back on May 5, in which he counted and personally inspected all 2,550 life preservers on the *Slocum*. He found 25 defective and ordered them destroyed. Garvan chose not to challenge this fanciful recollection by noting how it differed significantly from a statement Lundberg issued on the day of the fire claiming that he had counted 3,000 life preservers and rejected none. The district attorney was confident that the evidence, including Lundberg's admission that he passed the fire hose without running water through it, pointed to criminal negligence.

This surprise testimony was quickly followed by another remarkable announcement—that Captain Van Schaick wished to have his version of the disaster placed on the record. The drill room fell silent as a wheelchair bearing the slumped form of the captain was wheeled into the room and to the witness platform. The audience watched with a mixture of anger and pity as he gingerly hobbled to the witness chair. His face was partially covered in bandages and one foot bore a cast.

Van Schaick's testimony was simple and straightforward and it produced no surprises, except his admission that no new life preservers had come aboard the *Slocum* since 1894 and his insistence that fire drills were routinely held on the boat. As expected, the captain stood by his decision to run for North Brother Island and let it be known, with the help of leading questions from Attorney Dittenhoeffer, that he had safely carried some 30 million passengers before June 15 without a fatality. In fact, the captain exaggerated his record of safety by claiming, "I never had an accident."

Toward 5:00 P.M. the last witness stepped down and Coroner Berry proceeded to read his charge to the jury.

> *This great loss of life has shocked the entire world, and, it is hoped, has roused the United States authorities, as it has the city authorities, to take such steps as will prevent a like possibility in the future.*
>
> *The law requires a carrier of passengers to exercise the strictest vigilance in receiving a passenger, conveying him to his destination, and setting him down in safety—the strictest vigilance that the means of conveyance employed and the circumstances of the case will permit. Now, the reason of this rule is manifest. A passenger cannot know, nor is he presumed to know, anything about the machinery of a ship or its equipment or appliances. He has paid his passage, and he is wholly passive in the hands of and is at the mercy of the owners of the vessel, their agents and employees.*

The jurors returned to an adjacent room and the waiting began. Nearly three hours later, at 8:50 P.M., the jury returned and the foreman read the verdict. They found Frank A. Barnaby, James K. Atkinson, and five other directors of the Knickerbocker Steamboat Company guilty of criminal negligence; as were Capt. William Van Schaick, Capt. John A. Pease, Edward Flanagan, and Inspector Henry Lundberg. No cheers or jeers emanated from the audience of grieving survivors and relatives, only tears and sighs of relief. If there was anything positive to be found amid their harrowing ordeal, it was the certainty that justice would be served. One thousand innocent lives had been snuffed out by corruption and greed, but justice had been served.

As the participants in the coroner's jury left the Second Battery Armory and made for the trains to take them home, many stopped to pick up copies of the *Evening World* and its rivals. In them they found coverage of the final day of testimony, but all had hit the newsstands before the verdict came in. There was another story, however, that instantly grabbed their attention. Earlier in the day the Danish steamer *Norge,* traveling from Copenhagen to New York with 780 passengers and crew, struck some rocks off Scotland and sank. Early reports were sketchy, but hundreds were presumed dead. In the days that followed, they and the rest of the world learned the awful details of a captain whose poor judgment brought on the disaster, a boat outfitted with inadequate lifesaving equipment, and a crew that did nothing to help the passengers and instead fought them for places in the lifeboats. Only 129 were saved.

Part Four

FORGETTING

Well it has been said that there is no grief
like the grief which does not speak.

—LONGFELLOW

MEMORIAL

J ust as they had precisely one year earlier, the Liebenows awoke on
June 15, 1905, to a gorgeous spring day. A bright warm sun climbed
steadily upward into a sharp blue sky broken only by the occasional
puffy, fair-weather cloud. Through the windows of their apartment on
West 125th Street came a welcome breeze, along with the familiar sounds
of a city of 4 million people starting their day.

One year ago they were a family of five, up early and filled with excitement as they prepared to head downtown to meet their relatives, the Webers, at the pier on East Third Street. Today they were only three. Paul and
Anna Liebenow, along with their six-month-old baby Adella, had survived
the disaster aboard the *Slocum*. Their two other daughters, Helen and Annie, had perished, along with the Webers' two children and Paul's sister,
Martha. Now, one year later, they prepared to attend a memorial service at
the Lutheran cemetery in Queens.

Blissfully unaware of the ordeal she'd miraculously survived and the
sisters she'd lost, Adella, now eighteen months old, chattered away as she
romped around the apartment. Her parents put on their black mourning
clothes, most likely the same ones worn to all the funerals the year before.

On Adella, they put a new white dress. This adhered to the custom of the day that emphasized the purity and innocence of youth, but also stemmed from the fact that Adella, as the youngest person to survive the disaster, had been chosen by the Organization of the General Slocum Survivors to unveil the new monument erected in honor of the disaster's sixty-one unidentified dead.

Sometime after 8:00 A.M. they left their apartment to catch a train downtown to Little Germany. Unlike last year, they now had a choice between the elevated lines and the new subway that had opened the previous October. By 9:30 A.M., in accordance with the instructions issued by the organization, the Liebenows joined the Webers and hundreds of fellow members at Tompkins Square Park. Soon they boarded a series of specially arranged trolley cars that took them to the cemetery in Middle Village, Queens. After a group lunch at nearby Niederstein's Hotel, the Liebenows and their fellow organization members marched in solemn procession to the cemetery.

More than fifteen thousand people filled the cemetery by the time the service began at 3:00 P.M. Nearly all the adults wore black ribbons and pins that read "We Mourn Our Loss." Where long ago lay an enormous trench filled with coffins stacked three deep there now stood a twenty-foot-tall monument wrapped in an American flag and surrounded by grass and flowers. Close at hand was a grandstand built to hold one thousand members of the survivors' organization. Most of its seats were left empty by order of a police inspector, who at the last minute deemed the structure unsound. Because of Adella's special role, the Liebenows were one of the few families allowed to sit on it. Snapping in the breeze above the crowd were American and German flags with black streamers attached. The afternoon air was hot and several people fainted as they waited for the ceremony to begin.

The first mournful strains of Chopin's *Funeral March* brought a sudden hush to the crowd. As they listened, a group of children placed flowers around the base of the monument, including one wreath made of sixty-one roses, one for each of the unidentified dead. Paul and Anna Liebenow, like dozens of mourners around them, shed especially bitter tears at that moment, knowing—hoping, anyway—that the body of their

Helen was among them. Both were devastated by the loss of their two old-est daughters, but the fact that no trace of Helen was ever found inflicted an especially deep and lingering pain.

Bishop Henry C. Potter of the Episcopal Church offered an opening prayer and Rev. D. W. Peterson followed with an address in German. Charles Dersch, president of the Organization of the General Slocum Survivors and chief organizer of the day's events, then delivered the main ad-dress. Unlike the ministers who spoke before and after him, Dersch did not dwell on the unfathomable mysteries of God's ways, nor on the need for faith to help one carry on. Rather, he spoke to the anger and frustration of many who gathered that afternoon over the state of the prosecutions against the men indicted for their role in the disaster. One year after the event, not one had been convicted. Dersch had lost his wife and daughter, and the emotions underlying his words were palpable.

"For a year from this day we have known what it means to be without our loved ones. They were taken from us by the greed of those who loved money more than lives. The innocents died horrible deaths to fill the purses of the greedy." The Organization of the General Slocum Survivors demanded that justice be served and, equally important, that new laws be enacted so "that it will be impossible for such a horror to happen again."

Dersch's impassioned speech was followed by several more inter-spersed with musical selections sung by the United Singing Societies of New York and Brooklyn. Finally the appointed moment for the monument unveiling arrived. Anna Liebenow rose with Adella in her arms, descended the grandstand, and walked slowly across the grass to the shrouded monu-ment. As she did, soloist Miss Hattie Jacobi sang "The Holy City" over the soft weeping of the thousands of onlookers. Adella, to her mother's relief, sat quietly in her arms clutching her doll. As the last note of the song echoed out over the crowd, she hoisted Adella upward and helped her grasp a small rope. The effort likely caused her some pain, as she was still recovering from severe burns to one side of her body. Adella gave it a firm tug. Slowly the heavy American flag slipped away to reveal the monument, and the singing societies launched into another selection.

Nearly everyone in the crowd had contributed to the monument fund, and now for the first time they saw the fruits of their generosity. Two classically robed figures approximately six feet tall stood atop a fourteen-foot base of carved granite. One of them, symbolizing Faith, pointed upward to heaven while gazing knowingly at the other, who represented Courage. On either side of the base were two smaller sculptures representing Grief and Despair. Just below them was affixed a brass plaque depicting the burning boat and below that an inscription describing the disaster and the sixty-one unidentified dead. The words IN MEMORIAM at the lower end of the base completed the arrangement.

The dramatic unveiling by the baby survivor coupled with the stirring choral accompaniment unleashed a flood of emotion among the thousands gathered. Families and friends wept uncontrollably and held each other for support. Not since the funerals of a year ago had there been an occasion that invited such an uninhibited exhibition of sorrow. Still, there was a certain measure of joy beneath it all, inspired by the somber beauty of the monument and its message of hope. As young Adella looked at the monument she pointed upward and said, "See, pretty." Just then a crew member from the *Franklin Edson* stepped forward and handed her the doll she dropped while pulling the rope.

After another address and several more songs, including "Nearer, My God, To Thee," Reverend Archdeacon Nelson stepped forward and closed the ceremony with a benediction. Slowly the crowd began to dissipate as families headed for home or made one last stop at family burial plots where the rest of the *Slocum* victims rested. The Liebenows and Webers no doubt lingered over their lost children and Martha before making their way back to Manhattan.

The sadness that pervaded the first anniversary ceremonies was accentuated by several things only hinted at during the speeches that day. The most obvious was the absence of Pastor Haas. Sadly, it was not infirmity or emotion that kept him away from his flock, but rather a bitter controversy over the distribution of the relief funds.

It began only weeks after the disaster, when Charles Dersch and other members of the Organization of Slocum Survivors held a rally at Scheutzen Hall to protest the work of the relief committee. Many in the crowd of five hundred stood up and recounted their unsuccessful efforts to get the committee to pay funeral bills or provide relief to the destitute. Newspapers picked up on the controversy and ran stories of families on the verge of starvation. Dersch and the survivors' organization charged the committee with wasting money on consultants hired from Buffalo, including paying their railroad and hotel bills.

These charges lodged against the relief committee were understandable given the size of their task and the high expectations placed on them, but ultimately untrue. Out of a total of $124,205.80 collected by the end of August 1904, only $1,062 had been spent on operating expenses and not a dime of it on men hired from Buffalo—or anywhere else, for that matter. The great majority of the fund, $81,280, went to cover the expenses of 705 funerals. The rest went for things like temporary aid, medicine, and clothing. Approximately $18,000 was set aside in a fund to care for twenty-seven children left orphaned by the disaster.

The controversy originated when the committee refused to pay for lavish funerals that ran as high as one thousand dollars. In other instances they denied relief to families they believed able to sustain themselves through their own resources or with the help of extended family and friends. These tough decisions stemmed not from coldheartedness, but rather from the simple fact that the relief fund was not large enough to help everyone.

But what really sparked controversy and ultimately the schism between Reverend Haas and the Organization of Slocum Survivors was the relief committee's decision to hand over its balance of $20,000 to St. Mark's Parish. Haas had convinced the committee that his church was destitute after the loss of so many parishioners, especially its most prosperous ones. St. Mark's, he explained, would use the funds to help pay its bills and, more important in the eyes of the committee, carry out its long-standing charitable services to the community. With the relief committee expected to dissolve itself by the fall, Haas was concerned about the long-term care needs of his stricken parish.

Charles Dersch and other members of the survivors' organization were outraged. Haas, they noted, had already received $12,400 in private donations and needed no further assistance. They demanded that every penny of the $20,000 still in the relief fund be spent on the families still suffering from the disaster. Haas refused to surrender the money, and the rift became permanent, shattering the unity of the flock he'd spent decades building.

So while the thousands gathered in the Lutheran cemetery on the first anniversary of the disaster, they did so without Reverend Haas. That evening he presided over a memorial service at St. Mark's. Every seat in the church was filled, doubtless by more than a few who'd spent the day at the cemetery. They listened intently as Haas spoke of the need both to accept the tragedy and to make sure a like event never occurred.

The schism over the relief fund was not the only source of despair among the people directly affected by the *Slocum* disaster. By the time of the first anniversary memorial service, they were beset with the growing fear that no one responsible for the loss of their loved ones would go to jail. Only three weeks earlier, on May 25, 1905, USSIS assistant inspector of hulls Henry Lundberg walked out of federal court a free man. This was his third trial for manslaughter since January, and all had ended in mistrial with the juries hopelessly split (charges against Inspector Fleming had been dismissed at the outset of the first trial). Technically he could be tried again, but the chances of a fourth trial were remote. Worse, everyone knew that the subsequent trial of Barnaby and the directors of the Knickerbocker Steamboat Company depended heavily on Lundberg's being found guilty. So long as Lundberg remained innocent, Barnaby and his cronies could hide behind the USSIS certificate of approval issued after his inspection six weeks before the fire. As lawyer Terence McManus said during the coroner's inquest when conceding the issue of life preservers, the company "relied entirely on the inspection made by federal authorities that everything on the boat was in first-class condition." Eventually their fears would be realized as charges against Barnaby and the other officials of the company were dropped.

That left the prosecution of Capt. William Van Schaick. The case against him still seemed strong, but in the spring of 1905 no date had been set for any trial, and federal prosecutors seemed in no hurry to set one. Justice delayed indeed seemed justice denied.

Hand in hand with this fear that the guilty would go unpunished was the growing sense that the public had already begun to forget the tragedy. In the weeks following the announcement of guilty verdicts by the coroner's jury, the *Slocum* saga continued to demand front-page coverage. On June 29, for example, one day after the verdict, Secretary Cortelyou ordered every steamboat operating in New York harbor reinspected by a team of USSIS inspectors brought in from outside the New York office. News of the reinspections and their stunning results—one-third of all life preservers and one-quarter of all fire hoses found defective on inland steamers—made headlines in all the dailies. So too did the news on July 29 that the federal grand jury to which the coroner's jury verdict was referred voted to indict seven men (Van Schaick, Lundberg, and Fleming for manslaughter; Barnaby, Atkinson, Dexter, and Pease for aiding and abetting Van Schaick's crime).

But then as the wheels of justice slowed to a crawl, the public seemed to lose interest, especially as other events competed for attention. In late June and early July the Republican and Democratic national conventions were held, with Theodore Roosevelt and Judge Alton B. Parker gaining their respective nominations. News of the St. Louis World's Fair at home and the Russo-Japanese War abroad filled the dailies' columns on a regular basis, as did the sensational Nan Patterson murder story. The New York Giants baseball team made headlines not merely for finishing first in the National League but for refusing to play Boston, the American League champions, in the recently established World Series (Boston had won the first one in 1903). "We're the champions of the only real major league," sneered the Giants' John McGraw. In late October the city threw a massive party to celebrate the opening of its new subway. A few weeks later hometown hero Theodore Roosevelt was elected president. The *Slocum* story returned again and again to the dailies, but never to the degree that it had in the two weeks immediately following the disaster.

When they did make news, *Slocum*-related stories rarely made the front page. For example, in late August a new scandal broke when it was learned that a New Jersey cork manufacturer had inserted iron bars in blocks of cork it sold to the Kahnweiler life preserver company. This was done to fraudulently (and cheaply) raise the weight of the cork to the legal minimum. Although not directly related to the *Slocum* disaster, the incident immediately put it back in the news because of the role defective life preservers had played in it.

The *Slocum* again faded until several papers picked up on the unusual story of one man's ongoing search for his little boy. William Bandelow lost his wife and five-year-old daughter in the disaster. But stories from rescuers of a little blond boy saved and brought to the Brooklyn shore, coupled with the lack of a body, convinced him that his three-year-old son George was alive, living with a woman who believed he was an orphan. Bandelow had five hundred circulars printed with a photo and description of the boy, along with a promise. "I offer a reward of $100 for the recovery of my boy alive or dead." And if that was not incentive enough, he assured the reader, "If you can in any way assist me in finding the child you will help one who has lost all dear to him in this world." The story stayed alive well into the fall, fed by numerous alleged sightings, before disappearing for good.

Two events in October, one trivial, the other serious, briefly revived the *Slocum* story. On October 16 a showgirl named Fanny Baker began a week-long publicity scam designed to boost her flagging stage career. She claimed that her uncle, a Mr. A. P. Baker of Michigan, had been aboard the *Slocum*. Panicked at the outbreak of the fire, he put his will and deeds to his properties in a tin box and cast it into the East River. He survived the disaster, she claimed, long enough to tell her that she was named in the will as his sole beneficiary. And so after issuing press releases to the papers, Fanny Baker astonished onlookers as she donned a heavy diving suit and spent the afternoon on the bottom of the East River. No box or fortune was found, since neither had ever existed, but Fanny did succeed in garnering a priceless bit of fame.

On the very same day, the Federal Commission of Investigation established by President Roosevelt and Secretary Cortelyou issued its report.

The scathing sixty-two-page document pulled no punches in denouncing the conduct of Captain Van Schaick and his crew and condemning the gross negligence of the Knickerbocker Steamboat Company executives. Moreover, it castigated the New York bureau of the USSIS as corrupt and inept and recommended the firing of Rodie, Dumont, and Barrett. President Roosevelt, having seen the report a week earlier, agreed, and the three were immediately terminated. Finally, the report laid out a series of sweeping regulatory reforms, most of which would be subsequently enacted by Congress.

With no action on the prosecutions of the seven indicted men, the *Slocum* once again slipped out of the public eye. Then on December 1 the famed muckraking journal *Munsey's* magazine published a lengthy piece about the *Slocum* disaster. The article's tone and take on the affair was vividly conveyed by its subtitle: THE EXACT FACTS OF THE MOST SHOCKING AND PITIFUL TRAGEDY IN THE ANNALS OF THE SEA, WITH THE DAMNING EVIDENCE OF CRIMINAL INDIFFERENCE AND DESPICABLE DISHONESTY ON THE PART OF THE DIRECTORS AND INSPECTORS.

More to the point, the author, Herbert N. Casson, captured the sense of fear shared by many concerned people that the *Slocum* disaster was being forgotten and the guilty ones about to go free. "The article that follows," he wrote in his opening sentence, "is published to make people think." For the next twenty-one pages Casson laid out a no-holds-barred indictment of all involved and then closed with a poignant question.

This nation remembered the Maine. It was willing, even enthusiastic, to shoulder the ponderous burden of war because of the destruction of a battleship and two hundred and sixty men. But what about the Slocum? What about this loss of life that is almost four-fold greater and incomparably less excusable? How shall this mystery be explained—that we rush to battle to avenge the death of two hundred and sixty young men, who had knowingly enlisted in a perilous calling, and then sit as helpless as a colony of rabbits when a treacherous and law-breaking corporation burns and drowns a thousand of our women and children?

While no immediate answer was in the offing, another steamboat tragedy in New York gave added weight to Casson's impassioned plea for justice and reform. On December 17 the steamer *Glen Island* bound for New Haven, Connecticut, caught fire on Long Island Sound. The captain and crew performed admirably, as did the lifeboats, but seven crewmen and two passengers nonetheless died in the incident. It served to jog the public's fading memory of the *Slocum* disaster and to make clear the fact that serious reforms were needed in steamboat safety and regulation.

Then came the three consecutive mistrials of Inspector Henry Lundberg. For a time, as day after day the papers carried the testimony of crewmen, survivors, and witnesses ("*Slocum* Horror Retold" was a typical headline), it appeared that the story had once again taken center stage. Yet with each mistrial the stories grew smaller and appeared deeper and deeper in each edition, often only as a simple recap without details, quotes, or photographs. By the time of the first anniversary memorial service, the city's editors had all but shifted their coverage of the *Slocum* disaster from that of a news story to one of human interest. To their utter frustration, those who cared deeply about the *Slocum* story and its questions of justice and public safety were learning a hard lesson. As veteran city editor Stanley Walker would later write, "News is as hard to hold as quicksilver, and it fades more rapidly than any morning glory." Even the news of the needless loss of more than a thousand lives.

MEMORIES

The one place from which the details, emotions, and legacies of the *Slocum* disaster never faded, of course, was in the hearts and minds of the survivors and relatives of those killed. Like any traumatic, life-altering event, the disaster of June 15, 1904, permanently changed the way they viewed their world and themselves. For some it meant learning to live with the voids left behind by those who died. For others it meant wrestling with what modern psychologists term "survivor's guilt," the constant, nagging and maddeningly unanswerable questions: Why did I survive and they perish? What if I'd reacted differently when the fire broke out? Or held on tighter in the water? Often these challenges were made all the more difficult to meet by poverty, permanent injury, and the debilitating effects of post-traumatic stress syndrome. Ultimately, however, these people all asked the same fundamental question: How will I go on?

For men like Pastor Haas, the answer was simple. "We must continue our work," he admonished his flock in his first sermon following the disaster, "we must not give up." Their loved ones were gone, he acknowledged, but "we can hold our love as a memory of our dead." We can and must turn the calamity into "a blessing" and accept God's challenge to rebuild our lives and our parish.

For Haas, this was no silver-lining-trust-in-God's-ways blather. Rather, it was an expression of true conviction. His dead wife and daughter, he believed, did not want him to wallow in despair. He believed they would want him to continue his ministry to the stricken people of St. Mark's. And so he did, despite the painful memories that confronted him at every corner of the neighborhood and the many tempting offers from more prestigious parishes and colleges.

The task before him was enormous. The fire not only swept away half of St. Mark's membership, but also compelled scores of families to move away from a neighborhood so intimately linked with the death of their loved ones. Nearly one year after the fire, a survey produced by the city's Commissioners of Accounts reported to Mayor McClellan that 170 (28 percent) of the 622 families known to have been on the *Slocum* had moved out of Little Germany. It was a trend that only accelerated in the years to come, so that by 1910 only a handful remained and Little Germany was practically gone. The *Slocum* disaster did not cause the disintegration of Little Germany (the trend was well under way even in the 1890s), but it did make it happen more quickly.

Haas, nonetheless, pulled off a small miracle and saved the parish. Bolstered by his deep faith in God, he stayed on for seventeen years after the fire and ministered to an ever-shrinking congregation. He even remarried, choosing as his bride Clara Holthusen, the sister of John Holthusen, the former principal of St. Mark's Sunday school. In 1921, after thirty-nine years of faithful service to St. Mark's, the sixty-seven-year-old minister retired as pastor, moved to Staten Island, and joined the faculty of Wagner College. He died at his home September 29, 1927.

Catherine Gallagher's story of overcoming the devastating effect of the fire is equally compelling. Having lost her mother and two siblings in the fire, the eleven-year-old suffered another blow immediately after when her father, overcome with grief, abandoned her. She moved in with her poor, elderly grandparents and together they struggled to get by on savings and her twenty-five dollars per month from the relief fund. When her grandfather died two years later—from a broken heart, the family always believed—she and her grandmother moved in with her aunt and uncle. Soon Catherine was forced to quit school to work in a cigar box factory. All the while she carried in her heart both the sorrow of losing her mother and siblings and the feeling of guilt that somehow she had driven her father away.

Notwithstanding this harrowing childhood, Catherine managed to live what she described as "a very good life." At age twenty she married Thomas Connelly, a truck driver, and together they had eleven children. Every now and again she told her children about the fire. "I thought at first it was a terrible fairy tale that Mother made up. That it never happened," remembered her daughter Betty Reilly. As she got older, Catherine talked about the fire more frequently, as though she'd progressively lost her ability to repress her memories of the traumatic ordeal. "If I close my eyes," she told an interviewer at age 104 (93 years after the fire), "I can still see the whole thing." Right up to her death in November 2002 at age 109, she urged her family to always attend the annual memorial service. "Go," she told her daughter Betty Reilly a week before the ceremony in 2001, "make sure no one ever forgets the *General Slocum*."

Others left behind by the tragedy were unable to handle the pain with such fortitude and strength. Andrew Stiel was similarly overwhelmed by grief and painful memories, but he chose a very different response. A widower, he'd lost his four children, three sons and a daughter age six to sixteen, on the *Slocum*. Heartbroken by his loss and tormented by his decision to let them go on the excursion, he fell into despair. No amount of consoling from friends or relatives could diminish his agony and loneliness. Like at least half a dozen others, he soon committed suicide.

Thoughts of suicide no doubt crossed the mind of Paul Liebenow from time to time. But they were no doubt countered by his sense of responsibility to care for what remained of his family, his wife Anna and daughter Adella, the youngest survivor of the disaster and the toddler called upon to unveil the monument to the unidentified dead in the Lutheran cemetery. As a bartender in a popular Harlem restaurant, he earned a respectable working-class wage of twenty dollars per week. With a family to support and bills for his and his wife's ongoing medical care for injuries suffered in the fire, he had no choice but to press on with his life as best he could. He joined the Organization of the General Slocum Survivors, helped raise money for the monument in the cemetery, and testified at most of the hearings and trials related to the *Slocum* disaster.

But he gradually came to believe, no doubt in part as a result of the failed Lundberg trials and diminishing public interest in the story, that he needed to create a record of the *Slocum* disaster. It would not be for him or his wife, for neither seemed capable of forgetting any of the details of the ordeal. Rather, he would do it for his baby, Adella. Six months old at the time of the tragedy, she had no memory of the fire, the near-drowning, the funerals, or even her sisters. And yet he instinctually knew that the *Slocum* disaster had forever changed her parents and would forever shape her life.

So sometime in early May 1905, as plans for the first anniversary ceremony and monument dedication neared completion, Paul Liebenow bought a scrapbook. Then he began to clip *Slocum*-related articles from the daily newspapers like the *Times, Tribune, Journal,* and *World* as well as the German-language *Herold* and *Staats-Zeitung* and paste them into the book. The first were the stories related to the first anniversary service. Nearly all featured headlines and photographs referring to his beloved daughter as the "Youngest Slocum Survivor" and her role in unveiling the monument. These reflected the pride he felt in his daughter and her successful performance. But in the weeks, months, and years that followed, the scrapbook collection showed a man desperate to leave his daughter a chronicle of the event that had so utterly altered her life. He added page after page of articles related to the *Slocum* investigations and trials, but also anything remotely related to steamboat accidents or safety violations. "Passengers in Terror on Drifting Ferry-Boat," read one such piece from the *World*. But Liebenow also clipped, as if to suggest that all had not died in vain, any article about reforms in steamboat safety regulations—"New Law Will Make Life Preservers Safe" and "Era of Fireproof Steamboat Dawns."

Nothing seems to have escaped his eye, including postage-stamp-sized articles noting deckhand John Coakley's arrest for theft, Captain Van Schaick's marriage, Officer Scheuing's award for heroism in saving lives at

North Brother Island, and several stories about relatives of *Slocum* victims committing suicide or going insane. "Driven To Suicide, As Was His Brother, by Slocum Horror," read the headline of one.

As the project took on a life of its own, Liebenow began to include artifacts and documents related to the family's experience in the disaster. On one page he pasted in envelopes from the morgue that had held the personal effects of his nephew and niece Frank and Emma Weber. On the latter the morgue worker had scrawled: "Emma Weber, Body 765, Ring—diamond chip, Sterling Silver Chain bracelet—charred."

On another page he added the letters written to him by friends after they learned of the disaster. One came from an old friend, Conrad Haas, who was working at a restaurant on the grounds of the St. Louis World's Fair. He read about the fire and wrote inquiring about the Liebenows and offering his "sincere and heartfelt sympathy" in the event that any were among the dead. Elsewhere he included solicitation letters from florists on the eve of the first anniversary service urging customers to order early to avoid the rush and from lawyers offering their services should he decide to sue the Knickerbocker Steamboat Company.

Liebenow clearly wanted his daughter Adella to know of his role in the fight for justice. The scrapbook contains all of his subpoenas calling him to testify at the coroner's inquest and several of the subsequent trials, as well as countless letters and membership cards for the Organization of the General Slocum Survivors. He also wanted her to know of his ongoing effort to find and identify Helen's missing body, so he pasted in several letters from the Department of Charities responding to his requests for additional information.

Some of the most moving items included in the scrapbook are those Liebenow selected to convey the utter unexpectedness of the disaster. On one page, for example, he placed a single portrait photograph of Helen smiling while seated in a pram. It is a vision of innocence and beauty devoid of any suggestion of impending doom. Underneath, he wrote "Our Helen." Nearly as evocative are two haberdashery receipts pasted side by side on a page. On one showing his purchase of a new suit and hat for the St. Mark's excursion, he wrote "Before June 15/04." On the other showing the purchase of a mourning band, he wrote, "After June 15/04." The first succinctly captured the joyful anticipation of the excursion, the second the shocking result.

Liebenow added material to the scrapbook for four and a half years. On the last page used he pasted in two small stories. One, headlined "Death Welcome To Car Victim," told of August Bahr's death. After losing his wife and three children on the *Slocum* he was never the same. Struck by a street-car, he exhibited no will to live and died days later of relatively minor in-juries. The second article, "General Slocum in Port," told of the return of the ill-fated boat, its hull now used as a coal barge. The article was dated November 1908, only fourteen months before Liebenow died.

Liebenow's scrapbook accomplished its intended task. As his Adella grew up, his collection of articles and ephemera helped her understand the *Slocum* disaster in a way that no number of annual memorial services on June 15s or bits of information gleaned from her mother and other sur-vivors ever could.

But the scrapbook also provided a vivid portrait of her parents' suffer-ing. Both were reticent and rarely talked about the disaster and the loss of Anna, Helen, and Aunt Martha. Yet as Adella would say decades later when describing the book, "It was his therapy." As such it captures the in-expressible emotions of sorrow, anger, and guilt. Nowhere was this more evident than in his frequent inclusion of poems by Ella Wheeler Wilcox in the book. Wilcox was a very popular if not especially talented poet at the turn of the century whose works frequently appeared in the *New York Journal*. Much of her poetry consisted of melodramatic stanzas on nature, love, betrayal, and passion. Some, however, dwelt on themes of death, trial, and sorrow—poems influenced by her own experience of losing her only baby just hours after its birth. It was in these poems that Liebenow found a measure of comfort. One poem he clipped, entitled "Sympathy," asked

Is the way hard and thorny, oh, my brother?
Do tempests beat, and adverse wild winds blow?
And are you spent, and broken, at each nightfall,
Yet with each morn you rise and onward go?

Brother, I know, I know!
I, too, have journeyed so.

Another, entitled "Faith," prompted him to cut it out doubtless because it urged him to trust in God despite his trials.

I will not doubt, though sorrows fall like rain,
And troubles swarm like bees about a hive;
I shall believe the heights for which I strive
Are only reached by anguish and by pain;
And though I groan and tremble with my crosses,
I yet shall see, through my severest losses,
The greater gain . . .

None of the ten poems he clipped from the *Journal*, however, so fully captured the unending pain endured by a parent who loses a child as did "When a Baby Soul Sails Out." Although written from the perspective of a mother, it evidently spoke to the sorrow Liebenow (and his wife) carried with him after the loss of Anna, Helen, and a son who died soon after birth one year after the fire. In losing adult loved ones to death, writes Wilcox, it's not hard to imagine them enjoying the "delights" of heaven.

But when a child goes yonder
And leaves its mother here,
Its little feet must wander,
It seems to me, in fear.
What paths of Eden beauty
What scenes of peace and rest
Can bring content to one who went
Forth from a mother's breast.

In palace gardens, lonely,
A little child will roam,

And weep for pleasures only
  Found in its humble home—
It is not won by splendor,
  Nor bought by costly toys,
To hide from harm on mother's arm
  Makes all its sum of joys.

It must be when the baby
  Goes journeying off alone,
Some angel (Mary maybe),
  Adopts it for her own.
Yet when a child is taken
  Whose mother stays below
With weeping eyes, through Paradise,
  I seem to see it go.

With troops of angels trying
  To drive away its fear,
I seem to hear it crying
  "I want my mamma here."
I do not court the fancy,
  It is not based on doubt,
It is a thought that comes unsought
  When baby souls sail out.

In the twenty-first century, Wilcox's poetry is dismissed as mass-produced romantic pap. Indeed, Jenny Ballon, her only biographer, wrote in 1940, "She was not a minor poet, but a bad major one." Nonetheless, in 1904 some of her work clearly meant a great deal to men like Paul Liebenow as they struggled to press on with their lives under the weight of unspeakable tragedy. Though he frequently annotated his clippings for Adella's benefit, he wrote nothing next to the poems. He didn't need to.

SCAPEGOAT

One of the stories followed closely by Liebenow was the prosecution of Capt. William Van Schaick. As captain of the *General Slocum* he was the man most directly connected to the tragedy. Barnaby had failed to purchase adequate safety equipment and Lundberg had failed to properly inspect the vessel, but it was Van Schaick who seemingly tolerated this negligence and then compounded it by hiring an untrained crew and never holding fire drills. Moreover, it was Van Schaick who made the controversial decision to press ahead at full speed on the East River to North Brother Island instead of simply bringing the *Slocum* in at a nearby pier. With the likelihood of a trial, let alone a conviction, of Barnaby and the directors of the Knickerbocker Steamboat Company fading with the third Lundberg mistrial, all attention focused on the captain.

United States District Attorney for New York Henry L. Burnett promised in the days following Lundberg's third mistrial in late May 1905 that the prosecution of Van Schaick would begin immediately. But a crowded court calendar and other unforeseen delays pushed the day of reckoning off eight more months—fully one year and seven months after the *Slocum* disaster.

Jury selection began on January 10, 1906, and opening arguments followed five days later. As before, survivors and relatives of victims packed the courtroom, but they harbored expectations greatly diminished since the coroner's inquest in June 1904. The legal "procrastination," as the *Times* put it in an editorial that neatly captured the frustration shared by many, was "a most serious matter." It eroded the public's faith in the legal system and caused it to lose interest in the case.

> *There has been, not exactly a denial of justice, but something very like it, and all expectation that any real responsibility for criminal negligence involving so many has long since passed away. Not only has indignation cooled, but memories have grown dim in regard to the mute details of the affair, and many witnesses who would have been useful are beyond reach. What the end will be everybody knows—and comparatively few are much concerned about it.*

For those whose indignation had not cooled and memories remained distressingly clear there was great concern, and they packed the courtroom each day. Among them were the Liebenows, including young Adella, who with her mother appeared in a photograph in one of the dailies under the headline "Youngest Survivor At Slocum Trial." They listened intently to the testimony that commenced on January 16 and brought forth a by now familiar cast of witnesses—Van Wart, Weaver, and Conklin—and a few new ones, including Capt. William Van Schaick, Jr., son of the defendant and master of the steamboat *Cephus*. Although they searched high and low, officials were unable to find ex-Inspector Henry Lundberg, a witness Van Schaick's lawyer was eager to put on the stand.

Neither the Liebenows nor anyone else in the courtroom during the ten days of testimony heard anything new or startling. As in the previous investigations, the questions and answers continued to focus on life preservers, fire drills, and fire hoses. The matter of Van Schaick's decision to beach the boat on North Brother Island never came up. On January 26, attorneys for both sides presented closing arguments. Assistant United States District Attorney Ernest Baldwin exhorted the jury to find Van Schaick guilty of criminal negligence.

> *You can, from the evidence shown you, arrive at but one conclusion, and that is that the death of some of those unfortunate victims of the Slocum was due in whole or in part to the negligence of this man, Captain Van Schaick. Do you believe that if he had done his whole duty the hundred odd burned to death and the nine hundred and odd that were drowned would today be in their graves? You cannot from this mass of uncontradicted evidence arrive at any other conclusion.*

Abram Dittenhoefer, counsel for Van Schaick, then offered his plea for a verdict of not guilty. The USSIS, he argued, was the real culprit, having certified the *Slocum* as seaworthy six weeks before the disaster. There was no evidence, he continued, to prove intentional and willful neglect on the part of Van Schaick, only perhaps a bit of carelessness. Finally, he noted, life was full of perils that no amount of precaution could fully guard against. Nothing could have saved the forty thousand who perished in the 1902 Mount Pelée volcano eruptions on Martinique. "Even at the Hoboken pier fire," he said, recalling the June 1900 disaster involving four steamships, "300 lives were lost in spite of efforts of a competent fire department supplied with the most complete apparatus. No amount of apparatus and the perfection of fire drill would have saved the *Slocum* for the fire had become a raging inferno before it was discovered."

The next day, Judge Edward Thomas charged the jury and dismissed them to deliberate. Twenty-five minutes later they returned with a verdict. The swift decision surprised everyone, including Judge Thomas, who'd gone to lunch, and it was some time before the verdict was announced. While he waited anxiously, Van Schaick received congratulations from friends and supporters who believed the maxim that brief deliberations invariably mean acquittal. Also aware of this maxim, the Liebenows and other survivors sat tensely awaiting the official word.

"Has the jury reached a verdict?" asked the court clerk.

"We have," replied the foreman. On the first and second counts involving the death of the *Slocum*'s steward, Michael McGrann, and an anonymous passenger referred to as Rachel Roe, they found Van Schaick not guilty. On the third count of criminal negligence for failing to ensure that the *Slocum* had a crew properly trained in emergency procedures and an adequate supply of safety equipment, however, they found him "guilty as charged."

While murmurs of approval mixed with gasps of surprise among the spectators, the captain sat stoically. Given the vilification he had received since the disaster, he had prepared himself for the worst. But Lundberg's mistrials and the gradual cooling of the public's passions regarding the tragedy allowed him to harbor hopes of an acquittal. Now that he'd been found guilty, the only question that remained was the length of his sentence. A few minutes after the jury's announcement, Judge Thomas called the old captain up to the railing. "You have been convicted on a very serious neglect of your duty," intoned the judge. "I sentence you to ten years' imprisonment."

The harsh sentence of ten years in Sing Sing Prison prompted divergent responses among the public and press. Several jurors conceded that had they known what was in store for the captain, they would have voted for acquittal on all counts. "We felt sorry for the old man," one of them told a reporter. The *Times*, one of the loudest voices calling for justice to be served in the *Slocum* incident, declared the captain a scapegoat. The corrupt owners and inspectors who allowed the firetrap to carry passengers have eluded justice, while the captain "falls into the hands of justice, and he gets it untempered with any degree of mercy." Van Schaick simply declared, "The United States Government made me the scapegoat."

But nearly all the survivors and relatives of victims deemed the verdict and sentence appropriate, as did several papers. "The sentence pronounced yesterday upon Captain Van Schaick," opined the *World*, "is severe but just." It will send a message to all steamboat captains that negligence regarding passenger safety will not be tolerated. Still, the *World* demanded that prosecutors "punish the greater guilt of the owners."

The old captain was allowed to remain free on bail while his lawyers appealed the verdict. Two years would pass before the United States Circuit Court of Appeals upheld the verdict and ordered Van Schaick to prison. During that time Van Schaick moved to a farm in upstate New York and married Grace M. Spratt, the nurse and former love he'd been reunited with while recuperating in the hospital. On February 27, 1908, he kissed his bride and hugged his son and entered Sing Sing Prison. Although his sentence ended with the dramatic phrase "at hard labor," the aged mariner was quickly put to work in the prison greenhouse. Prisoner 57855 grew to be well-liked by fellow inmates and guards whose companionship, coupled with hopes of an early release, kept him in good health.

Meanwhile, his defenders, led by his indefatigable wife, launched a campaign to have him pardoned. "Anyone who thinks we're throwing in the sponge is dead wrong," she told a reporter. "We'll battle to the last gasp, take another breath and go on fighting." Joining her in the struggle was the American Association of Masters, Mates, and Pilots, the group that in 1903 had presented Van Schaick with an award for his exemplary safety record. The captain was one of their own, and the association felt duty bound to stop what they viewed as his unjust persecution. Their letter-writing appeal brought a flood of correspondence to President Roosevelt from citizens across the country, including prominent clerics, newspaper editors, labor union leaders, and reformers. Their petition drive garnered a quarter million signatures, which they promptly sent to the president. Charles Dersch and the Organization of the General Slocum Survivors countered with a campaign of their own, but mobilized only a fraction of the number. Roosevelt mulled the pardon request over, and after consulting with the Justice Department, rejected it. Van Schaick's supporters never flagged, however, and kept up their campaign until August 26, 1911, when the federal parole board voted to release Van Schaick.

It was a Saturday morning, and Van Schaick was working in the greenhouse when word arrived that the warden wanted to see him. "Captain," the warden greeted him, "I've got good news for you." The old man, aware that he was up for parole consideration, looked at him with anticipation. "Here are the papers making you a free man," the warden continued. "You can leave the prison whenever you like."

Several hours later, Van Schaick stepped off a train in Grand Central Station and proceeded immediately to a West 98th Street boardinghouse for a tearful reunion with his wife.

The next day reporters came calling, and Van Schaick was eager to talk about everything—the fire, the trial, prison, and his plans. At one point a reporter asked him if he harbored any ill will toward those who had put him in prison and fought to keep him there. "Lord bless you, not a soul," he replied without hesitation. "I haven't a grudge against anyone."

Weeks later Van Schaick and his wife moved to a farm near Troy, New York, purchased for him by his supporters in the National Board of Steam Navigation and the American Association of Masters, Mates and Pilots. He lived there another fifteen years and died at the Masonic Home in Utica, New York, on December 9, 1927, at the age of ninety.

GHOSTS OF DREAMS
PASSED AWAY

Captain Van Schaick's parole was yet another bitter disappointment to Dersch and the Organization of Slocum Survivors in their quest for justice. More than a thousand of their loved ones were gone and now no one—not Lundberg, not Van Schaick, and not Barnaby (charges against him were dropped in 1908)—would be made to pay for their role in the disaster. The public side of the ordeal was rapidly coming to a close and they were powerless to stop it.

On December 4 the hull of the *General Slocum*, now a coal barge named *Maryland*, foundered and sank to its final resting place off Atlantic City, New Jersey. "Ill fortune always followed her," remarked her owner. "I'm glad she's gone."

Three weeks later, as the survivors and relatives of the victims of the *Slocum* disaster endured their seventh Christmas Day without their loved ones, President Taft's formal pardon of Van Schaick became official. Exonerated of all guilt in the disaster and restored to full citizenship, he was free to live out his days in peace. No such remedy awaited the people whose lives were destroyed by the horror of June 15, 1904. Theirs was an ordeal not ended by the stroke of a pen. Nothing—neither time, nor fortune, nor faith, nor new love—would remove the painful memories of the disaster that swept away friends, spouses, and children. All they could hope for were the moments when happy memories of those now gone temporarily brightened what poet Ella Wheeler Wilcox called the perpetual "midnight of sorrow." In this sense, their memories were not merely a burden to bear, but also a source of strength that enabled them to persevere in spite of their experience. As Wilcox put it in one of her poems:

> *I would not forget you. I live to remember*
> *The beautiful hopes that bloomed but to decay,*
> *And brighter than June glows the bleakest December,*
> *When peopled with ghosts of the dreams passed away.*

LEGACY

Despite the best efforts of Charles Dersch and the Organization of the General Slocum Survivors, public memory of the disaster faded with astonishing speed. Only seven years later it was replaced as the city's *great* fire when the Triangle Shirtwaist Factory burned. There were similarities between the two fires—both involved immigrants and mostly female victims and both aroused public wrath. But the Triangle fire's death toll was 85 percent lower than the *Slocum*'s. How then did it become the "fire of fires" in New York's and the nation's memory?

Several factors begin to explain this remarkable legacy. First, there was the context. The Triangle Shirtwaist Factory fire occurred at a time of intense labor struggle, especially in the garment trades. Only a year before, tens of thousands of shirtwaist makers had staged a huge strike for better wages, hours, and conditions. Now 146 of them lay dead and there was no question as to who was to blame. This conclusion was reinforced when the public learned that the factory owners had locked the exits to keep the women at their machines, an act that seemed more sinister and nakedly greedy than cutting corners with safety equipment as with the owners of the *Slocum*.

Second, the *Slocum* disaster was, in the words of several newspaper reporters at the time, a "concentrated tragedy." The great majority of those killed were from a single parish and lived within a forty-block area. Their fellow New Yorkers were horrified and outraged by the tragedy, but only a relative handful were directly affected.

Third, the onset of World War I eradicated sympathy for anything German, including the innocent victims of the *General Slocum* fire. Newspaper articles covering the annual June 15 commemoration ceased abruptly in 1914 and did not reappear until 1920. By then, as the Triangle fire became firmly entrenched in the American memory, all that remained of the *General Slocum* fire was an ever-shrinking annual commemoration at the Lutheran cemetery in Middle Village, Queens.

Still, the *Slocum* didn't disappear entirely. Now and again the story resurfaced, usually in the aftermath of a succeeding catastrophe like the sinking of the *Titanic* in April 1912 (ca. 1,500 killed), the sinking of the *Empress of Ireland* in May 1914 (1,012 killed), and the capsizing of the *Eastland* in Chicago in July 1915 (844 killed). The latter incident was eerily reminiscent of the *Slocum* disaster because it was a charter excursion for Western Electric employees and their families. The top-heavy steamer rolled over at the pier and sank in minutes. Ironically, it was the addition of extra lifeboats on the top deck in the wake of the *Titanic* sinking that led to the disaster. Even in the news coverage of this event, the *Slocum* received only passing mention, generally for death toll comparisons and discussions of corporate liability.

In the 1920s the *Slocum* story achieved a bit of immortality when James Joyce included a half-page reference to it in his monumental work *Ulysses*, first published in 1922. The novel is set in a single day, June 16, 1904, the day following the *Slocum* horror, and chronicles the misadventures of Leopold Bloom, a Jewish Dubliner. At one point one of the characters walks into a bar and strikes up a conversation with the bartender about news of the day.

Terrible affair that General Slocum explosion. Terrible, terrible! A thousand casualties. And heartrending scenes. Men trampling down

women and children. Most brutal thing. What do they say was the
cause? Spontaneous combustion. Most scandalous revelation. Not a
single lifeboat would float and the firehose all burst. What I can't
understand is how the inspectors ever allowed a boat like that. . . .
Now, you're talking straight, Mr Crimmins. You know why? Palm oil.
Is that a fact? Without a doubt. Well now, look at that. And America
they say is the land of the free. I thought we were bad here.

I smiled at him. America, I said quietly, just like that. What is it?
The sweepings of every country including our own. Isn't that true?
That's a fact.

Graft, my dear sir. Well, of course, where there's money going
there's always someone to pick it up.

Joyce's stream-of-consciousness masterpiece has fascinated and frustrated readers ever since its publication. Scholars have pored over every word and phrase in an attempt to decipher their meaning. Joyce's reference to the *Slocum* disaster is one of the most overt clues as to the day in which it takes place. As a result, each year on June 16, Joyce devotees around the world celebrate "Bloomsday" with readings, festivals, and plays in honor of the Dublin writer and his most famous work.

The *Slocum* story gained a different sort of immortality in 1934 when it was splashed upon the silver screens all across America in the film *Manhattan Melodrama*. It opened with a stunning (by 1934 special effects standards) reenactment of the fire as a setup for a story about the lives of two East Side boys. Orphaned by the disaster, they face an upbringing of hardship and trial. One boy (played by William Powell) achieves Horatio Alger success, becoming a crusading district attorney. The other, "Blackie" Gallagher (played by Clark Gable), however, turns to a life of crime. Ultimately there is a showdown between the *Slocum* orphans. The most striking thing about the treatment of the *Slocum* story in the film is its transformation from a German church outing to an Irish neighborhood excursion. Passengers are seen enjoying food and drink aboard the boat, listening to the wistful melody of the Irish-American favorite "The Sidewalks of New York." One of the many film fans who turned out in July 1934 to see *Manhattan Melodrama* was gangster John Dillinger (accompanied by the "Lady in Red"). He went down in a hail of FBI bullets as he exited the theater.

In 1940, after holding out longer than anyone could have imagined possible, St. Mark's parish on East Sixth Street closed its doors for good. It soon reopened as a Jewish synagogue, an institution more reflective of the neighborhood's population. The remnant of the St. Mark's congregation worshiped in several Lutheran churches uptown before formally merging with Zion Lutheran on East 84th Street. Zion-St. Mark's parish still exists today (as does the synagogue on East Sixth Street), though its congregation once again numbers only about one hundred.

No doubt at the prompting of the Organization of the General Slocum Survivors, the New-York Historical Society decided in 1954 to curate a small exhibit to mark the fiftieth anniversary of the disaster. It opened Friday, June 11, with a ceremony that included twelve survivors. An article in the *Herald Tribune* included a large photograph of them, now aged 51 to 85, standing in formal attire around a ship's wheel. The reporter observed how the men and women mainly talked about how beautiful the weather had been on June 15, 1904, and about wearing fancy clothes, playing bean ball, and eagerly awaiting the opening of the picnic baskets being guarded by their mothers. "They all recalled the holocaust all right," he noted, "—and some still have horrible scars from it—but they discussed the fire as if it seemed unreal fifty years afterwards."

Perhaps it was the news coverage that attended the fiftieth anniversary or a chance conversation with some relatives, but not long after the New-York Historical Society exhibit closed, Claude Rust began to research the *Slocum* disaster and conduct interviews with survivors. His maternal grandmother, Charlotte May, was killed on the excursion, and he developed a passionate desire to know more about it. After more than twenty years of research, he published in 1981 *The Burning of the General Slocum*, the first credible account of the disaster.

By then only a dozen or so survivors were still alive, and membership in the Organization of the General Slocum Survivors had so dwindled, it had all but ceased to function. The Queens Historical Society formed a Slocum Memorial Committee to keep the annual June 15 commemorations going. The disaster's eightieth anniversary in 1984 prompted the *Times* to send a reporter to the service in Queens. His article, "Years After Ship Fire, Captain's Role Debated," included interviews with survivors who both blamed and sympathized with Captain Van Schaick. For the former, eight decades had done little to erase the bitterness of the ordeal.

In the early 1990s the job of preserving the memory of the *Slocum* disaster increasingly fell to men and women with no connection to the event other than sympathy and fascination. Frank Duffy, executive vice president of the Maritime Industry Museum at the SUNY Maritime College, got involved as a result of his love of maritime history. Soon the *Slocum* story became a major part of his research and writing, a development that led him to spearhead a drive in the late 1980s to restore a memorial fountain erected long ago in Tompkins Square Park in honor of the children who died on the *Slocum*. Ever since its rededication in 1991, Duffy has remained active in the effort to keep the *Slocum* story alive. In 1997, Duffy convinced the Parks Department to hold an annual memorial ceremony at the fountain on June 15. The short, moving ceremony usually draws fifty or so people, most of whom are members of the media and the curious, plus a handful of descendants of survivors and victims.

The 1990s also saw the establishment of a new organization, the General Slocum Memorial Association, for the planning of the annual commemoration at Trinity Lutheran Church and the nearby cemetery in Middle Village, Queens. Ken Leib, a German-American with no connection to the tragedy (though he recently began researching a possible relative), joined the association in 1998 and soon became its president. He successfully steered the annual memorial service in Queens in a more ecumenical direction where not only victims and survivors are remembered, but also the heroes and caregivers. Leib has also involved the children of nearby Intermediate School 93, who over the past few years have written a poem and play (each read and performed at the annual memorial service), designed and made a memorial quilt, developed a pop-up book, and recorded a radio feature about the *Slocum*. Participants in the memorial service seem especially taken with the fact that nearly all the children are of immigrant or minority heritage.

The Queens ceremony tends to draw more people than its Tompkins Square counterpart, though Duffy and Leib do not see their respective events as competitive. They work closely together to plan them and generally hold them on separate days. Even with a larger turnout, the Queens ceremony draws only a small number of descendants of survivors. The only living survivor, Adella Liebenow Wotherspoon, despite her advanced age (ninety-eight at the 2002 event), almost always makes it.

The release of the 1997 blockbuster film *Titanic* sparked renewed interest in the *Slocum* story as many newspapers and magazines drew the inevitable comparisons between the events. This was also a time when, as a result of New York City's giddy emergence from three decades of rising crime, budget crises, and crumbling infrastructure, New Yorkers and Americans in general were taking a growing interest in the city's history. Suddenly a city that had long prided itself on paying no attention to the past was awash in books, museum exhibitions, walking tours, and documentaries chronicling its history. The apotheosis of this trend came in late 2000 with the release of Ric Burns's *New York: A Documentary Film*, a twelve-hour PBS special. While it made no mention of the *Slocum* fire, the film's companion book did include a special feature on the tragedy.

One month before the Burns documentary aired, in October 2000, internationally recognized marine explorer and fiction writer Clive Cussler located the wreck of the *Slocum*, a.k.a. the barge *Maryland*, off the New Jersey shore near Atlantic City where it sank in 1911. Cussler, whose discovery of the Confederate submarine *Hunley* off South Carolina is considered one of the great marine archaeology finds of the twentieth century, is not interested in treasure or artifacts. His organization, the National Underwater Marine Agency, or NUMA, is a nonprofit committed "to preserving our maritime heritage through the discovery, archaeological survey and conservation of shipwreck artifacts." The wrecked boat, he hopes, will remain undisturbed for all time.

The most recent event to bring the *Slocum* story back before the public, of course, was the terrorist attack on the World Trade Center on September 11, 2001. Journalists scrambled to find events with which to compare the devastation and loss of life. Inevitably, the most obvious comparison in national history was with the Japanese surprise attack on Pearl Harbor in December 1941.

Closer to home, however, it was the *General Slocum* disaster that journalists, politicians, and historians turned to for comparisons—especially when it came to considering what type of memorial to build. Ultimately the WTC attack and *Slocum* fire were quite different events. One was a willful act of destruction and murder akin to a military strike except that all the victims were civilians. The other was a tragedy born of negligence, greed, and just plain bad luck. Still, there were too many parallels to ignore. The most obvious was the profound shock and horror felt by the people of New York, especially those who lost loved ones. No tragedy in the city's four-hundred-year history comes close to the carnage of these two events, and no others produced a greater outpouring of sympathy and sorrow. Another obvious parallel was the selfless heroism exhibited both by uniformed personnel and everyday people on the scene. Although no rescuers died in the *Slocum* fire, many risked their lives so that others might live. Such was the case on a larger scale and with more dire consequences on 9/11.

Other parallels emerged the closer one looked. In both cases, relatives of those missing rushed to find and display photographs of their loved ones. In 1904, photo reproduction technology was slow and expensive, so searchers carried their original photos and held them out to people, hoping someone could provide some information. In 2001 the city was awash in color copies of broadsheets showing photos of the missing and contact information. Both proved futile.

In both 9/11 and the *Slocum* fire people turned to poetry as a way to express their pain, sorrow, and anger. In the former case, thousands of poems began appearing on websites, in newspapers, and at curbside memorials just hours after the towers collapsed. In the latter, we know that at least one man, a simple bartender named Paul Liebenow, turned to the emotive poems of Ella Wheeler Wilcox for solace. Doubtless many more did as well.

The public reaction to the tragedies was likewise similar: they opened their wallets. Both 1904 and 2001 saw huge amounts of money garnered from New Yorkers as well as Americans across the nation. For people wanting to do something tangible to aid the sufferers, giving to the relief funds became the obvious choice. Sadly, this shared aspect produced still another point of similarity—embarrassing squabbles over the distribution of relief money.

In both September 2001 and June 1904 the city's mayor emerged as a central figure to whom people looked for leadership and reassurance. The nation, indeed the world, marveled at Mayor Rudolph Giuliani's superb handling of the crisis, both from an operational standpoint in coordinating the relief effort and from a symbolic and rhetorical one through his words of resolve. George B. McClellan, Jr., provided much the same dual service to the people of New York in the summer of 1904, but with a far lower profile in keeping with the strict standards of propriety that governed the actions of public officials in that era. Still, McClellan, like Giuliani, was widely hailed for his leadership during the crisis.

Both events left behind thousands of people whose lives would never again be the same. As in the aftermath of any disaster, people who lost children, sisters, brothers, parents, and extended family, not to mention friends, colleagues, and neighbors, were left to struggle with the pain and sorrow of their loss. For some this emotional trauma was compounded by "survivor's guilt," condemning the living to forever ask *why them and not me?* Just as most *Slocum* survivors and relatives of victims somehow found the strength to carry on with their lives, those directly affected by 9/11 are striving to do the same. Not all succeeded in the case of the *Slocum*, as evidenced by the many suicides and cases of people drinking themselves to death. Not surprisingly, the devastation of 9/11 has already produced its first reports of suicides.

A final parallel between the catastrophes of 1904 and 2001 concerns the effort to build fitting memorials to the victims. Two memorials were constructed in the wake of the *Slocum* tragedy, the monument in the Lutheran cemetery unveiled in 1905 and a small fountain placed in Tompkins Square Park (in Little Germany) in 1906. While final questions of design and form regarding a 9/11 memorial remain unresolved, it is certain that one will be built on the site of the World Trade Center towers.

Behind these and all similar initiatives lies a threefold goal: to honor the dead, provide the living with a place of contemplation and remembrance, and ensure that society never forgets what happened. Yet as the *Slocum* survivors discovered, as will someday the descendants of 9/11 victims, all three are honorable goals, but only the first two are ultimately achievable. Monuments can keep alive the *historical* memory of events like the Johnstown Flood, Pearl Harbor, and 9/11 for centuries to come. The actual memory of these and other traumatic events like the *Slocum* fire, however, lives on only in the hearts and minds of those who experienced them. They are not transferable—despite the best efforts of survivors and descendants—from one generation to the next. Given the fact that the only real memory of the *Slocum* fire resides with the last living survivor, ninety-nine-year old Adella Liebenow Wotherspoon, it's only a matter of time before the tragedy of the steamboat *General Slocum* ceases to be remembered in any real way. Then it will exist for succeeding generations not as a memory, but rather as a cautionary tale of greed and carelessness and a story of unspeakable loss and extraordinary courage.

ACKNOWLEDGMENTS

Where to begin when it comes to thanking all the people who helped make this book possible? I'll start with my diligent team of researchers led by the indefatigable and extraordinary April White of KnowMore Research.com and also including Joan Koster-Morales, Reza Tehranifar, and Catherine Sarubbi. No request, no matter how obscure, seemed beyond their ability to track down an answer. Ursula Pawlowski and Mary Beth Snodgrass deserve recognition for their work compiling an exhaustive database of *General Slocum* victims and survivors, as do Sean Costello and Ryan Shanahan for their work building the website www.General-Slocum.com. I also need to thank Kathy Kirk Rooney and Joan Banach for their typing services and Joel Villa and John Buckingham for help with scanning pictures.

My research into the *Slocum* tragedy benefited immeasurably from the extraordinary resources and research staffs at the National Archives and Records Administration, New-York Historical Society, Queens Historical Society, New York City Municipal Archives, and New York Public Library. I especially want to thank Warren Platt at the NYPL for his help in tracking down answers to several important questions.

I was very fortunate to come into contact with several people involved in *Slocum*-related projects who proved very generous with their time. Documentary filmmakers Hank Linhart and Phil Dray took time from making the definitive documentary on the *Slocum* tragedy to answer many questions and provide me with invaluable tapes of interviews with survivors they conducted over the years. Frank Duffy and Ken Leib, leaders in the ongoing effort to hold annual memorial services in honor of the *Slocum* victims and heroes, answered all my questions and provided me with important research leads. The same must be said for Kathy Jolowicz and Karen Lamberton, two women engaged in their own research into the *Slocum* story.

Enough cannot be said of the vital role played by survivor Adella Liebenow Wotherspoon in the writing of this book. She graciously welcomed me into her home and answered every question I put to her. She also let me look at the scrapbook her father, Paul Liebenow, made in the wake of the tragedy that claimed his two older daughters. Similarly, Betty Reilly and Maureen Enright, the daughter and granddaughter of *Slocum* survivor Catherine Gallagher Connelly, endured my many phone calls and answered all my questions.

Many descendants of victims and survivors likewise offered much valuable information. These include: William H. Manz (for information on the Mueller family), Eugene F. Kelleher (Police Officer John A. Scheuing), Judith Loebel (the Halley family), Richard K. Cross (Wilhelmina Rauch), Candy Twynham (the Rheinfrank family), Joan Colvin (the Knell family), Patricia Lawrence (Michael McGrann), Charles C. Bothur (James C. Ward), Linda Slocum (the Oellrich family), Robert J. Zipse (the Zipse family), Marion Andrews (the Firneisen family), Mark Rosenholz (Sylvia Harris), and Joann Schmidt, Carol Bollinger, and Karen Lamberton (the Muth, Hessel, and Schnitzler families). Claude Rust, who lost his grandmother in the *Slocum* tragedy and wrote the first credible book about the event, wrote to offer me help in the spring of 2002, but died before we could meet.

Others deserving of thanks include Elliott Wilshaw and Robert Wilson for providing photographs from their personal collections, Reverend Wolf and Stella Kaufmann of Zion-St. Mark's Parish for information about the history of St. Mark's Church, Rev. Ed Vodoklys, S.J., for help with some difficult German translations, Dennis R. Yeager, Esq., for assistance in understanding the legal process ca. 1904, and Dr. Paige Reynolds for answering questions pertaining to James Joyce and *Ulysses*. I am similarly indebted to New York City firefighters Tom Cashin and Frank Thurlow, who, along with Dr. Vytenis Babrauskas of Fire Science and Technology, Inc., and Jonathan Klopman, an independent marine surveyor based in Marblehead, Massachusetts, shared with me their vital knowledge of the nature of fires and firefighting. I also need to thank my graduate school mentor, Kenneth T. Jackson of Columbia University and the New-York Historical Society, under whose tutelage I developed a love of New York City history and first learned of the story of the *General Slocum*.

Recognition must also go to Juan Valdez for supplying the coffee, without which this book would never have been written.

I must also thank my editor at Broadway Books, Charlie Conrad, and his able assistant, Alison Presley, for all their insight, guidance, and last-minute troubleshooting. Special thanks must also go to my agent, friend, and mentor John Wright, who despite suffering terrible loss on 9/11, saw the project through to completion.

And most important of all, I must thank my wife, Stephanie, whose love and faith carried me along through the many late nights and lost weekends sacrificed in writing this book. I didn't have to write a book about a terrible tragedy in order to be reminded how truly blessed I am.

ABOUT THE SOURCES

A complete and detailed set of footnotes for this book is available at www.general-slocum.com and in hard copy format at the New-York Historical Society, New York Public Library, Queens Historical Society, Museum of the City of New York, and City University of New York, Gotham Center.

This book is based almost entirely on primary sources—that is, documents and records generated around the time of the *General Slocum* disaster in June 1904. Despite the fact that no victim, survivor, or rescuer left a diary or significant set of personal papers, I was able to draw upon a vast array of documents and sources that allowed me to piece together not just the overall story but several personal portraits. The foundational resources for my research were New York City's daily newspapers, in particular the *World, Times, Tribune, Sun, Herald, Journal,* and the German-language *Staats-Zeitung.* Owing to the enormity of the event, they provided exhaustive coverage of the fire, rescues, recovery effort, funerals, and trials. Throughout the disaster and its aftermath, the papers competed with each other to provide the most

minute details, often in the form of lengthy interviews with survivors and rescuers. Later, when the legal proceedings against the *Slocum*'s captain, crew,
and owners took place, the daily press printed lengthy transcripts of the testimony in which witnesses described their ordeals in great detail (indeed, these
are the *only* transcripts of the hearings and trials that survive, as all the original
records were destroyed). It is from these personal accounts, from people like
Annie Weber and Reverend George Haas, that I was able to reconstruct a nar-
rative that included vivid details and extensive dialogue (all dialogue comes
from these sources, or interviews; none is manufactured) of the fire, rescues,
scenes at the morgue, funerals, and trials. Remarkably, many of these newspaper accounts are collected in three "instant" books published in 1904 and accompanied by numerous photographs: John Wesley Hanson, Jr., *New York's
Awful Excursion Boat Horror* (Chicago, 1904); Henry Davenport Northrup,
New York's Awful Steamboat Horror (Philadelphia, 1904); and John S.
Ogilvie, *History of the General Slocum Disaster* (New York, 1904).

Even though the *Slocum* fire is nearly a century old, I was able to draw
upon the memories of two survivors, Adella Liebenow Wotherspoon and
Catherine Gallagher Connelly. The latter, aged 107 by the time I began my
research, was too frail to interview, but the details of her ordeal as an
eleven-year-old aboard the ill-fated ship were captured in two video interviews I was fortunate enough to gain access to. Her daughter, Mrs. Betty
Reilly, and granddaughter, Maureen Enright, were able to provide additional detail. Wotherspoon, only six months old at the time of the fire, obviously has no specific "memory" of the fire, but she grew up in a
household shattered by the event (her two older sisters, two cousins, and
an aunt were killed). More important, she possessed a scrapbook of news
clippings and personal records compiled by her father—as close to a diary
as I came in trying to understand the inner pain of those who survived.
Nearly as important was the information provided by the many descendants of victims, survivors, and rescuers. Death and birth certificates, federal census tracts, and city directories filled in the remaining details.

I also relied on a vast amount of information contained in a number of
published government reports related to the fire. The *Annual Report* of the
New York City Department of Public Charities for 1904, for example, in-

cluded the most comprehensive record of those on the *General Slocum* on June 15, 1904, and their fate. Included in this report were full names, addresses, death certificate numbers, and the names of hospitals to which survivors were admitted. The *Report of the United States Commission of the Investigation upon the Disaster to the Steamer* General Slocum, *October 8, 1904* (Washington, D.C.: Government Printing Office, 1904), the product of an investigation ordered by President Theodore Roosevelt in the wake of the tragedy, offered a careful summary of the fire as well as a stinging indictment of the United States Steamboat Inspection Service and its shortcomings. A later document, "Bill H.R. 4154 for the Relief of the Victims of the *General Slocum* Disaster," published by the U.S. Congress, House Committee on Claims in 1910, likewise provided a detailed catalog of information regarding each family (including occupations and incomes) and its fate. Because this document was compiled six years after the fire, it added new information such as the fact that certain survivors had subsequently died of their injuries, committed suicide, or gone insane. Annual reports of the New York City Board of Health, Fire Department, and Police Department (all New York: Martin Brown Press, 1905) also added important perspectives and details.

Since the flawed inspection of the *General Slocum* was a crucial element of the story, I pored over the records of the U.S. Steamboat Inspection Service found at the Library of Congress in Washington, D.C. These included voluminous correspondence received and generated by the USSIS both before and after the *Slocum* fire—letters that provided a window into the agency's culture of corruption and overall ineffectiveness in protecting lives and property. Other important records included the *Annual Report of the Supervising Inspector General, 1900–1910* (Washington, D.C.: Government Printing Office, 1900–1910), U.S. Civil Service Commission, *Information Concerning Examination for Entrance to the Steamboat Inspection Service* (Washington, D.C.: Government Printing Office, 1910), and the U.S. Steamboat Inspection Service, *General Rules and Regulations* (Washington, D.C.: Government Printing Office, 1904).

My insight into St. Mark's Evangelical Lutheran Church and the surrounding German community was based upon the parish archives now housed at Zion-St. Mark's in Manhattan. Of particular importance in this collection was a brief history of the parish, *Zion-St. Mark's Lutheran Church: A History* (published privately by the church, 1992), and biographical information of Reverend George Haas. Additional information on Haas came from the archives at Wagner College on Staten Island. The New-York Historical Society possesses an original copy of the *Journal for the Seventeenth Annual Excursion St. Mark's Evan. Lutheran Church, June 15, 1904,* the program for the ill-fated trip that contained many significant details about the St. Mark's community and the plans for the excursion. The N-YHS also holds a partial collection of the minutes of the regular meetings of the Organization of the General Slocum Survivors (1951–63), as well as a scrapbook of newspaper clippings relating to the disaster and records pertaining to rescuer Sam Berg, and the original (and significantly larger) manuscript of the autobiography of Mayor George B. McClellan, Jr., later published as *The Gentleman and the Tiger: The Autobiography of George B. McClellan, Jr.*, edited by Harold C. Syrett (Philadelphia: Lippincott, 1956). Details about the annual memorial services came from newspaper coverage and the collections of the Organization of the General Slocum Survivors, *Annual Memorial Service Program, 1905+,* held at the New York Public Library.

Secondary sources also proved essential to the writing of this book. Three previously published books (in addition to the aforementioned three "instant books" published in 1904)—Werner Braatz and Joseph Starr, *Fire on the River: The Story of the Burning of the General Slocum* (n.p., 2000), Irving Werstein, *The General Slocum Incident: Story of an Ill-Fated Ship* (John Day Company, 1965), and Claude Rust, *The Burning of the General Slocum* (Elsevier/Nelson Books, 1981)—provided solid overviews of the disaster story. Books such as Bernard Dumpleton, *The Story of the Paddle Steamer* (Molksham, Venton, 1973), and William H. Ewen, *Days of the Steamboats* (Connecticut, 1988), likewise supplied valuable details on the emergence of the steamboat in the nineteenth century. Jerry O. Potter, *The Sultana Tragedy: America's Greatest Maritime Disaster* (Pelican Pub Co., 1992), offered a key retelling of the ship catastrophe that occurred in 1865.

For information regarding New York's German community, I relied upon Stanley Nadol, *Little Germany: Ethnicity, Religion, and Class in New York City, 1845-80* (Urbana, 1990); Jay P. Dolan, *The Immigrant Church: New York's Irish and German Catholics, 1820-1865* (South Bend, 1975); and Mario Maffi, *Gateway to the Promised Land: Ethnicity and Culture in New York's Lower East Side* (New York, 1995). Much valuable insight into the German immigrant experience in America came from Don Heinrich Tolzmann, *The German-American Experience* (Humanity Books, 2000). Contemporary articles such as Edward Steiner's "The German Immigrant in America," *The Outlook*, January 1903, shed light on the increasingly positive view Americans held of Germans by the turn of the century.

Acquiring a deeper understanding of New York City at the turn of the twentieth century led me to Mike Wallace and Edwin Burroughs, *Gotham: A History of New York City to 1898* (Oxford, 1999), and David Hammack, *Power and Society: Great New York at the Turn of the Century* (New York, 1991). For specifies on the East River, Hell Gate, and the major maritime catastrophes that preceded the *Slocum* disaster, I turned to Jeanette Edwards Rattray, *The Perils of the Port of New York* (New York, 1973). Stanley Walker, *City Editor* (Frederick A. Stokes Company, 1934), and James Wyman Barrett, *Joseph Pulitzer and His World* (Vanguard, 1941), likewise illuminated the world of big-city newspapers in 1904.

Terry Golway, *So That Others Might Live: A History of New York's Bravest, The FDNY from 1700 to the Present* (Basic Books, 2002), offers the most valuable source on the larger history of fires and firefighting in New York City. Margaret Hindle Hazen and Robert M. Hazen's book, *Keepers of the Flame: The Role of Fire in American Culture, 1775-1925* (Princeton, 1992), proved invaluable in developing my awareness of the deep-seated fear of and obsession with fire most Americans had in 1904. Leon Stein, *The Triangle Fire* (Lippincott, 1962), remains the best source for the most famous fire in the city's history, while books by Richard Snow and John F. Kasson detail the rise of disaster spectacles at Coney Island, especially Fire and Flames.

For details on the characteristics and behavior of fires, I relied upon the

National Fire Protection Association's *NFPA 921, Guide for Fire and Explosion Investigations* (1995).

I must add that some of my greatest insights into the nature of fire derived from interviews with Dr. Vytenis Babrauskas of Fire Science and Technology, Inc., and Jonathan Klopman, an independent marine surveyor based in Marblehead, Massachusetts.

A NOTE ABOUT THE AUTHOR

Edward T. O'Donnell is Associate Professor of American history at the College of the Holy Cross in Worcester, Massachusetts. He is the author of *1001 Things Everyone Should Know About Irish American History* (Broadway Books, 2002). He lives in Holden, Massachusetts, with his wife, Stephanie, and four daughters, Erin, Kelly, Michelle, and Katherine (and their dog, Sammy). To learn more, please visit his website: www.EdwardTODonnell.com.